Personality Development in Sanskrit Literature

Personality Development in Sanskrit Literature

Editor

K.B. ARCHAK

Kaveri Books
New Delhi-110002

First Published in 2014
ISBN 978-81-7479-157-3

Published by
Kaveri Books
4832/24, Ansari Road
New Delhi - 110 002 (India)
Tel.: 011-2328 8140, 2324 5799
E-mail: kaveribooks@vsnl.com
kaveribooks@gmail.com
Website: www.kaveribooks.com

Laser Typesetting by : Deep Graphics, Delhi

PRINTED IN INDIA

Preface

Ancient Indian Sages had an intense desire for the well-being of the whole mankind. They held universal welfare as *summum bonum* of their life for which they exclaimed- "*Lokāḥ Samastāḥ Sukhino Bhavantu*". They had realized the truth of life, examined its ins and outs, advised the beneficial secrets and showed pathway to the truth of life. This itself is the Indian view. Their precepts if be followed and brought into practice, there would be global happiness, peace and prosperity. And the history of the mankind has been the witness to it.

Perhaps, every human being is capable of executing dos and don'ts. Since the time immemorial, human being is alone responsible for all incidents constructive or destructive, in the past and present. Despite, Indians of the past showed the splendid pathway to the well-being of human beings, by treading which, one can remove bad qualities and develop beneficial ones. This of course is the main goal of personality development. In fact personality development consists of three instrumental facets such as intellect, mind and body. Of them, one's intellect if be stronger than both mind and sense-organs, starts functioning properly in its capacity. In otherwise case, the human being becomes a slave to passions, loses his individuality, behaves wantonly to fulfil his evil aspirations, becomes hatred to the society, banished from the society and finally sorrow-strikened for ever.

On the other hand a person of sharp intellect is identified as a strong one, as such, our ancestors have proclaimed 'बुद्धिनाशात् प्रणश्यति' and so on. A man of such intellect has to have the realization of 'माता भूमि+ पुत्रोऽहं पृथिव्याः, वसुधैव कुटुम्बकम्, सर्वेऽत्र सुखिनः सन्तु, सर्वे सन्तु निरामयाः, सर्वे भद्राणि पश्यन्तु, मा कश्चिद् दुःखभाग् भवेत्' – etc. These declarations emphatically adjudicate broad mindedness of our Indians of past and show their being developed psychologically, socially and ethically. Treading their foot-steps of successful life, one should lead the life and let others live. Such a man has to have confidence and love for his wife driving the chariot of his life. Such a couple can alone lead happy life. Therefore, Manu states: 'सन्तुष्टो भार्यया भर्ता, भर्त्रा भार्या तथैव च।' Moreover he should look after his brothers and sisters, lest they should be envious of each other. He should protect peace and harmony among all members of his family. "मा भ्राता भ्रातरं द्विक्षन् मा स्वसारमुत स्वसा". In maintaining peace and harmony of the family, if any obstacle comes in the way, he should not lag behind, but step ahead with unstinted will power. In this way, the person should lift himself up without becoming a puppet in the hands of *kāma, krōdha, lōbha, mōha, mada, matsara* the six internal enemies.

Further, that which causes beneficiary effects to himself, to his relatives and the society around him, becomes the very truth of life. So is the declaration: "यत्सतां हितमत्यन्तं तत्सत्यं यद्भूतहितमत्यन्तं तत्सत्यम्". It is to be noted here that just as a surgeon operates a defective part of the body to save patient's life, so too one's performance of even undo act yielding good fruit, is borne by the society. Telling lie for the benefit of other, does not incur sin. Therefore Indian code of Law allows it. To illustrate, thieves were running after a cow to catch hold of it in a forest. On the way, they saw brahmin whom they asked about the cow. For a while, he contemplated on himself whether he should tell the truth. But he observed telling truth would result in the death of cow; and willed to speak lie and said that he has not seen a cow. As a result, effort of thieves renders in vain. This is substantiated - "अनृतं जीवितस्यार्थे वदन्न स्पृश्यतेऽनृतैः". Therefore truth may be avoided to maintain non-violence. Thus *ahiṁsācaraṇa is* one of the facets of Dharma. On the other hand, it is said "आततायिनमायान्तं हन्यादेवाविचारयन्" i.e. without entertaining second thought, that person आततायी should be killed, who would obstruct the path of a beneficient one.

पुण्यस्य फलमिच्छन्ति पुण्यं नेच्छन्ति सेवितुम्।
न पापफलमिच्छन्ति पापं कुर्वन्ति यत्रतः।।

Since persons wicked by nature like Duryodhana are always harmful to others, yet they don't want to undergo the fruits thereof. They cannot be brought on the path of righteousness. In addition, they desire to enjoy fruit of meritorious deeds, yet they are averse to any such deeds. One should keep away himself from the company of such person, because the latter one makes the former vile, brings him under his thumb and brings back to his track. This is the downfall of his personality. So too is the downfall of the king Kaṁsa a wretched person, as read in the Bhāgavata Purāṇa.

A person aspiring for his development should inculcate the disciplines of *Dharma, Artha* and *Kāma* for which, he should always remain in the company of good people. In addition,

प्रत्यहं पर्यवेक्षेत नरः चरितमात्मनः ।
किं नु मे पशुभिस्तुल्यं किं नु सत्पुरुषैरिति ।।

He has to introspect himself every day, what he has done like animal and what in association with good people. He requires to correct himself and look for his development. This is what the fellowship sectors now-a-days follow the discipline.

The imperative aspects of personality development have been emphasized in the vedic canons and the texts of classical Sanskrit literature. Even so, the life history of high-souled persons recorded in the respective works, is evident to show that Indians of the past achieved the success of their life reaching the zenith of personality development. Despite such strong support of culture, our Indian youths in the fast changing world today, being influenced by foreign culture, are attracted by transitory physical luxuries and suffer a lot. This is what an acute situation our society is facing. Alas, the glory of then Bharata-bhumi, is today densely clouded!

With a view to warding off such thick curtain over the Indian culture, to creating awareness of various ethical disciplines for one's development and to showing the height of its brilliant glory, a small effort was made by means of organizing the National seminar on 'Personality Development in Sanskrit Literature' for two days (24-25 March 2011) by the P.G. Dept. of Studies in Sanskrit, Karnatak University, Dharwad (Karnataka State).

The National Seminar was inaugurated by Sri Sri His Holiness Dr. Kotturu Mahaswamiji of Gangavati. Dr. (Smt.) Meena Chandavarkar, Director, UGC Academic Staff College, K. U. Dharwad, as the chief guest spoke on the role and importance of personality development in ancient literature and emphasized how everybody should develop oneself for the betterment of the society now-a-days. Dr. K. Pratap Professor of Sanskrit, S.V. University Tirupati (A.P.) delivered significant key-note address. Basing on the central theme of the seminar more than twenty research papers were presented by scholars from inside and outside Karnataka State, followed by useful discussion. The seminar was concluded with Valedictory address by Dr. Ashok Chachadi Professor and Director of Kousali Institute of Management Studies, K. U. Dharwad.

The task of editing such work was possible due to the help rendered by my colleagues and student-friends. I express my heartfelt thanks to them. Further, I am grateful to all authors of respective papers as. they co-operated in sending the revised copies well in time. Similarly my gratitudes are due to Kaveri Books, New Delhi, which expressed its readiness to publish the proceedings of the Seminar and which magnificiently did the job within a scheduled period.

12-12-2012 **Dr. K. B. Archak**

Contents

1

Nature of Personality Development

K. B. Archak

As is evident from the title, this paper addresses the purpose, scope and way of understanding personality development. It is classified into four sections designed to orient the personality development amidst other fields. The first section deals with the understanding of personality development – what is personality? Motivation for the study of personality ? The second section deals with the meaning of the term '*personality*' and third section speaks about the connotative aspects personality according Indian and Western views. Further, the determinants of personality in Indian view are explained in the fourth section.

The personality is certainly a complex and fascinating phenomenon. Because every individual hungers for attention, for self-insight, and for inner peace. Hence everybody now-a-days show much concern to under-standing the word '*personality*'. The parent wants to understand the personality of his child; the teacher of his student; the executive of his employee; and all desire to know about their own personality. As a torch-bearer the study of the science of personality certainly promises these gains.

The layman uses the term '*personality*' in two senses : some times he describes an acquaintance as having a good or strong personality, meaning that he has qualities enabling him to win friends and influence people, i.e., in terms of social attractiveness. At other times he describes people in terms of their most striking characteristics, i.e., submissiveness, impulsiveness, aggressiveness etc. Beauty contestants are typically judged on their physical attractiveness, talent and personality. Here the judgement of a good personality is based upon their social poise and sophistication.

No two persons are exactly the same, not even identical twins. Some people are anxious, some are risk-taking; some are phlegmatic, some highly-strong; some are confident, some shy; and some are quiet and some are talkative. This issue of differences is fundamental to the study of personality.

The fundamental questions which motivate to study personality are about 'Who am I ?', which reflect an important extension of the question 'Who am I in the eyes of others ?' Indeed the answer to 'Who am I ?' is dependent on understanding the relation of the person asking others in relation to him or her.

Personality is one of the most abstract words in any language. Though its connotative significance is very broad, its denotative significance is acute. Nothing can be more abstract. It is neither male nor female, neither young nor old. As a noun, '*person*' is hardly more than what 'to be'. In French, it may even come to mean 'nobody'.

It would therefore, be justified to look at the word '*personality*' in two different approaches namely Indian approach and the Western approach. With the under-standing of the word *personality* from both the approaches, one can perhaps conclude the true meaning of the word *personality* and *personality development*.

Indian Connotation of "Personality"

The term *personality* in Sanskrit, means 'व्यक्तित्वम्', which is *bhāvavācaka* of 'व्यक्तिः'. The term 'व्यक्तिः' derived from the root 'अञ्जू' with 'वि-उपसर्ग' and the suffix 'क्तिन्'. This word is generally used in the sense of manifestation, evident, individuality, specific appearance and so on. In precise, this term व्यक्तिः carries four types of meanings :

i) Following the statement – तं संतः - श्रोतुमर्हन्ति सदसद्-व्यक्तिहेतवः (*Raghuvaṁśa* 1.10), it means distinction or discrimination implied by exposition.

ii) On the basis of the statement :
सन्तानस्तनुभावनष्टसलिला व्यक्तिं भजन्त्यापगाः ।
(*Abhijñāna Śākuntala*, VII.8), it means visible appearance or clear perception.

iii) It means real nature – this is substanciated by the statement from the *Bhagavadgītā* – 'न हि ते भगवन् व्यक्तिं विदुर्देवा न दानवाः' (10.14)

iv) Separateness, individuality, distinctness, etc. This meaning is supported by the *Bhagavadgītā* – अव्यक्ताद्व्यक्तयः सर्वाः प्रभवन्त्यहरागमे । (VIII.18)[1]

Besides, the signs denoting the gender of the word, such as, पुल्लिङ्ग, स्त्रीलिङ्ग, नपुंसकलिङ्ग are collectively called *Vyakti*. In this context it may be noted that the grammarians consider the meaning of *Vyakti* as an eliment supporting the correct meaning of the term. However, this meaning is not relevant to the present context with which the study is undertaken.

Further another term '*development*' read along with *personality* is synonymous with Sanskrit word विकसनम् which is derived from the root 'कस्' *to move* with a prefix 'वि' and the suffix 'घञ्'. Its meaning is quite emphatic which means *Vṛddhi* i.e., increase, pervasion, lustrous, auspicious, etc. Keeping these meanings in view, the reading of 'व्यक्तित्वविकसनम्' suggests revealing the real nature of a person is auspicious and qualitative, it tends to the increase of happiness for himself and for the society around him. Thus, व्यक्तित्वविकसनम् implies a sort of responsibility to be borne for achieving the goal.

The element of विकसन is naturally endowed by some persons, while some others possess this quality due to his association with good people. On any count व्यक्तिवविकसन yields a sense of homogeneity through both individuals and unification in the society.

Western Connotation of "Personality"

The word '*personality*' is derived from a latin word '*persona*', which means '*mask*'. Significantly, in the theatre of the ancient latin-speaking world, the mask was used as a plot device to disguise the identity of character; but it rather was a convention employed to respresent the character.

'*Persona*' originally denotes the theatrical mask first used in Greek drama and adopted about hundred years before Christ by Romans. These are the personas that people project and display, but also include the inner parts of psychological experience which are collectively called the '*self*'. The Greek designation for mask was *prosopon*, a word having vague resemblence to *persona*. Several authorities regard the latin term as a direct derivation from the Greek.[2]

Crisis of this theory point to the probability of such a marked alteration occuring in the form of the word. To escape this difficulty other philologists favour its derivation from the

Etruscan and old Latin word *Persum* (head or face), some trace its origin from Latin *Per se una* (self-containing).

The term '*personality*' in English, '*Personnalite*' in French and '*Personlichkeit*' in German closely resemble the '*personalitas*' of Medieval Latin. In classical Latin '*persona*' alone was used, but its meanings in many respects are equivalent to those of modern that commence with '*persona*' itself.[3]

In the writings of Cicero (106-43 B.C) probably not long after the word first appeared, are found at least four distinct meanings of '*persona*'.

a) As one appears to others (but not as one really is);
b) The part someone plays in life (e.g., a philosophy);
c) An assemblage of personal qualities that fit a man for his work;
d) Distinction and dignity (as in a style of writing).

The *first* meaning, of course, has the original significance of the mask; the *second* suggests real status; not the mere pretence; the *third* meaning – signifies the inner psychic qualities of the player himself; and the *final* meaning connotes importance and prestige which later were conveyed by the derivative term *personage.*[4]

Starting with *Persona* as Mask, the four earliest derivative meanings are listed and numbered. Each serves as a radiant point for later semantic change.

(1) The first logical extension of *persona* as Mask refers then to "external appearance (not the true self)". The objective *personatus* meant provided with, or wearing, a mask. Unlike *persona*, it never took on the meaning of the true self. It was always fictitious, counterfit, a pretense.

(2) The second root meaning signifies the "character or role which the player assumes in the drama".

(3) Further the next derivation – "An individual possessed of distinctive personal qualities". This meaning, of greatest importance in the development of psychological definitions, appears as the third usage in Cicero's writings.

(4) The fourth derivation, likewise found in Cicero, has the significance of "prestige and dignity". This meaning was eagerly assimitated into the Roman caste system, wherein some individuals had legal rights and obligations, and others did not.

(5) Hence *persona* was used to indicate, "the free born citizen (as distinguished from the slave)."

(6) Still in classical Latin, the term came to mean Ṣa representative (one who stands for a group or institution)."

(7) Whence the Latin expression *persona grata*. The representative of the church came later to be called its "*parson* (Anglo-Saxon, persoun)."

(8) Important persons, possessed of prestige and dignity came also to be known as "*personage*". As a later day example, the family name McPherson is derived from the cluster of meanings expressed in definitions (5), (6), (7) and (8).

(9) A by-path was created by the Latin grammarian Varro (116-26 B.C.) who early spoke of the "person in grammar", a metaphor based upon the resemblance between dramatic and synta-ctical roles.

These definitions, can be placed in order according to their position in a continum of meanings ranging from the external (false, mask-like) manner to the internal (true) self.

Keeping these meanings in view, *personality* can be defined as a dynamic and organized set of characteristics possessed by a person that uniquely influences his or her cognitions, motivations and behaviours in various situations.

According to *Morton Prince* (1924)[5], "Personality is the sum total of all the biological innate dispositions, impulses, tendencies, appetites, and instincts of the individual, and the acquired dispositions and tendencies." This definition places a potentially useful emphasis on the inner aspect of personality. Like Kempf's, however, it seems to cover virtually all of psychology, rather than to delimit a particular field.

Floyd Allport (1924)[6] states that "personality traits may be considered as so many important dimensions in which people may be found to differ." This seems much too inclusive. For example, it includes physical dimensions, which are only indirectly of importance for personality. Elsewhere he offers a more useful formulation, "Personality is the individual's characteristic reactions to social stimuli and the quality of his adaptation to the social features of his environment."

Munn states that personality may be defined "as the most characteristic integration of an individual's structures, modes of behaviour, interests, attitudes, abilities and aptitudes especially from the stand point of adjustment in social situations". *Eysenk* defines that, "Personality is the more or less stable and enduring organisation of a person's character, temperament, intellect and physique, which determines his unique adjustment to the environment.

According to this author, Personality is the dynamic organisation and integration of the various innate and acquired psychological traits into a harmonious unit which facilitates the individual, to protect or to restore the physiological and psychological homeostasis, by interaction with the physical and socio-cultural environ-ment. Man in order to protect or to restore the homeostasis, employs the innate abilities like intelligence, learning ability, creative ability, perceptual ability and emotions, and in the course of interaction acquires certain value morals and other qualities, which give him satisfaction and thereby become part and parcel of the self due to frequent use. The self armed with these qualities, values, morals, and various behaviours constitute the personality, which in turn determines his unique adjustment to his internal and external environment.[7]

Despite these variant Western approach, one does entertain a feeling that Western content of personality is hardly comprehensive, and hence throw dim light on the tough path of life, as comparing to the Indian approach. Therefore, the latter approach holds better acceptability.

Determinants of Personality

Generally, no individual is born with personality, but with the inherited characteristics or tendencies leading to personality development. If the environment is conducive, these tendencies tend to develop into strong and obviously good behavioural patterns. Approximately, fifty percent of one's character is inherited. To an equal extent, environment determines it too. If the characteristic is weak and environment is good, the inherited factor is not developed or expressed in bad or harmful actions. However, if the environment is bad, even the good characteristics cannot attain their genetic potential and the bad characteristics become part of personality. The influence of books, films, parents, friends and education may have certain beneficial as well as very harmful effects on the personality of an individual.

The human personality is unique and is determined by five aspects viz., physical, mental, intellectual, socio-moral, spiritual which are influenced by both *Heredity* and *Environment*.

Physical Determinant

A person is born with a certain characteristics that determines his personality. This involves the heredity component. Physical development of an individual starts from the movement of its conception. Therefore, Indian tradition ordains that a woman advanced in pregnancy requires to be in healthy atmosphere, to eat good food and to listen to the ethico-philosophical stories. In addition she has to have positive thinking in all the affairs of family life. These functions of a woman bring forth much impact on the baby conceived.

With this background the personality development in Indian tradition is spoken off through prescribed stages of *brahmacarya – gṛhastha – vānaprastha* and *sanyāsa*. However during the span of agewise two stages, *Kaumāra* and *Yauvana*, an individual should inculcate and perform the vows of the *brahmacarya* and *gṛhastha*. Thereby, he can achieve *dharma, artha* and *kāma*, first three goals of life. No doubt the achievement of *dharma, artha* and *kāma – puruṣārthas* is not possible all at once.

For an embodied individual requires to fulfill the preliminaries regarding food, behaviour, education, etc. The foremost of all these essentialities is the discipline of feeding one's embodiment with prescribed food. In this regard the *Bhagavadgītā* in 17th chapter explains at length about the food acceptable for one's own well-being. There in, it is said, food conduceive to health, strength and purity of mind, and is pleasant as *sattvika*. On the contrary, foods that are very bitter, sour or saltish, pungent and produce diseases are *rājasika*. Old and stale food, food that has lost its taste and flavour, petrified, spoiled and impure is *tamasika*. Thus, *sāttvika* food is most important factor contributing to one's development in his day to day activities. In the consiquent of accepting *sātvika* food the person develops the qualities of *sātvika* discipline. This practice has to be continued incessently through the walks of his life, during the observance of *brahmacarya āśrama*.

Being well-supported by the intrinsic qualities he requires to undergo some ritualistic *saṁskāras* like *Upanayana*, which certainly boosts up his hidden lustre and promotes his education systematically. It leads to emphasize that the education is one of the essentialities of personality development. To undergo a course of education both mental and intellectual faculties have to be firm substatums, without which education renders no fruit. Here arises a curiosity to know the nature of both mental and intellectual faculties determining the fundamentals of personality development.

Mental Determinant

The mind is superior to the body. It is the mind that makes the body, but not *vice-versa*. Mind is a repository of thoughts. Negative and evil thoughts make the mind weak. Weak and uncontrolled mind always succumbs to temptations, creating havoc with a person. The habit of brooding over failures gives rise to negative thoughts.

There are a few fortunate souls who are lucky enough to attain success without pitfalls; the rest have to pass through the hurdles and difficulties. But the real hero is he who welcomes challenges in life and faces them with boldness and courage.

A strong mind always remains calm even in adversities. It never succumbs to temptations, and develops tremendous courages to say 'No' to immoral thoughts and actions. It always remains free from prejudice, suspicion, and jealousy. Clarity of thinking makes it possible to take right decisions and come to right judgements. Such a mind will never indulge in wrong actions, prompted by evil emotions, such as desire, anger, greed, fear, hatred, etc., but will be always guided by serious, deep and right thinking. Positive thinking, concentration, fearlessness, adventurous nature, and self-confidence are the vital qualities of a strong mind.

The mind can be controlled by applying strong will-power and regular training. The body needs nutritious food, so does the mind need good ideas. Thought-power is a great source for strengthening the mind.

Intellectual Determinant

Intellectual strength is superior to physical and mental strength, and hence it forms an important part of our personality. Though this intellectual faculty is present in everyone, in most of the cases it remains dormant due to lack of proper training and intellectual exercise. Escessive use of modern electronic gadgets has converted man into a machine.

Originality, creativity, and deep thinking are taking leave of mankind; and artificiality, imitation and shallow and superficial thinking are making their presence felt everywhere.

To cultivate different talents creative thinking is absolutely necessary. Deep thinking brings out the hidden talents in man or woman in the form of inspiration, which is possible only through the power of concentration. The power of concentration helps to grasp subtle and higher things. And here comes the role of the intellect. Our senses and mind are restless. Since the intellect is superior to them, it alone can bring them under control. And, therefore, one must develop tremendous will power to control the mind and to fix it on higher things, to achieve success in life.

The other function of the intellect is to discriminate between right and wrong. The mind does not have that capacity. It can provide you a number of solutions for your problem, but it is for the intellect to choose the right one. This world is a mixture of good and bad; and, therefore, unless one cultivates this power of discrimi-nation, he will not be in a position to discriminate between the right and the wrong.

Once the mind gets addicted to such things, it is difficult to get out of their clutches. Hence, tremendous intellectual strength is needed to control the vagaries of the mind.

Intellectual strength is that which brings happiness to oneself and to the others. Otherwise, it is only cleverness or crooked intellect, which ruins oneself and the society.

Therefore, to develop a strong, discriminative and determinative intellect, it is necessary to cultivate intellectual faculty.

Socio-moral Determinant

The system of personality development regards socio-moral discipline as an indispensable priliminaries to the fulfilment of the life. An individual aspiring for personality development should be ethically equiped in the society in which he lives. He should influence the society with his ideal virtues. Ofcourse the *Śikṣāvalli* of the *Taittirīya Upaniṣad* grafically explains ethical codes of one's life. So to, other *Upaniṣads* like the *Īśāvāsya,* the *Kāṭhaka, Chāndogya,* the *Bṛhadāraṇyaka* among others enjoine the moral presepts in a significant manner. For instance, the *Īśāvāsya Upaniṣad* in its opening *mantra* मा गृधः कस्यस्वित् धनम्,

asks an individual to live the life of contentment without being greedy of other's wealth. Really, this is the right definition of *Vairāgya* or detatchment. Such many other precepts have been laid down in the *Upaniṣads* and the *Bhagavadgītā* too.

Similarly, truthfulness, non-stealing, non-violence etc. are essential qualities to be possessed by the person along the path of personality development. However, the *Yogadarśana* of Patañjali substantiates this view while enumerating the eight divisions of *Yoga*. As said their in, the discipline of *yama*[8] includes non-violence, truthfullness, non-stealing, continence and non-receiving of gift, likewise, another constituent i.e., *Niyama*[9] includes cleanliness (internal and external), contentment, mortification, study and self-surrenderness. Infact, the cultivation of all such qualities brings about the power of self-concentration in all his dealings. The term *svādhyāya* under *niyama* comprises one's duty conscious-ness. Conspicuously enough, the second *mantra* of *Īśāvāsya Upaniṣad* reiterates as below :

कुर्वन्नेवेह कर्माणि जिजिविशेच्छतं समाः ।
एवं त्वयि नान्यथेतोऽस्ति न कर्म लिप्यते नरे ।।

Īśāvāsyopaniṣad, *Mantra*-2

And the *Bhagavadgītā*[10] too expresses the same idea. The regulation of one's own duties promotes psychological spirit within oneself and reinforces the person to tread the path of his life without any disturbance due to mental distress. The mental energy gained by him makes a way to overcome all evil thoughts. With the *Saṁskāras* of all these qualities he remains in the society for its well-being by practice of compassion over it. Looking after the well-being of the society with the sense of universal brotherhood an individual should protect others to the best of his capacity, and show the path of righteousness to the extent of his satisfaction. At this juncture the foremost *puruṣārtha* i.e., *dharma* plays an important role in the life of an individual. Undoubtedly, following the path of righteousness contributes a lot to one's psychological growth.

As a matter of fact, spiritualism of Indian tradition has been a singular solution to overcome all such impediments. under the shade of spiritualism one should know the whole world, but unless it is realized one's own knowledge becomes destitute of significance. Wisdom consists in knowing oneself, i.e., one's mind and the living spirit and also in understanding why one seek it. And it is the wisdom that is essential for happiness.

As was already pointed out, one's personality development from physical to spiritual sphere primarily depends on the prescribed food he takes. In this connection the *Taittirīya Upaniṣad*[11] puts forth the doctrine of *five sheaths* (*pañcakośa*) of every individual. It is worthy to note here that, Vedic psychological philosophy, as interpreted by Yatīśwarānand,[12] the famous disciple of Śrī Rāma Kṛṣṇa, regards consiousness Ṣas the essence of personality" and the secret of strengthening of personality lies in its proper integration of one's body, mind, ego and spirit in a harmonious, intelligent and spontaneous way. Here, 'integration' does not mean the fractional unity in the Western sense, but a complete unity, to form into a perfect whole. Every cell in our body is like a tiny solar system and an organisation by itself. All such units form a part of the greater unit which we call a body. To impart movement to the body, these units must co-ordinate with the general movement; when this is not the case, disharmony or illness is definitely a result. So the body must be nourished with pure food, fresh air and good amount of physical activities which brings energy, strength, health and cheerfulness. Similarly, our mind is a 'synthetic whole' consisting of the faculties of cognition, feeling and willing. These faculties of mind are often at war with one another and create terrible confusion within the individual. There are conflicts of duties, conflicts of moral standards, conflicts of spiritual ideals. The individual may become the whirlpool of emotions struggling together if there is no integration which stands of purity, strength and harmony.

A Path from Physical to Spiritual Sphere

As said before the five sheaths of the soul have been described in Taittirīya Upaniṣad. The person consists of the essence of food. The gross physical body is the product of food. This is the first sheath. Different from and within it is the self that consists of life (*prāṇa*). The breath (*prāṇa*) is the life of all beings. Different from and within it is the self consisting of mind (*manas*). Different from and within it is the self consisting of intellect (*vijñāna*) which direct all deeds. Different from and within that which consists of intellect is the self consisting of bliss (*ānanda*). The true self is beyond the five sheaths : material (*anna*), life (*prāṇa*), mind (*manas*), intellect (*vijñāna*) and bliss (*ānanda*). This is the hierarchy of the factors of individual personality.

Thus 'integration', has its physical aspects, its mental aspects and also its spiritual aspects. In a properly integrated personality the 'ego' or individual's consciousness which directs and guides the mind and the body in a harmonious, intelligent and spontenious way. The individual feels harmonized and integrated when one is master of one's own mind and sponteniously follows the spiritual life without conflicts. The process of mental purification is called 'sublimation' in psychological terms. It is a process of giving a higher turn to the desires of primary instincts. Such a blessed personality sees the supreme spirit in himself and in all beings. His mind is neither shaken by misery nor upset by happiness. He becomes free from attachment, fear and anger and thus he is one with the 'supreme consciousness'. For the realisation of supreme consciousness one is bound to practise the yogic methods.

The predominant aspects of yogic methods fascilitating one's personality development are taken here into account.

Patañjali's Aṣṭāṅga Yoga

Patañjali has described eight steps in the pursuit of the path of his yoga. They are : 1. *Yama* (Abstinences), 2. *Niyama* (Observances), 3. *āsana* (Postual patterns), 4. *Prāṇāyāma* (Regulation and control of breath), 5. *Pratyāhāra* (Abstraction), 6. *Dhāraṇa* (Concentration), 7. *Dhyāna* (Meditation), 8. *Samādhi* (Absorption or Trance).[13]

These are the eight steps first five, namely, *Yama, Niyama, āsana, Prāṇāyāma* and *Pratyāhāra* have been graded as *Bahiraṅga Yoga* or external *yoga* practices, while the last three steps, namely, *Dhāraṇa, Dhyāna* and *Samādhi* are considered as *Antaraṅga* or internal *yoga*. Among these, *Pratyāhāra* is actually the link between the *bahiraṅga* and *antaraṅga yoga*.

Bahiraṅgayoga

Yama (Abstinences or rules of social conduct)

The word Yama, literally means control. Thus, this principle requires an individual to control his day-to-day behavior in relation to his environment without which moral behavior is not possible. The *yoga* system of Patañjali admits the following five *yamas* in abstinences[14] :

Ahiṁsā[15] or non-violence ensures that an aspirant should not injure any living being through body (काया), mind (मनसा), or speech (वाचा), i.e., by action, thought or speech.

When a man becomes steadfast in his abstention from harming others, then all living creatures will cease to feel animity in his presence.

Satya[16] The observance of non-violence indirectly implies the observance of truthfulness. When a person observes truthfulness, he gets the power of obtaining for himself and others the fruits of good deeds without having to perform the deeds themselves.

āsteya[17] or nonstealing, broadly means non-appropriation i.e., restrain from appropriating the property of other persons for personal use.

Brahmacarya[18] or continence or non-indulgence in sex refers to non-deviation from *Svadharma*, the law of one's being. However, the observance of celibecy is an important aspect as it plays a significant role in purification of mind and helps in conserving the energy and keeps physically and mentally fit.

Aparigraha[19] or non-possessiveness essentially refers to the restraint on a yogi for limiting his requirements. When a man becomes steadfast in his obstention from greed, he gains knowledge of his past, present and future existance.

Niyama[20] (observances or rules of personal hygiene)

The *Niyamas* which form the routine code of conduct consist of –

Śauca[21] refers to the practice of purity in every sphere of the bodily and mental activity.

Saṁtoṣa[22] means contentment. A mind which is in the state of contentment, one gains supreme happiness. Thus, he can concentrate and meditate.

Tapas[23] or austerity refers to the perfection of the sense organs and body often destruction of impurities by austerities.

Svādhyāya[24] or self study consists of developing a habit of devoting - regular time to the study of philosophy and spiritual texts, which remind the aspirant that the spiritual self is the reality.

Īśvarapraṇidhāha[25] consists of complete surrender to the God and the constant meditation. As a result, one achieves *samādhi*.

Āsana[26]

Āsana according to Patañjali is defined as '*sthira-sukham āsanam*'. Thus asana means seating oneself in comfortable sitting position. The practice of asanas have multidimentional roles to play in the practice of *yoga* and welfare of the mankind, namely, relaxation, meditation as well as correction and culture of physical body. *Yogāsana* is to assume a certain bodily position in order to encourage various vital organs and glands to function more efficiently leading in turn to an overall development of body and the mind.

The postures have been described in detail in different texts on *Haṭhayoga* such as *Gheraṇàa Saṁhitā, Haṭhayoga-Pradīpikā, Śivasaṁhitā* etc. Various postures appear to have been devised to rehabilitate various parts of the body or to provide appropriately stable and comfortable postures facilitating *Dhyāna* and *Samādhi*.

Prāṇāyāma[27]

Prāṇāyāma [(*Prāṇa* = breath) + (*āyāma* = pause)] is concerned with the control and regulation of breath and in a broader sense the control and regulation of vital force i.e., *prāṇa*. In Patanjali's concept, basically *prāṇāyāma* consists of four phases, viz.,

i) *Pūraka* (Inhalation)

ii) *Kuṁbhaka* (Pause or breath holding inside)

iii) *Recaka* (Exhalation)

iv) *Śūnyaka* (breath holding outside)

Ṭ *Pratyāhāra*[28] has been considered as an act of withdrawal of mind from sensory objects meaning thereby an inhibition of the mind from the sensorial perceptions.

Antaraṅgayoga

❐ *Dhāraṇa*[29] as prescribed by Patañjali, is a part of *Antaraṅga yoga* and includes it as a constituent of *Saṁyama*, a term applied to the composite entity of the three higher practices of *Antaraṅgayoga* namely, *Dhāraṇa, Dhyāna* and *Samādhi*. Patañjali considers *Dhāraṇa* (*concentration*) as the act of confining the mind within a limited mental area i.e., the object of concentration.

❐ *Dhyāna*[30] – Meditation is an unbroken flow of thought toward the object of concentration. As mentioned earlier *Dhāraṇa*, *Dhyāna, Samādhi* are the developed states of mind and are collectively designated as *Saṁyama*.[31] *Dhāraṇa* is the process of concentrating the mind in a particular area which is followed by *Dhyāna*, when the mental waves attain equillibrium under the influence of *Dhāraṇa* and *Samādhi* is the state of trance.

❐ *Samādhi*[32] as described by Patañjali, is that state when there is consciousness only of the object of meditation and not of the mind itself. This is the last state of concentration of the mind.

The different stages of *Samādhi* such as *samprajñatā* and *asamprajñatā*, represent progressive release of consciousness from its limitations and *Kaivalya* is that state in which it can again function in perfect freedom.

Among the various means of personality development in the spiritual sphere, numerous energy structures within and around the physical body play an important role. The energy channels (*nāàis*) function through subtle body, within which six *cakras* are situated. The most important of these *nāàis* are called *suṣumnā*, *iàā* and *piṅgalā*. Through these various *nāàis*, the *cakras* being boosted up by control over breath take up the vital energy from the subtle body of the person. By means of this energy system, the human being achieves higher levels of spiritual status.

This is how *yoga* is considered as the means or methods of getting the ultimate awareness or a means of approaching realization of the self by way of yogic methods. Identifying the retrospective effect on personality development, it is necessary to know the very basis of all the yogic methods culminating in the fulfilment of one's life. These are fundamentals of personality development in the context of Indian tradition and culture, are four-fold *puruṣārthas – Dharma, Artha, Kāma,* and *Mokṣa*. These *puruṣārthas* have been dealt with in the Vedic texts, *Rāmāyaṇa Mahābhārata* and other Sanskrit classical works. Without the knowledge, and the practice of these *puruṣārthas* one's personality development is null and void.

The personality development in the ancient literature speaks of multi-dimensional disciplines of personality development in a perfect symphony of human achievement. Many historic examples illustrate this point. No doubt, in the present days too, great philosophers and social reformers like Ramakrishna Paramahamsa, Vivekananda and Mahatma Gandhi among others, have achieved their goals to the best extent of their capacity. But after a gap of some decades, there prevailed a great lacuna in human disciplines throughout one's life and because of which, great politicians, scientists, philosophers of the present day, have met with many difficulties and their achievement fell in dismay. Hence, one can conclude that due to one's indifference or disinterestedness in the ancient practices that mould a man righteous, one keeps away oneself from one's success in one's particular endeavour. Hence, the practice of personality development in the fervor of ancient lore is of dire need of the day.

Adjudication of Eastern and Western Views

The opinions of the western thinkers like Hegel etc., regarding personality are given above to find out compatibility with those of Indian scholars, past and present. Whatever may be the width and depth of the opinions of the western philosophers, their thinking lies through four perspectives. Such as, physical, mental, intellectual and social. Yet, after an introspection of western opinions one need not be hesitant to state that western opinions, undergo certain changes according to the changes in world phenomena. While, howsoever the number of concepts are woven in the womb of personality development according to Indian thinkers, they have remained unchanged even after the lapse of thousands of years. Hence, it is evident, the concept of personality development as framed by Indian scholars has been flawless, unambiguous, effective, eternal and ever applicable. The reason behind it is that, the Indian scholars of the past, due to their meditative will-power, had supra-natural vision of the universal truths contributing to the well-being of his own and the society around him.

Although, *Varṇa* system as stated in the *Bhagavad-gītā* was prevailing strictly in the ancient period, the preceptors then did not consider any such social differences, but propounded the theory of personality development as accessible to the people then. In the consequent of this, the whole of the mankind had been benefitted at large, by bringing into practice all the disciplines of the personality development. Right from the Vedic age the aspect of duty-consciousness contributing to one's culture has been emphasized not only in the works of *Dharmaśāstra* but also in the philosophical works, which however are co-relative with each other. In fine, the Indian concept of personality development is all eternal and ever beneficial to the whole of the universe, with sound cultural background.

It is known to one and all that though the foreign culture is quite attractive now-a-days, it lays no impact on the people so far as one's own ethical development is concerned. On the other hand, Western thinkers have given wide scope for self-confidence and self-creativity, but such aspects have given no heed to the cultural aspects of their life. In turn, the elements of self-confidence, creativity and so on have encouraged the egoism in all the individuals whosoever is attracted among the children too. This growth of egoism resulted in the loneliness and hence dipression.

The luxurious, pleasure-seeking life-culture of foreign countries devastate their own life of ethics. In addition, the Indian culture at present, being much influenced by their luxurious culture suffers from essential need of ethics.

Thus, the mundane life of transitory pleasures naturally leads to unending desires of new scientific and technological developments; and causes conflict, tension and stress which disturb the equillibrium of life. To ward off such disturbed condition, Indian scriptures like *Vedas, Upaniṣads,* the *Bhagavadgītā* etc. teach the aspirants how to maintain equanimity, harmony through duty consciousness, righteousness meditation truthfulness, yogic practices. Such practice makes one free from stress as well as strain and finally leads to bliss of personality development of life.

Though the Westerns have excelled in developing the faculty of outer science, the Indians since the Vedic age struggled hard to understand, improve and to inculcate the faculty of inner science of their personality. This is however, has been witnessed by one and all.

With a view to lifting up the persons roaped into the cavern of luxurious foreign culture. Indian sages at present like Śrī Ramana Maharshi, Śrī Ramakrishna Paramahamsa, Swami Vivekananda and so on had and have been making efferts for the development of the society. The teachings and philosophy of these great personalities are positively based on the course of ethical life explained in the texts of ancient sages. Thus, it becomes clear that Indian concept of personality development is unfathomable and ever truth.

Reference

1. i) cf. V.S. Apte, *The Practicle Sanskrit English Dictionary*, Motilal Banarsidass, Delhi, 1978, p.893

   ii) Radhakantadev Bahadur, *Áabdakalpadruma*, Vol. 4, Motilal Banarsidas, Delhi 1961, p.529.

   iii) Brahmavadhuta Shrisukhanandanatha, *Áabdärthacintämaçiå*, Printwell, Jaipur, 1992, p.461.

   iv) Taranatha Tarkavachaspati, *Väcaspatyam*, Vol. VI, Choukhamba Sanskrit Series, Varanasi, 2002, p.4979.

2. H.Rheinfolder, "Das wart 'Persona' " Zsch f roman philol, Beiheff, 1928 77- pp 22 ff.

   Q– Gordon W. Allport, Personality – A Psychological Interpretation, Constable & Com. Ltd., London, 1955, pp.25-26

3. These various theories may be readily traced through Rheinfelder, op-cit. and Mulks op-cit.

   Q– Gardon W. Allport, *Personality A Psychological Interpretation,* Constable & Com. Ltd., London, 1955, p.25

4. Q– Ibid., p.26
5. Ross Stagner, *Psychology of Personality,* McGraw Hill Book Company, p.5
6. Ibid.,
7. Prof. P.Nataraj, *Psychology*, Srinivasa Publications, Mysore, 2005, pp.95-96.
8. अहिंसासत्यास्तेयब्रह्मचर्यापरिग्रहा यमाः । *Pätañjala Yogadaráana* - II-30
9. शौचसन्तोषतपः स्वाध्यायेश्वरप्रणिधानानि नियमाः ॥ Ibid - II-32.
10. कर्मण्येवाधिकारस्ते मा फलेषु कदाचन ।
मा कर्मफलहेतुर्भूः मा ते संगोस्त्व कर्मणि ॥ *Bhagavadgïtä* - II.47
11. अन्नाद्वै प्रजाः प्रजायन्ते । याः का श्च पृथिवीꣳश्रिताः अथो अन्नेनैव जीवन्ति । अथैनदपि यन्त्यन्ततः । अन्नꣳहि भूतानां ज्येष्ठम् । तस्मात्सर्वौषधमुच्यते । सर्वं वै तेऽन्नमाप्नुवन्ति । येऽन्नं ब्रह्मोपासते । अन्नाद्भूतानि जायन्ते । जातान्यन्नेन वर्धन्ते । अद्यतेऽत्ति च भूतानि । तस्मादन्नं तदुच्यत इति । तस्माद्वा एतस्मादन्नरसमयात् ।

    प्राणं देवा अनु प्राणन्ति । मनुष्याः पशवश्च ये । प्राणो हि भूतानामायुः । तस्मात्सर्वायुषमुच्यते । सर्वमेव त आयुर्यन्ति । ये प्राणं ब्रह्मोपासते । प्राणो हि भूतानामायुः । तस्मात्सर्वायुषमुच्यत इति । तस्यैव एव शारीर आत्मा । यः पूर्वस्य । तस्माद्वा एतस्मात्प्राणमयात् ।

    यतो वाचो निवर्तन्ते । अप्राप्य मनसा सह । आनन्दं ब्रह्मणो विद्वान् । न बिभेति कदाचनेति । तस्यैव एव शारीर आत्मा । यः पूर्वस्य । तस्माद्वा एतस्मान्मनोमयात् ।

    विज्ञानं यज्ञं तनुते । कर्मणि तनुतेऽपि च । विज्ञानं देवाः सर्वे । ब्रह्मज्येष्ठमुपासते । विज्ञानं ब्रह्म चेद्वेद । तस्माच्चेन्न प्रमाद्यति । शरीरे प्राप्मनो हित्वा । सर्वान्कामान्समश्नुत इति । तस्यैव एव शरीर आत्मा ।

    यः पूर्वस्य । तस्याद्वा एतस्माद्विज्ञानमयात् । अन्योऽन्तर आत्मानन्दमयः । तेनैव पूर्वः । स वा एष पुरुषविध एव । तस्य पुरुषविधताम् । अन्वयं पुरुषविधः । तस्य प्रियमेव शिरः । मोदो दक्षिणः पक्षः । प्रमादे उत्तरः पक्षः । आनन्द आत्मा । ब्रह्मं पुच्छं प्रतिष्ठां । तदप्येष श्लोको भवति ॥ *Taittirïyopanièad – Brahmanandavalli* – Anuväka 2-5
12. Yatïáwaränanda, *"How to integrate personality"*, contribution in *Vedänta for the Western world*, Ed., Christopher Ishwerwood, Allen and Unwin Ltd., London, 1948.
13. यम - नियमासन - प्राणायाम - प्रत्याहार - धारणा - ध्यान - समाधयोऽष्टावङ्गानि ॥ *Patañjali Yoga Sùtra* - II-29
14. अहिंसा - सत्यास्तेय - ब्रह्मचर्यापरिग्रहा यमाः ॥ Ibid - II - 30
15. अहिंसाप्रतिष्ठायां तत्सन्निधौ वैरत्यागः ॥ Ibid - II - 35
16. सत्यप्रतिष्ठायां क्रियाफलाश्रयत्वम् ॥ Ibid - II - 36

17. अस्तेयप्रतिष्ठायां सर्वरत्नोपस्थानम् ॥ Ibid - II - 37
18. ब्रह्मचर्यप्रतिष्ठायां वीर्यलाभः ॥ Ibid - II - 38
19. अपरिग्रहस्थैर्ये जन्मकथन्तासंबोधः ॥ Ibid - II - 39
20. शौच-सन्तोष-तपः स्वाध्यायेश्वरप्रणिधानानि नियमाः ॥ Ibid - II - 32
21. शौचात्स्वाङ्गजुगुप्सां परैरसंसर्गः ॥ Ibid - II - 40
22. सन्तोषादनुत्तमः सुखलाभः ॥ Ibid - II - 42
23. कायेन्द्रियसिद्धिरशुद्धिक्षया-तपसः ॥ Ibid - II - 43
24. स्वाध्यायादिष्टदेवतासम्प्रयोगः ॥ Ibid - II - 44
25. समाधिसिद्धिरीश्वरप्रणिधानात् ॥ Ibid - II - 45
26. स्थिरसुखमासनम् ॥ Ibid - II - 46
27. तस्मिन् सति श्वासप्रश्वासयोर्गतिविच्छेदः प्राणायामः ॥ Ibid - II - 49
28. स्वविषयासम्प्रयोगे चित्तस्वरूपानुकार इवेन्द्रियाणां प्रत्याहारः ॥ Ibid - II-54
29. a) धारणासु च योग्यता मनसः ॥ Ibid - II-53

    b) देशबन्धचित्तस्य धारणा ॥ Ibid - III-1
30. तत्र प्रत्ययैकतानता ध्यानम् ॥ Ibid - III-2
31. त्रयमेकत्र संयमः ॥ Ibid - III-4
32. तदेवार्थमात्रनिर्भासं स्वरूपशून्यमिव समाधिः ॥ Ibid - III - 3

2

Upaniṣadic Thought on Human Values and Personality

S. Ranganath

Upaniṣads known as Śruti prasthāna are the treasure trove of Indian wisdom which has made an indelible impression on the oriental scholars from times immemorial by highlighting the human values for the development of personality; and especially they are relevant in the twenty first century when modern man knows the price of every commodity and value of none.

Man who has no value sense, changes his behaviour according to moods. Man is not an object among objects but is the subject. He is the creator and bearer of values. He is no longer regarded as the "Crown of Creation" nor as made in the "Image of God". The value of man as a spiritual being of infinite worth is under fire today. Disbelief in this value has resulted in the attack on all attendant values; and hence a serious discussion on values and their relevance to modern youth in shaping their Personality becomes imperative at this stage.

The present paper intends to discuss some of the Upaniṣadic thoughts on human values like Truth or *Satya*, Faith or Śraddhā, Charity or Dāna, respecting the teachers or *Acharyas*, honoring the guests or *atithi*, sublimation of pride or *Ahaṁkāra*, to adopt humility or *Vinaya* and so on, in the light of *Bṛhadāraṇyaka*, Śvetāśwatara, *Taittirīya*, Muṇḍaka, Kaṭha, *Kena*, *Praśna*, *Chāndogya* and other principal Upaniṣads.

I. Satya or Truth

Taittiriya Upaniṣad belonging to **Krishna Yajurveda** narrates the importance of Satya by adopting the tow parameters of *Vidhi* and *Niṣeda*. Not only it states "*Satyaṁ Vada*" – speak the truth, but at the same time states – "*Satyānna Pramaditavyam*". There should be no inadvertence about truth. "*Muṇḍakopaniṣad*" emphatically states – *Satyameva Jayate* – only truth triumphs which has become our national emblem. To stress this point *Taittiriya* comes forth with the statement – सत्यं च स्वाध्यायप्रवचने च सत्यमिति सत्यवाचाराथीतरः – Truth, learning and teaching should be practiced. Truth is the thing what *Satyavacha* of the line of Rathiyara thinks. *Bṛhadaranyaka Upaniṣad* states that "The name of Brahman is Truth of Truths – अथ नामधेयं सत्यस्य सत्यमिति (1.3.6). Again, the oft quoted statement "Asatoma Sadgamaya" (1.3.28) lead me from unreal to real occurs in Brihadaranyaka. (1.3.28). Again Bṛhadāraṇyaka beautifully brings out the intermingling of Truth and Honey in a Poetic way which substantiates Shelly's statement – "Poetry beautifies Philosophy and Philosophy edifies poetry."

इदं सत्यं सर्वेषां भूतानां मध्वस्य सत्यस्य सर्वाणि भूतानि मधु (2.5.12) – This truth is like honey to all beings and all beings are like honey to this truth. Muṇḍakopaniṣad (2.2.2) states that Brahman is true. This is immortal. This is to be penetrated. O Good looking one! Shoot at it – तदेतत्सत्यं तदमृतं तद् वेद्धं सोम्य विद्धि. The immortal entity is covered by truth points out Bṛhadaraṇyaka with the following two statements.

1. तदेतदमृतं सत्येन छन्नम् (1.63.) and
2. नामरूपे सत्यं ताभ्यामयं प्राणच्छन्नः (1.6.2)

This immortal entity is covered by Truth. The name and form are Truth. The vital force is covered by them. This Truth leads us to the divine path states Muṇḍakopaniṣad (3.1.6): सत्येन पन्था विततो देवयानः (3.1.6). One know truth through the heart, therefore it is on the heart that Truth rests points out Bṛhadāraṇyaka:

हृदयेन हि सत्यं जानाति, हृदये ह्येव सत्यं प्रतिष्ठितं भवति (3.9.23).

The entrance to the Truth (Brahman) is covered by the Golden disc of Sun states Īśāvāsya . Do thou O Sun open it so as to be seen by me who am by nature truthful:-

हिरण्मयेन पात्रेण सत्यस्यापिहितं मुखम् ।
तत्त्वं पूषन्नपावृणु सत्यधर्माय दृष्यये ।। (Mantra 15)

While commenting on this verse, Swami Ranganathananda, the most effective speaker in the order of Ramakrishna after Swami Vivekananda, states – "Until and unless the Devil in us dies, the Divine in us will not shineforth."

II. Faith or Śraddhā

Śraddhā or faith is defined as

शास्त्रस्य गुरुवाक्यस्य सत्यबुद्ध्यावधारणा ।
सा श्रद्धा कथिता सद्भिः यया वस्तु उपलभ्यते ।।

Śaṅkarāchārya in his Vivekachūḍāmaṇi states - Śraddhā is that which is the total belief in the statements of the scripture's and the words of the peerless masters. This Śraddhā or Faith took possession of Nachiketa when his father was presenting gifts to the Brahmins:-

तं ह कुमारं सन्तं दक्षिणासु नीयमानासु श्रद्धा विवेश सोऽमन्यत । (1.1.2)

Taittiriya Upaniṣad states – *Śraddhayā deyam, Aśraddhayā Adeyam* – Give with reverence. Don't give with irreverence. The latter statement could be best described the way in which the father of Naciketa was gifting away useless barren cows as gifts:-

पीतोदका जग्धतृणा दुग्धदोहा निरिन्द्रियाः ।
अनन्दा नाम ते लोकाः तान् स गच्छति ता ददत ।।

He goes to those worlds that are known as joyless, who gives away the cows that have drunk water and eaten grass, whose milk has been milked for the last time.

This faith comes on account of trust; and hence Gandhiji states that "faith sees no disappointments in life". "It is the faith in the doctor which cures the patient more than the actual medicine which he prescribes" – states Radhakrishnan. Ramakrishna Paramahamsa opines that" One can acquire one's object of desire with faith".

III. Charity or Dāna

Charity or *Dāna* forms an important aspect of our value system. One should give with reverence and not with irreverence states *Taittiriya Upaniṣad*:-

श्रद्धया देयम् । अश्रद्धयाऽदेयम् । श्रिया देयम् । ह्रिया देयम् । भिया देयम् । संविदा देयम् । - The offering should be with honor, the offering should be with honor, the offering should not be with dishonor, the offering should be in plenty, the offering should be with modesty. The offering should be with awe. The offering should be with sympathy which is almost like a *Danamimamsa*. The *Chāndogyopaniṣad* states that one of the three branches of Dharma is Dana – त्रायो धर्मस्कन्धाः यज्ञः, अध्ययनं दानं चेति. Infact, Kathopaniṣad begins with the gifting away of useless barren cows.

IV. Respecting the Teachers or Guru

"GURU" is unique to Indian Tradition. The word Guru cannot be translated into any other language. The letter "GU" indicates ignorance and "RU" indicates remover. Hence Guru is one who removes the ignorance in the form of darkness and instills light in the form of knowledge. To, understand the nature of the Self one has to approach a Guru, states *Muṇḍakopaniṣad*:-

तद्विज्ञानार्थं स गुरुमेवाभिगच्छेत् समित्पाणिः श्रोत्रियं ब्रह्मनिष्ठम् ।

This was narrated in reality in Praśnopaniṣad :-

सुकेशा च भारद्वाजः, शैब्यश्च सत्यकामः, सौर्यायाणि च गार्ग्यः, कौसल्यश्च आश्वलायनो, भार्गवो वैदर्भिः, कबन्धी कात्यायनः हि एते ब्रह्मपरा ब्रह्मनिष्ठाः, परंब्रह्म अन्वेषमाणः एष ह वै तत्सर्वं वक्ष्यतीति ते समित्पाणयो भगवन्तं पिप्पलादमुपसन्नाः ।। (I.i)

The six students in search of the self approached the master Pippalada in keeping with the tradition. Here, the conversation between the teacher and the taught is narrated to highlight the quality of Humility which is a must to acquire knowledge.

Varahi Upaniṣad emphatically states that without the grace of Guru a disciple cannot attain his natural state. He cannot get Self Realization and cannot have control over his senses:-

दुर्लभा सहजावस्तः दुर्लभं तत्त्वदर्शनम् ।
दुर्लभो विषयत्यागो सद्गुरोः कृपया विना ।।

The pupil with the earnest desire of getting emancipation through self realisation used to approach a Guru and through a dialogue by adopting the mode of conversation used to be benefitted from a Guru as could be evinced in the Shilaka Dalbhya conversation, Ushasti – King conversation, Jānaśruthi – Raikva, Satyakāma – Haridruma conversation, Upakosala – Jābāli conversation, Nārada – Sanatkumāra conversation, as depicted in *Chāndogya Upaniṣad* or Usasti – Yajnavalkya conversation, Artabhaga - Yajnavalkya conversation, Kabandhi Yajnavalkya conversation, Gārgi - Yajnavalkya conversation, and so on as narrated in Bṛhadāraṇyaka Upaniṣad.

Taittiriya Upaniṣad states – *Ācarya devo bhava* – considered Acharya as god. The word Acharya is defined as:-

आचिनोति हि शास्त्रार्थान् आचारे स्थापयत्यपि ।
स्वयमाचरते यस्तु स तु आचार्य इति श्रुतिः ।।

The same Upaniṣad continues – "*Achāryāya priyam dhanam āhṛtya Prajatantum ma Vyava chetsih.*

Having offered the desirable wealth to the teacher, continue line of progeny, but don't cut off.

The teacher is the first form (of knowledge) and the pupil the second form – *Acāryaḥ Pūrvarūpam, Antevāsi Uttararūpam.*

Bṛhadāraṇyakopaniṣad. points out that one should not accept wealth from a disciple without fully instructing him:- (*nānariuśiṣya hareteta*) (4.1.2)

Śvetāśvatara Upaniṣad states that if the truths are told to a high minded person, who feels the highest devotion for god and his teacher as for god, then they will surely shine forth:

यस्य देवे परा भक्तिः यथा देवे तथा गुरौ ।
तस्यैते कथिता ह्यर्थाः प्रकाशन्ते महात्मनः ।। (6.23)

A Guru is supposed to instruct a *Siṣya* thus – whatever good works have been performed by our preceptors, only those should be performed by you, not the others as stated in *Taittirīya Upaniṣad* – यान्यस्माकं सुचरितानि तानि त्वयोपास्यानि नो इतराणि ।। (1.11)

Only Guru can make a Sisya cross over the bondage of *Avidyā*, thus points out *Praśnopaniṣad* :-

त्वं हि नः पिता योऽस्माकमविद्यायाः परं पारं तारयसि । (6.8)

V. Honouring the Guests or Atithi

A Guest is to be respected as a god, states *Taittiriya Upaniṣad: Atithidevo bhava*. From *Kathopaniṣad*, we know Yama treated Nachiketa as a worthy guest when Nachiketa went to Yamaloka to keep up the words of his father:-

तिस्रो रात्रीर्यदवात्सीगृहि मे अनश्नन् ब्रह्मन् अतिथिर्नमस्यः ।
नमस्तेऽस्तु ब्रह्मन् स्वस्ति मेऽस्तु तस्मात्प्रति त्रीन् वरान् वृणीष्व ।।
(1.1.9)

O Brahman, since you have lived in my house for three nights without food, a guest and an adorable person and let good accrue to me (By averting the fault arising) from that lapse. Ask for three boons – One in respect of each night.

Nachiketa like fire entered the abode of Yama says Katopaniṣad :-

वैश्वानरः प्रविशति अतिथिर्ब्राह्मणो गृहान् । (1.1.7)

Taittiriya Upaniṣad points out – न कञ्चन वसतो प्रत्याचक्षीत (3.10) Let him not utter unpleasant words to any one, who has come for shelter. Further *Taittirīya* states – अतिथयश्च स्वाध्यायप्रवचने च (1.9) Hospitality to guests and also the learning and teaching of the Vedas are to be practiced simultaneously.

VI. Sublimation of Pride or Ahaṅkāra

Pride comes before fall. This is nicely narrated in the Yakṣopakhyana of Kenopaniṣad which commences as – Brahma ha devebhyo vijigye tasya ha brāhmaṇo vijaye deva amahīyanta – It was Brahman indeed. That achieved victory for the sake of the Gods. In that victory, that was in fact Brahman's, the gods became elated.

> ब्रह्म ह देवेभ्यो विजिग्ये तस्य ह ब्रह्मणो विजये देवा अमहीयन्त त
> ऐक्षन्तास्माकमेवायं विजयोऽस्माकमेवायं महिमेति । तद्धैषां विजज्ञौ
> तेभ्यो ह प्रादुर्बभूव तन्न व्यजानत किमिदं यक्षमिति । (III.i)

They thought "Ours indeed is this victory. Ours indeed is this glory".

Brahman knew their pretension. He did appear to them. They could not make out about that thing as to what the Yakṣya might be. They said to fire, O Jataveda, find out thoroughly about this thing, as to what this Yakṣa is. He went to Yakṣa. Yakṣa interrogated him- "Who are you ? fire said – I am Jātaveda and I can burn down all that is on the earth. Yakṣa placed a straw and asked him to burn it.

Jātaveda approached It with vigour but could not do any thing and returned. Then it was the turn of Vāyu, and what happened to Agni also happened to Vayu. His pride was shattered that he could blow away anything and everything. Next, it was the turn of Indra who could not even see Yaksha. Thus, all the gods learnt a lesson that arrogance will lead them nowhere.

In the sixth chapter of *Chāndogya Upaniṣad* we have the illustration of the arrogant and highheaded Svetaketu returning from Gurukula and unable to answer a simple question posed by his father. Further, he was instructed by his father regarding the Mahavākya "*Tat Tvam Asi*" with nine examples.

VII. To Adopt Humility and Vinaya

Here, we have the classic example of a Guru as narrated in *Praśnopaniṣad*. When the six students pose questions to Pippalāda he humbly states that he wants some time to think about. If he finds answers, he would answer them otherwise he would join with them and ready to approach his own master to get clarification. This should be the attitude of a true seeker of knowledge.

Conclusion

One can remark on the above illustrations that a modern student can be successful in his career in building up a good personality if one follows the values such as practicing Truth, having indomitable faith, cultivating a sense of charity, respecting the elders and teachers, honouring the Guests, sublimating pride, adopting humility in one's life and so on.

References

1. Īśavasyopaniṣad
2. Kenopaniṣad
3. Kathopaniṣad
4. Taittiriyopaniṣad
5. Mundakopaniṣad
6. Chandogyopaniṣad
7. Praśnopaniṣad
8. Bṛhadāraṇyakopaniṣad
9. Śvetāsvataropaniṣad
10. Vivekacūḍāmaṇi

3

मनुस्मृतौ स्त्रीव्यक्तित्वविकासपरिकल्पना

Sujata M.N.

मनुस्मृतिः मनुमहार्षिणा विरचितः स्मृतिग्रन्थः। वेदकालीनसमाजे ये नियमाः आचरणयोग्याः आसन् तान् मनसि निधाय विरचितः ग्रन्थः इति सम्भावयितुं, शक्यते, इतिहासादवगम्यते च इति ह हास इत्युक्ते पूर्वम् एवं किल आसीत् इति। अत्र पूर्वमित्युक्ते स्मृतियुगे। स्मुतियुगः (क्रि. पू. 400) क्रि पू. पञ्चमशातकादारभ्यते। श्रुतेरनन्तरं स्मृतिः। स्मृतयः बह्व्यः सन्ति। तासु पाराशरस्मृतिः, याज्ञवलक्यस्मृतिः मनुस्मृतिश्च प्रसिद्धास्सन्ति। कत्तौ पाराशरः स्मृताः इति कलौ युगे पाराशरस्मृतिरेव वेदविदैरपि आद्रियते। मनु-याज्ञवल्वयस्मृतिभ्यां मेधातिथिः, कुल्लूकः, भारूचिः, विश्वरूपः, विज्ञानेश्वरादयः विस्तृतं व्याख्यानं व्यरचयन्। किन्तु पराशारस्मृतिव्याख्या विस्तरेण श्रीविद्यारण्यैः विरचिता। पराशरमाधवीयम् इति प्रसिद्धं च वर्तते।

मनुस्मृतिरपि प्रसिद्धा एवं। मनुमहर्षिविषये एवमुच्यते-

य: कश्चित्कस्यचिद्धर्मो मनुना परिकीर्तितः।

स सर्वोऽभिहितो वेदे सर्वज्ञानमयो हि सः।। 2-7 मनुस्मृतिः

आदरः, गौरवः, प्रीतिः, प्रसन्नता इत्यादिसझ्गुणैः उत्तमव्यक्तित्त्वं रूपते। व्यवहारे तस्य अभिव्यक्तिः व्यक्तित्वविकासाय कारणं भवति व्यक्तेः भावः

व्यक्तित्वम्। तस्य विकासः व्यक्तित्वविकासः अस्य सामान्यार्थस्यापेक्षया अर्थव्याप्तिः विस्तृता वर्तते। विभिन्नक्षेत्रेषु, उद्योगेषु, शालासु च व्यक्तित्वविकासार्थमेव कार्यक्रमाः परिणामकारिणः भवन्ति इति वक्तुं न शाक्यते। यतः अनुकरणं मनुष्यस्य स्वभावः। अतः महात्मा गान्धी महोदयः उक्तवान् दुष्टं न श्रोतव्यं, न द्रष्टव्यं, न वक्तव्यञ्च। परिसरेण अधिकाः जनाः प्रभाविताः भवन्ति। शैशवादारभ्य यौवनावस्थापर्यन्तं दिनस्य अधिककालं गृहे यापयति मनुष्यः तेर्हि गृहस्य परिसरः निर्मलः निर्दुष्टः च भवेत्। गृहे ज्येष्ठाः सर्वदा शुचिनः, उत्तमकार्येषु निरताः, संस्कारसम्पन्नाः, मधुरभषिणः, अध्ययनशीलाः, स्नेहशीलाश्चेत्यादिसद्गुणिनः भवन्ति चेत् पुत्राः अपि तर्थव वर्धयेयुः। पुत्राणां पालने, लालने पोषणे च स्त्रीणां दायित्त्वं पात्रं कर्तव्यञ्च महत्त्वपूर्णमेवा

अतएव गृहिणी गृहमुच्यते इति आर्योक्तिः तस्मादेव मनुस्मृतौ मनुमहर्षिणा स्त्रीणां रक्षणे, पोषणे, सम्माने च आद्यता दत्ता वर्तते तथैव तेषां नियमने निग्रहणे च नियमाः उग्राः वर्तन्ते। यत्र नार्यस्तु पूज्यन्ते रमन्ते तत्र देवता इति सः एकत्र वदति। अपरत्र।

'न स्त्री स्वातन्त्र्यमर्हति' इत्यपि स एव वदति। सामान्यतया इदानीन्तनदिनेषु इंद वाक्यं गृहीत्वैव बहवः मनुस्मृतिम् आक्षिपन्ति। सम्पूर्णश्लोकः एवमस्ति–

पिता रक्षति कौमारे भर्ता रक्षति यौवने।
रक्षन्ति स्थविरे पुत्रा न स्त्री स्वातन्त्र्यमर्हति।। इति

रक्षा नाम अनर्थप्रतीधातः इति मेधातिथिभाष्ये वर्तते। अनर्थस्तु अनाचारवृत्ततिक्रमेण - अप्रवृत्तिपरेण च अन्यायतो धन-हरणादिना परिभवः। तस्य प्रतीधातो निवारणम्। तत् पित्रादिभिः कर्तव्यम्। अस्वतन्त्रा इत्युक्ते सर्वकार्ये न स्वतन्त्रा इति न। यतः तत्र स्पष्टं उच्चते - नानेन सर्वक्रियाविषयमस्वातन्त्र्यं विधीयते, किन्तु स्वतः शक्तिविकलत्वात् स्वात्मसंरक्षणाय न प्रभवतीति कारणं सूचितम्।

1) स्वातन्त्र्यम्:- Every rule has an exception इति आङ्ग्लोक्ति:। यत्र नार्य: आत्मरक्षणसमर्था: तत्र तादृशा: स्त्रिय: स्वातन्त्र्यं नार्हन्ति इति वक्तुं न शक्यते। वेदकाले एव गार्गी मैत्रेयी इत्याद्या: ब्रह्मवादिन्यश्च आसन्। तथा चेत् इदानीन्तनकाले (क्रिश. प्रथम) शतकानन्तरं लक्ष्मीबाई राज्ञी भवितुं नासीत्। कित्तुरू राज्ञी चन्नम्मा, मल्लम्मा इत्याद्या: प्रजाभि: प्राशंसार्हा: न भवन्ति स्म। तथापि सर्वा: स्त्रिय: एता:इव सर्वदा धैर्योत्साहं प्रदशयितुं न प्रभवन्ति इति तु अवधेयांश एव। अन्यदेकमुदाहरणम् अभिज्ञानशाकुन्तलात् उद्धर्तुमिच्छामि, शकुन्तला स्वेच्छया गान्धर्वेण विधिना दु:ष्यन्तेन सा विवाहिता, किन्तु यदा पतिगृहं प्रेषिता तदा दु:ष्यन्तेन पत्नीत्वेन नाङ्गीकृता। अनन्तरं पतिविरहिता दु:खिता च भविष्यति। इदानीन्तन समाजेऽपि बहूनि एताहशान्युदाहरणानि हश्यन्ते एव। सुसंस्कृत समाजं मनसि निधाय स्त्रीस्वातन्त्र्यविषये भाषामहे। किन्तु मनु: चातुर्वर्ण्य समाजं मनसि विचारयन्नेव नियमान् रचितवान् स्यात् इत्यापि चिन्तयितृं शक्यते।

2) **सम्मानम्** - अपर: विचार: अस्माभि: अवगन्तव्य: यत् गृहे स्त्रिया दासीत्वेन वर्तितव्यम् इत्यपि तेन न उक्तम् 'पूजार्हा गृहदीप्तय: ? इति अभिप्रैति स:। अपि च यत्रैतास्तु न पूज्यन्ते सर्वास्तत्राफला: क्रिया: इत्यापि तेनैव उक्तम्।

यस्मिन् कुले तया दु:खमनुभूयते शीघ्रमेव तत्कुलस्य नाश: सम्भवति। अत: गृहे सा सन्तोषेण वसेत्। तदैव कुलस्याभिवृद्धि: इति तस्य विचार: वर्तते।

समाजस्य अभिवृद्धि: कथं सम्भवति। यदि तत्र उत्तमा: प्रजा: सज्जना: शिष्टा: विद्यावन्त: भवन्ति तर्हि उत्तम-समाजनिर्माणं साध्यम्। प्रतिगृहमपि तर्थव। अत: स: एवमभिप्रौति-

याशं भजते हि स्त्री सुतं सूते तथाविधं।
तस्मात्थजाविशुद्धयर्थं स्त्रियं रक्षेत्प्रयत्नतः।। 9-9

न केवलं शास्त्रोपदेशादेव स्त्री रक्षितव्या। तस्याः रक्षणात् स्वं, स्वस्य आत्मनः पुत्रान् च रक्षति। (अत्र पुरूषः एव अपमार्ग गच्छेत् किं कुर्यात? इति भावना उत्पद्येत। तस्यापि दण्डः सूचितम् किन्तु अत्र तु विषयः स्त्रीव्यक्तित्वविकासः)

व्यवहारदक्षता- आर्थिकविषये तस्याः सम्बन्धः आसीत् वा उत वेदकालादारभ्य एतावत्पर्यन्तमपि स्त्री गृहस्य आर्थिक-विषये चतुरा दृश्यते। सामान्यतया आये व्यये च तस्याः अवधानं विद्यते एव।

अतः उच्चते-

अर्थस्य सङ्ग्रहे चैनां व्यये चैव नियोजयेत्। 9-12
शौचे धर्मे ऽ तपक्स्यां च पारिणाहस्य चेक्षणे।।
गृहस्य सर्व-व्यवस्थानां दायित्वं सामान्यतया स्त्रीणामेव।

प्रसन्नता- कुलस्य शान्तिः, सन्तोषादयः गृहिण्याधारितं वर्तते-अतः सा सन्तुष्टा भवेत्-सुखी भवेत्। (विद्या ददाति इति उक्तम्-)

स्त्रियां तु शोचमानायां सर्वं तच्छोचते कुलम्।
तस्यां त्वशोचमानायां सर्वमेव न शोचते।। 3-62
सर्वे तस्याः तुष्टीकरणार्थं प्रयत्नं कुर्युः इति भावः न।

प्रीत्यादरौ - प्रीत्या, आदरेण व्यवहारः अपेक्षणीयः
सन्तुष्टो भार्यया भर्ता भर्त्रा भार्या तथैव च।
यस्मिन्नेव कुले नित्यं कल्याणं तत्र वै ध्रुवम्।। 2-60

स्त्रिय अपि स्वसन्तोषेण गृहे भांयम्। अन्यत्र क्रोध-शोकवशगे सत्यपि भर्तूर्दर्शने मुखप्रसादस्मित-नर्म-वचनादिना प्रहर्षो दर्शनीयः। इति व्याख्यायां उक्तमस्ति।

विवाहमन्त्रेऽपि वधूं आशीर्ववचनपूर्वकमेवं वदन्ति- सम्राज्ञी श्वशुरे भव। सम्राज्ञी श्वश्रुवां भव, सम्राज्ञी भव ननान्दरि, भव सम्राज्ञी अधि देवृषु।-इति

त्वां श्वशुरः श्वश्रुः, ननान्दाः देवरः आदरेण यथा तथा त्वया तैः सह वर्त्तितव्यं, व्यवहर्तव्यम् इति अत्र आशयः स्यात्।

महाभारते द्रौपद्याः वचने सेवा अयं भावः दर्शितः- नित्यमार्यामहं कुन्तीं वीरसूं सत्यवादिनीं।

स्वयं परिचराम्येतां पानाच्छादनभोजनैः।
नैतामतिशये जातु वस्त्रभूषणभोजनैः।
नापि परिवादे चाहं ता वृथां प्रथिव्या समाम्।।

सर्वमेव अभिज्ञानशाकुन्तले कण्धोपदेशस्तु प्रसिद्ध एव।

शुश्रूषस्व गुरून् (कुरू प्रियसखीवृन्तिं सपत्नीजने)
भर्तुर्विप्रकृतापि शोषणतया मा स्म प्रतीपं गमः।
भूयिष्ठं भव दक्षिणा परिजने भाग्येष्वनुत्सेकिनी
यान्त्येव गृहिणीपदं युवतयो वामाः कुलस्याधयः।। 4-28

मातरि भक्तिः- माता गर्भात्प्रभृति दशमवर्षपर्यन्तं जातस्य संवर्धने क्लेशं सहते। तस्य कलेशस्य निष्कृतिः वर्षशतैरपि कर्तुं न शक्यते इति मनुमहर्षेः स्त्रीविषयक-उदात्ताभिप्रायः अस्मिन् श्लोकद्वये हश्यते।

यं मातापितरौ क्लेशं सहेते सम्भवे नृणाम्।
न तस्य निष्कृतिः शक्या कर्तुं वर्षशतैरपि।। 2-227
अपि च तयोर्नित्यं प्रियं कुर्यादाचार्यस्य च सर्वदा।
तेष्वेव त्रिषु तुष्टेषु तपः सर्वं समाप्यते।। 2-228

मौल्यैर्विना व्यक्तित्वविकासः न भविष्यति इति उक्तम्। अहमपि तदङ्गीकरोमि। अतः अत्र मनुस्मृत्याधारेण स्त्रियः रूतरदायित्वम् प्रदर्श्य आदरः,

प्रीतिः, गौरवम्, श्रद्धा, सौहार्दमित्यादयः सद्गुणाः स्त्रीणां गृहस्य, समाजस्यपि स्वास्थ्यं साधयति इति।

1) अस्माकं व्यक्तित्वविकासाय निष्पक्षपातातया प्रामाणिकतया आत्मावलोकनम् कृत्वा यत्र दोषः तस्य अपनयने प्रयत्नं कर्तुं शक्यते।

2) अडङ्कारत्यागेन सरलभावः सम्पद्यते। तेन सद्गुणश्रेष्ठानां अनुसरणं कर्तुं शक्यते। गुणाः पूजास्थानम्।

3) किन्तु बालानां, पुत्राणां व्यक्तित्वविकासाय सर्वैः यत्नः करणीयः समाजहिताय।

4) तदर्थं तैः सह व्यवहारे जागरूकता आवश्यकी। यतः

    1) तैः सह सम्भाषणसमये उदासीनता दर्शिता चेत् ते ततः परं आसक्तिं न दर्शयन्ति

    2) न अवगच्छामत् ततः परं अस्माभिः सह विचाराविनिमये अनासक्ता भवन्ति।

तेषां भाषणेन व्यवहारेण क्रुद्धाः भवाम चेत् ततः परं अनिवार्यतया अस्माभिः सह समयं यापयन्ति।

एवं कुरु एवं मा कुरु इति उपदिशाम चेत् ज्यामितां दर्शन्ति अतः तेषां रूचिं, व्यवधानं च ज्ञात्वा एव प्रीत्या प्रशंसानुस्सरं दोषापनयने प्रयत्नं क्रियते चेत् (लघुबालकाश्चेत् कथाद्वारा एतत्तु संस्कृतसाहित्ये प्रसिद्धः एव – पञ्चतन्त्रादयः) उत्तमव्यक्तित्त्वनिर्माणं साध्यं इति चिन्तनीयम्

संदर्भग्रन्थसूची

1. स्मर्यते वेदार्थोऽनया इति स्मृतिः स्मृ-(आध्याने) क्तिन् (3.3.94); दाब्दार्थकौस्तुभः-6 सहित्यविद्वान् श्री चक्रवर्ति श्रीनिवासगोपालाचार्यः बाको प्रकाशन – बेंगलूरू

2. शोचन्ति जामयो यत्र विनश्यत्याशु तत्कुलं।
   न शोचान्ति तु यत्रैता वर्धन्ते ताद्धि सर्वदा।। मनुस्मृतिः 3-57
3. स्वां प्रसूतिं चरित्रं च कुलमात्मानमेव च।
   स्वं च धर्मं प्रयत्नेन जायां रक्षन् हि रक्षति।। 9-7
4. विवाहविधिप्रयोगः-होम्बालि प्रिन्टर्स - गदग
5. अभिज्ञानशाकुन्तलम् - Publisher Bharatiya Book Corporation, Delhi-1996.

4

Yājñavalkya's View of Personality Development

C. Shivaraju

स्मृतिर्नाम स्मर्यते वेदार्थः अनया इति। वेदोदित आचार व्यवहार-प्रायश्चित्तादि कर्म स्वरूप-प्रतिपादकं ब्रह्मस्वरूप-प्रतिपादकं च शास्त्रम्

-मंडिकल् विद्वान् रामाशास्त्री - आर्यधर्मप्रकाशिका

The Treatise which enunciates and defines and at some time, admonishingly instructs, Etiquettes (Ācāras), Behaviour (Vyavahāra), Atonement (Prāyaścitta), etc., in keeping with the spirit of the injunctions of Vedas and thus helps an Individual to become one with the 'Absolute-Parabramha', after having attained and developed the allround personality is named as "Smṛti" It is a manual of ethics and describes at length about various laws, such as laws relating to purification, laws relating to treasure-finds, laws about witnesses, laws about thefts, rules for house-holders, duties of the king, written document, breach of service contract, the duties of an ascetic, etc. The Smṛti text owes its existence to the Śrutis or Vedas. If Srauta karma directly refers to Śruti, the Smṛti text refers to the same indirectly.

प्रत्यक्षाः हि श्रुतयः श्रौतेषु स्मार्तेषु पुनः... स्मार्तानामपि वेदमूलत्वमुक्तम्
- मंडिकल् विद्वान् रामाशास्त्रि - आर्यधर्मप्रकाशिका

There are 18 Smṛti Texts written by 18 different authors, viz., Manu, Bṛhaspati, Dakṣa, Gautama, Yama, Angiras, Yogisvara Yajnavalkya, Pracetas, Satatapa, Parasara, Samvarta, Usanas, Sankha,- Likhita, Atri, Visnu, Apastamba and Harita.

एते हि अष्टादश प्रोक्ताः मुनयो नियतव्रता इति।
वैद्यनाथीयः - अध्याय 1

There are 18 Upa-Smṛtis also, written by Jabali-Naciketas, Skanda, Jatukarni, Paithinas, Gobhila etc. These Smrti Texts have been held in high esteem, right from the Vedic period, as they are authentically used as law-books in the administration of Justice, including social – religious and political problems.

Yajnavalkya-Smrti is one of such texts, written by Yajña-valkya, said to be a nephew and disciple of Sage Vaisampayana, and undoubtedly the greatest representative of the later Vedic-age. Vaiśampayana is said to be one of the four pupils of Veda-Vyasa, the other three being Paila, Jaimini and Sumanta. By studying these texts, one can become free from misconception and misdirection, etc., with reference to the eternal values of life.

Personality Development and Smṛti-Texts

One may ask the pertinent question that what is the good of giving advice from the texts, when people are trodden with the problem of basic needs like food-shelter and clothing ? But we should not forget that even the Smṛti texts advocate and uphold the charity of food to the needy as the paramount Dharma, instead of giving sermons on the code of conduct. This can be substantiated by an Upanisadic line-

अन्नं न निंद्यात्, अन्नं बहु कुर्वीत, तद् व्रतं, अन्नं ब्रह्म।
–तैत्तिरीय उपनिषत्

Endeavour to secure an abundance of Anna, etc., following and practicing the precepts of Dharma, is the only path to Sreyas (well-being), for mankind. This can be followed by those who have strong and healthy bodies. This is possible through proper food and proper living. This form of Tapas helps to understand one's own self which amounts to the Personality Development, right from Anna-maya-kosa to Ananda-maya-kosa.

One should daily offer food to manes and human beings, atleast water should be definitely offered. He should seldom cook the food only for himself.

बाल–स्ववासिनी–वृद्ध–गर्भिण्यातुर–कन्यकाः।
संभोज्य अतिथिभृत्यांश्च दम्पत्योः शेषभोजनम्।।
–आचाराध्याय–पु–38, 1–105

"The householder should offer the food among the children, married woman, old people, pregnant woman, the diseased, the maiden, servant and guests. Then the couple should eat what remains."

In a nutshell, what has been explained by Upanisad, has been fully explained by this Smrti text, taking into account both Anna-saksatkara and Daiva- saksatkara which makes an individual a complete man.

Personality Development – These is no discrimination at all among the Varnas to aim at total development of a person as such, for example, the classical texts make it clear that the practice of Pañca-mahāyajña, especially, feeding of guests arriving at one's door, is enjoined upon Gṛhasthas of all Varnas. Yājñavalkya-Smṛti specifically asserts that a Śūdra-gṛhastha should never neglect the performance of Pañca-mahāyajñā observance, though he may abbreviate the ritual associated with the offerings of food to only the recitation of Namaskāra-Mantra:

भार्यारतिः शुचिः भृत्यः भर्ता श्राद्धक्रियारतः।
नमस्कारेण मंत्रेण पंचयज्ञान्न हापयेत्।।
-आचाराध्याय-पु-43, 1-121

A man should be devotedly attached to his wife, but should shun *Parastri* and *Veśyāgamana*. He should be pure both internally and externally. Proper maintenance and care for the attendants, parents and children, should be given. He should perform all religious rites including the Yajnas or sacrifices while reciting the saluting hymns to gods. This is the most significant aspect of the precept of Pañca-mahāyajña.

One who desires to develop and maintain good personality must adhere to the principles of good conduct: *Acarāh paramo dharmah.*. According to Yājñavalkya, Kama (desire), is not merely a passion, but born out of good determination. This is being guided by Śruti, Smṛti, Sadācāra, an act that pleases one's soul and a desire arisen with outright resolution to complete the accepted work.

श्रुतिः स्मृतिः सदाचारः स्वस्य च प्रियमात्मनः।
सम्यक् संकल्पजो कामः धर्ममूलमिदं स्मृतम्।।
- आचाराध्याय-पु-5, 1-7

Dharma is nothing different from the manner of right living. It is also a desire born of due deliberation in addition to other meanings such as – "to uphold, to sustain privileges, duties and obligations of a man". These are the things which make a person ideal as well as practical.

Personality Development with Reference to Women

Personality does not mean an unbridled independence. This is very much true with reference to the protection of a woman. It is in the fitness of things that an "abata" should be protected at any cost. It is also the firm conviction of Yājñavalkya that she should be protected by her father during adolescence, by her husband after marriage and by her son in old age. In the absence of these, she should be protected by her relatives.

रक्षेत् कन्यां पिता, विना पतिः, पुत्रास्तु वार्धके।
अभावे ज्ञातयः तेषां न स्वातंत्र्यं क्वचित् स्त्रियः।।
-आचाराध्याय-पु-31, 1-84

In the absence of the last two sources, the king should protect her:

पक्षद्वयावसाने तु राजा भर्ता प्रभुः स्त्रियाः।
-आचाराध्याय-पु-51, मिताक्षर

Thus restraining the self-willed act of a woman, amounts to the good personality development, according to Yajnavalkya, one of the most remarkable sages, known for his scholarship, experience, liberality, etc.

The True Personality Development cult boils down to the view expressed by a wise – saying-

अयं निजः परो वेत्ति गणना लघुचेतसाम्।
उदारचरितानां तु वसुधैव कुटुंबकम्।।

This is fully substantiated by Yājñavalkya while enumerating the duties of a house holder. One of such duties is to feed the needy and disabled and finally the Yajamāna should take the residual food -I-105. One can notice through this example, Yajnavalkya's concern with the whole creation as such. This concern with reference to all beings is echoed by Manu also in what he says as:

तृणांनि भूमिरुदकं वाक् चतुर्थी च सूनृता।
एतान्यपि सतां गेहे नोच्छिद्यंते कदाचन।।

The idea is, even a poverty trodden person can honour a guest. The houses of Good men never lack in these four things, namely, grass, shelter, water and good speech.

The all-round personality of a king is described while prescribing various duties for a king:

शास्त्राणि चिंतयेद् बुद्ध्या सर्वकर्तव्यता तथा।
ब्राह्मणेषु क्षमी, स्निग्धेषु अजिह्मः, क्रोधना रिषु,
स्याद्राजा भृत्यवर्गेषु प्रजासु च यथा पिता।।

The king should ponder over all duties and scriptures with self-application of mind. He should behave with Brahmhanas with forgiveness, the relations and the affectionate with simplicity, the enemies with wrath (or anger) and should be like a father to his attendants and the subjects (in the form of 'hitakāraka' and ahitanivartaka, as Mitaksara interprets).

अति सर्वत्र वर्जयेत् is a dictum. While describing the administration of king Atithi, Kalidāsa enlightens us as follows: World gets agitated, if the ruler become too cruel; he gets humiliated, if he becomes too soft or lenient; thus avoiding these two extremities, he should resort to the golden media of these two, being impartial. Thus indication how the king's personality should be:

The same being echoed by Yājñavalkya:

रिपौ मित्रे च ये समाः ... 2 व्यवहार प्रकरणम्

The prakarana deals with lending of Money (Ṛṇadhana prakarana which should be based on sound legal concepts and righteous practice, according to Yājñavalkya. For example, loan taken by the father is to be repaid by sons and grandsons, if the former becomes unable to pay on account of his death. This amounts to both character-ethic and personal ethic, under the shade of personality development.

अविभक्तैः कुटुंबार्थे यद् ऋणं तु कृतं भवेत्।
दद्युः तत् रिक्थिनः प्रेते प्रोषिते वा कुटुंबिनि।।
-व्यवहाराध्यायः, 2-45, पु-129

Personality development often involves strict measures. The following may be cited as a pointer to it: Money taken on lending, but spent on immoral things and vices need not be returned by borrower's dependents. That non-payment of borrowed money" does not constitute "the breach of law and violation of good personality".

सुराकामद्यूतकृतं दंडशुल्कावशिष्टकम्।
वृथादानं तथैवेह पुत्रो दद्यात् न पैतृकम्।।
-व्यवहाराध्यायः, - 2-47, पु-129

A son should not make any repayment of the loans taken by his father for drinking, for debauchery, for gambling, for arrears of the tax and fine, a futile gift to a rogue, ill-reputed doctor, cheater, etc., for any fine, fee and the gifts pertaining to his father. Thus it is an exception to the Rule-"Putra-pautraihṛṇam deyam"- according to Mitaksara. He also adds-

धूर्ते कितवे शठे... दत्तं दानं भवति निष्फलम्।
न दातव्यं तु प्रत्रेण यच्च न व्यावहारिकम्।।
-पु-399, मिताक्षरा

This is the timely advice to the parents, that they should not make their children liable and answerable for their illegal affairs, thereby the future legacy may develop good personality.

Similarly, the personality and image of some of the cultured house wives remain untarnished, if they become unable to repay the debt that they personally incurred, to uplift their respective families.

गोपशौंडिकशैलूषरजकव्याधयोषिताम्।
ऋणं दद्यात् पतिस्तेषां यस्माद् वृत्तिस्तदाश्रया।।
-व्यवहार अध्याय- 48, पु-130

As the livelihood of cowherds, brewers, actors, washermen and hunters depend on their wives, the husband should repay the loan, if any, raised by their wives, because their livelihoods are depending on him. Another nicety of Yajnavalkya's view is, how he views the duties and privileges of an individual, in a holistic way, without curbing their individual rights may be illustrated by this stanza-

पितृभ्यां यस्य यद्दत्तं तत् तस्यैव धनं भवेत्।
पितुरूर्ध्वं विभजतां माताप्यंशं समं हरेत्।।
-व्यवहार अध्याय-123, पु-154

Whatever money is given by the parents to any of the sons, if permissible under law, becomes the property of that son only. If the partition takes place among the sons after the death of their father and their mother without Stridhana, she is also entitled to get equal share in the property that is, whatever gift given by parents out of love, before partition of the property, that cannot be further divided and shared by all sons. Mitākṣara says:

a) न्यायसाम्यात् विभागात् प्रागपि यस्य यद् दत्तं, तत् तस्यैव, न विभागार्हम्; समं = स्वपुत्रांशसमं अंशम् -

-मिताक्षर, पु-657

b) असंस्कृतास्तु संस्कार्या भ्रातृभिः पूर्वसंस्कृतैः।
भगिन्याश्च निजाद् अंशाद् दत्वांशं तु तुरीयकम्॥

-व्यवहार अध्याय-124, पु-154

If partition is made among the sons after the death of their father, it is the duty of the elder brothers to co-operate with the younger brothers in their auspicious ceremonies, if the same has not been done. If the sisters are not married at the time of partition, each brother should give one fourth part of his share, or money equal to the value of one fourth of the share, for the marriage of those sisters.

Indeed all these matters are indispensable for life. Yājñavakya was one of the best judges of his time's, in addition to being a great philosopher, a true and ideal house-holder, coupled with rare virtues like unsophisticated generosity, clemency, learning, simplicity, and spirit of tolerance towards the customs and manners of others. He is more liberal in having given us, a comprehensive view on all Desa-dharmas and Kala-dharmas.

All these examples, though not seem to be referring to the cult of personality development, yet they suggestively highlight the respective sublime personalities who contributed their might and share, not only for the uplift of an individual, but of the society as a whole, amidst where they lived and left their impression for the futures to imbibe, irrespective of parents or children or brothers and sisters.

Opportunities for Personality Development

Many opportunities are provided for any individual right from a lower person up to the highest authority, to get enlarged his personality by rendering timely service to the community as a whole. This may be illustrated as follows:

The public utility must be kept in mind by a person who aspires for a good personality. In this context, Yajnavalkya, emphatically advices, that whatever the gifts in the form of token of appreciation, an individual receives, it must be surrendered to the group (leader) as a whole entity. Even the name and fame of a king gets magnified if he honours the representatives, on the priority basis, by giving suitable gifts and refreshments, since it envisages public interest. The gifts given by the king or any government officer does not amount to "bribing"; on the other hand, both the king and the representatives become covetable in the eyes of public for their yeoman service, just like the legend of king Raghu of Ayodhya and the rare disciple of sage Varatantu – Kautsa. This is how a good personality should be cherished.

A deep need of personal congruency and effectiveness and for healthy relationships with other people is intended here along with integrating i) Integrity ii) Humility, iii) Fidelity, iv) Modesty, v) Courage and other principles into our basic character

समूहकार्यं आयातान् कृतकार्यान् विसर्जयेत्।
स दानमानसत्कारैः पूजयित्वा महीपतिः।।
-व्यवहार अध्याय-2-189, पु-176

"The king should give priority to the representatives of public (because, they deal with projects of public welfare). They should be welcomed, given appropriate time to hear their grievances. Some gifts, refreshments etc. can also be offered to these representatives."

समूहकार्यं प्रहितो यल्लभेत तदर्पयेत्।
एकादशगुणं दाप्यो यद्यसौ नार्पयेत् स्वयम्।।
-व्यवहार अध्याय-2-190, पु-176

It is binding on a person, sent for some work of a group, that he should surrender to his group, whatever he has received there as a gift document etc. on his return. In case he does not surrender the same to his group, he shall be punished with fine not lesser than eleven times the cost of goods, things, document, prize, etc., so received (III-190).

While discussing stri-sangraha-prakarana- (A chapter on Adultery with women), Yājñavalkya gives a timely warning to a person who is bent upon attaining a noble personality, that holding an untimely and unreasonable talk with an unknown woman at an improper place and sharing the same seat with her, goes to establish the charge of Adultery. So a sensitive and wise man should avoid such incidents, which bring disgrace and unrepairable damages to his personality":

नीवीस्तनप्रावरणसक्थिकेशावमर्दनम्।
अदेशकालसंभाषं सहएकासनमेव च।।
-व्यवहार अध्याय-2-284, पु-205

The holding of a cloth, covering her breast, catching her by the hair, sitting on the same seat with her, establish the charge of adultery.

Views of Personality Development with reference to a Sanyāsin

An individual who desires to become an ideal ascetic should first fullfil his obligatory duties and then he may adorn the seat of a Yati.

अधीतवेदो जपकृत् अन्नवान् अन्नदो अग्निमान्।
शक्त्या तु यज्ञकृत् मोक्षे मनः कुर्यात्तु नान्यथा।।
प्रायश्चित्ताध्यायः, -3-57, पु-230

He alone is qualified who has studied the Vedas, practiced Japa and Tapa, who has begot a son, who has given food to the needy, conducted the sacrifices and finally concentrated his mind on emancipation or Mokṣa. A Yati becomes loveable and respectable by his discipline, austerities and by his kind disposition towards all living beings, begs alms after controlling the senses, by not entering the house where there are domestic animals in addition to the presence of other hermits who have come before.

This is how a person becomes duly qualified to become an Ascetic. External features like Daṇḍa, Kamaṇḍalu are not of much importance, and they do not really make a person, a true Sanyāsin.

नाश्रमः कारणं धर्मे क्रियमाणो भवेत् हि सः।
प्रायश्चित्ताध्यायः, -3-65, पु-232

That is, he becomes qualified and venerable due to his constant practice on the Eternal Truth called Parabrahma. He should be an abode of the following principles in addition to their practice namely.

सत्यं अस्तेयं अक्रोधो ह्रीः शौचं धीः धृतिः दमः।
संयतेंद्रियता विद्या धर्मः सर्व उदाहृतः।।
प्रायश्चित्ताध्यायः, -3-66, पु-232

Through these statements, one can get a glimpse of what makes Sanyāsa as an ideal personality, during Vānaprastha and Sanyāsāśrama.

These are some of the views of Yajnavalkya on personality development which embraces all aspects of human life. He is very precise, impartial and unambiguous while mentioning the characteristic features of any particular system, without harming the interest of male or female or any living being.

It is not a mere conjecture or hypothesis, but a "veritable-fact" that Yogiśvara-Yājñavalkya was a 'ture dharmajna' He was a practical sanyasin as well as a śrotriya-yajamāna. He was a parivrat in spirit and a true house holder, performing many sacrifices. To him, there was no distinction between the two Asramas. He specifically states that even Sanyasa, the last stage of life is not superior to the other Asramas. All the stages are of equal importance, so far as the object of life is concerned

आत्मलाभात् न परं विद्यते

To summarize, according to Yajnavalkya, "what lies behind us" and "what lies before us," are tiny matters, compared to "what lies within us".

This "within us" is indeed the nucleus and kernel of his work which amounts to true personality which may be called as Ātma - darśana through Yoga-darśana. This is a deliberate integration of life and principles, squaring with inner thought and outward behavior resulting in personal as well as public integrity. This is nothing but self-introspection without which no ideal personality can be seen. Really the seer Yājñavalkya is "neither an optimist, nor a pessimist but a "POSSIBILIST".

Bibliography

1. THE MITAKSHARA with Visvarupa and Commentaries of Subodhini and Balambhatti, Edited by – S.S. Setlur, B.A;LL.B., Brahmavadin Press, George Town, Madras. Year -1912.

2. Yajnavalkya. Smṛti of yogisvara-Maharsi. Yājñavalya [Sanskrit Text, English Translation with copious notes] Tr. By-B.S.Bist with an Introduction By- Dr. Urmila Rustagi, Published By-The Vrajajivan Indological studies and Chaukhamba Sanskrit publications.
3. Yājñavalkya. Smrti:- Published by- Nag publishers, II.A./W.A, Jawahar Nagar, Delhi.
4. Yājñavalkya. Smrti:- Tr. Nagesha Rango Kulakarni, Samaja Pustakalaya, Dharwad.
5. Foundations of Indian culture by Chidambara Kulkarni.
6. Arya Dharma Prakashika by Mandikal-Vidwan Rama Sastry Mysore.
7. History of Dharma Shastra, Vol-I By P.V. Kane, BORI, Pune, 1999.

References

1. The pages referred to here, belong to the Text-Book, Translated by B.S. Bist.
2. Mitakshara commentary- edited by S.S. Setlur.

5

Gleanings from Rāmāyaṇa on Personality Development

Shankar Bhat

Personality development is the mantra of modern world. In the modern context, concept of personality development is originated in western world as result of industrialization and liberal democratic system. In this background, we have to analyze the concept of personality development in Indian context.

This chapter is divided into four units, i.e.:

1. What is development?
2. What is personality development?
3. Personality development in Rāmāyaṇa
4. Conclusion

According to Leonard Frank, "Development is in third world, development is a debauched word, a whore of a word. It's users can't look you in the face. It is an empty word which can be filled by any user to conceal any intention, a trojan horse of a word. It implies that what is done to people by those more powerful than themselves is their fate, their potential, their fault. (Leonard Frank in '*The Development Game*')

Ashis Nandy says, "In the last eighty years few words have been as intensely discussed, glorified or attacked as 'Development'. Development has come into the southern world as an analogue of two process, modern science and modern colonialism, seeking legitimacy in a new civilizing mission. The ideology of development has come to faithfully mirror the key ideas of the colonial world view. (Ashis Nandy 2004)

This development projection is added to personality, and it became personality development. Thus the concept of personality development is also the product of liberal democratic view of the west. Its main intention is the protection of the interests of the capitalists.

Personality means a lot of different things to a lot of different people. Our personality actually plays a huge part in how we perceive the world and how the world perceives us.

Personality is dervied from the Latin word '*persona*', which means mask. Thus personality stands for the way we present ourselves to others or the others view us.

Western psychologists tried to define personality on psychological basis. Sigmund Freud attempted to explain individual differences by examining how our unconscious mental forces affect our thoughts, feelings and behaviours. Freud analysed personality with the help of three concepts namely, Id, Ego and Superego. There are mental concepts referring to certain processes or activities.

Neo Freudians like Alfred Adler, Carl Jung and Karan Horney have proposed theories of their own. Adler's theory is known as 'Individual psychology'. He believed that our behaviour is purposeful and goal directed. Horney disagreed with Freud on his extreme emphasis on biological detriments. She gave the concept of anxiety as a basic factor in understanding about personality. Jung termed his approach as 'Analytical psychology' and proposed collective consciousness and archetype. He believed that the collective consciousness is identical in the people of a given community and is inherited.

All these thinkers defined personality as behaviour, and referred only the outward characteristics of the person. When they talk about personality they refer to important behavioural or dispositional characteristics which distinguish one individual from other.

In Indian context, our sacred books like Vedas, Upanishads and Epics are worth studying; there is no mention of personality development as defined by western scholars, but we can see several illustrations about developed personalities. Our texts have given much importance to inner quality of the individual. We used the term '*Vyaktitva Vikasana*' in the place of personality development. According to our sacred books, human personality develops as a result of the meaningful interactions of the body, mind and spirit and evolves normally from lower to a higher state, i.e. Tāmasic to Sāttvik.

Thus in Indian context personality development means integrated individuality. Cultures and values are the base on which a person builds his personality and character. Epics like Rāmāyaṇa and Mahābhārata teach an individual the way to life enriching his personality. Similarly personalities are built on these values and cultures.

Rāmāyaṇa acts as the training ground and preparing individual soul for its eternal pilgrimage. The study of Rāmāyaṇa contributes to an integrated development of a human being, a vigorous body, a strong will, a powerful intellect and chastened and mellowed spirit.

The ideologies, beliefs, motives, actions and reactions symbolized in the epic are applicable for all times and for all ages. They have taught man for several centuries how life should be led and what should be the ultimate goal of life, socio-moral values. Values also elevate a man to spiritual level by purifying him both internally and externally, though the observance of social and moral discipline after studying this book.

Personality development in Rāmāyaṇa lies with the ideal relationship between individuals and performance of one's duty. i.e. Dharma. From the study Rāmāyaṇa we can see all these ideals are incorporated in day to day life. Rama is the repository of all that is noble and virtues, truths, charity, penance, detachment, friendliness, purity, straightforwardness, service to his precptors and help to the needy in adversity are the real ideal characters.

Daśaratha and Kausalyā stands for the ideals or parental affection and self sacrifice. Lakśmaṇa and Bharata epitomize fraternal love; Sita exposes the value of chastity, wifely fidelity. Sugreeva represents true friendship, Hanuman is unique in devotion and service to his master.

Rāmāyaṇa begins with the question by Valmiki to Nārada that, 'Is there anyone in this world at present who is full of virtues and at the same time possessed of great prowess, who knows what is right, is well versed in Dharma, who is conscious of service done, truthful and of firm resolve?.

कोन्वस्मिन्साम्प्रतं लोके गुणवान्कश्च वीर्यवान्
धर्मज्ञश्च कृतज्ञश्च सत्यवाक्यो दृढव्रतः (रा. बा. 1-5)

Nārada was delighted by this question and addressed the following words.

श्रुत्वा चैतत्त्रिलोकज्ञो वाल्मीकेर्नारदो वचः
श्रूयतामिति चामन्त्र्य प्रहृष्टो वाक्यमब्रवीत् (रा. बा. 1.6.20)

There is one born in the race of Ikshvāku and known by the name of Rāma. He has fully controlled his mind, is very powerful, radiant and resolve and has brought his senses under control. He is intelligent, sagacious, eloquent, glorious and an exterminator of foes. He knows the secret of virtues and is true to his promise. He is intent on the good of the people. He is illustrious full of wisdom, pure in his dealings, a man of self control and sharp mind. He is protector of all living beings and a staunch defender of righteousness (Dharma). He is well principled and protects his people. He knows the truth. He possessed of a bright intellect and good memory. He is gentle, noble and shrewd and is loved by all. He is a replica of Lord Vishnu in prowess and soothing like the moon. In anger he resembles the conflagration at dissolution. He is a counterpart of mother earth in forbearance, steadfast in truth like Lord Dharma. These qualities which Rama possessed are the attributes of good personality.

There are several instances which give us the idea of ideal behaviour or character of a person.

During the time of Rāma's coronation, Daśaratha advises Rāma as constantly keep your senses under control. Avoid vices born of lust and anger. Further he advises on administration. Here importance attached to personal discipline and farsightedness in matters of efficient administration will be evident from foregoing.

कामतस्त्वं प्रकृत्यैव विनीतो गुणवानसि
गुणवत्यपि तु स्नेहात् पुत्र वक्ष्यामि ते हितम् (रा.अ. 3-42-46)

When Bharata approaches to Rāma at Chitrakuta, Rāma advises Bharata, which highlight the duties and responsibilities of kingship covering all aspects and the entire range of administration in which king should attain proficiency if he was really concerned with the happiness and welfare of his subjects.

आघ्राय रामस्तं मूर्ध्नि परिष्वज्य च राघवः
अंके भरतमारोप्य पर्यपृच्छत्समाहितः (रा.अ. 100-3-76)

Starting with human relations at home and Bharata's personal conduct and self discipline, the questions cover his reverence and service to his parents, teachers and elders to ensure domestic harmony. it embraces all departments of government activity like home affairs, defense, foreign affairs, finance, labor relations, agriculture etc. Since each stanza begins with the word 'kācit' it is known as the *kācit sarga* of Rāmāyaṇa.

Śūrpaṇakhā's advice to Rāvaṇa is very surprising to note that she talks on administration. After her mutilation by Lakshmana for her foolish misadventure, she rushes to Ravana's court and criticises him on his lapses in public administration and tenders him advise on good administration.

ततः शूर्पणखा दीना रावणं लोकरावणम्
अमात्यमध्ये संक्रुध्दा परुषं वाक्यमब्रवीत् (रा. अर. 33-123)

Rāma is the man of duty conscious and adherence to Dharma is the essence of good personality. When mother Kauśalya and also the citizens of Ayodhya plead with Rama not to go to the forest, Rāma replies that Dharma lies in obeying the words of the father and that he being devoted to Dharma, cannot transgress the words of his father. Rāma says, 'I can renounce my life, Lakshmaṇa and Sita but I cannot break my promise'.

मया चैव भवत्या च कर्तव्यं वचनं पितुः
राजा भर्ता गुरुः श्रेष्ठः सर्वेषामीश्वरः प्रभुः (रा.अयो. 24-14)

When Vibhishana comes to Rāma he says, 'when the oppressed seeks relief at the hands of a virtuous and capable person, it is supreme Dharma to protect the surrendered even at the cost of one's life'. Rāma revealed his supreme Dharma by saying that even if the surrendered person is Rāvaṇa himself, he would save even those that deserve to be killed'.

अतो वा यदि वा दृप्तः परेषां शरणं गतः ।
अपि प्राणान्परित्यज्य रक्षितव्यः कृतात्मना (यु. 18-28)
आनयैनं हरिश्रेष्ठ दत्तमस्याभयं मया ।
विभीषणो वा सुग्रीव यदि वा रावणः स्वयम् (यु. 18-34)

The essence of an individual is manifested through his action. The character exhibits itself in action mental, verbal and physical. Therefore Dharma of an individual operates through every action of an individual. It is that basis from which personality springs.

Valmiki presented the functional aspect of Dharma throughout Rāmāyaṇa to show how it opertaes in the life of a person.

Rāma justifies his action on the basis of the sole principle of Dharma. He says, 'I am not introducing some such righteousness and Dharma unfavourable to thee, that has never been practiced before. I am simply treading that path that had been approved and followed by the predecessors.

नाहं धर्ममपूर्वं ते प्रतिकूलं प्रवर्तये।
पूर्वैरयमभिप्रेतो गतो मार्गोऽनुगम्यते (रा.अयो. 21-36)

Vālmiki often refers to Rāma's behaviour that was exemplary and served as a model to any one who would like to tread the path of Dharma. Quite often Vālmiki uses such expressions as –

Rāma always devoted to the welfare of the subjects

He does not injure any one
He is the protector of living things
He is beloved to the whole world
He is devoted to the well-being of the whole world.

Any such expressions are used to describe Rama and his behaviour which is Dharma itself in essence.

Conclusion – The philosophers of ethics identify four specific stages of the development of personality within a person, They are –

1. Strength of will
2. Extending the mental horizon and developing a better insight
3. Cultivating a sense of discipline and regular performance of one's own duties and
4. Developing the attitude of honesty in thought, nobility in feeling and sincerity in action.

Rāma exhibited all these at every stage of his action. Therefore he is rightly called '*Dharma personified*'.

The world today is experiencing a period where relationship based on the economy, individualism and greed is at an all time high. This is because success is productivity driven and allows business and corporate life to take precedence over family life and personal goals. Rāmāyaṇa assimilates principles of science and psychology within its broader fold of spirituality and wisdom and thus affords an all inclusive solution.

Bibliography

1. Ashis Nandy: Development, Science and Colonialism, Winter,1996
2. Jan Nederveen Picterse: Development Theory/Deconstruction/ Reconstruction, Sage Delhi 2001
3. J.S.Rajput: Need for moral values to Indian youth, The Ramakrishna Mission Institute of Culture
4. M.G. Prasad: Relevance of Ramayana, Osborne Terrace, Maplewood
5. Valmiki Ramayana: The Educational Supplies Depot, Palghat.

6

विदुरनीत्यां व्यक्तित्वविकसनम्

भीमसेनाचार्य पाण्डुरङ्गि

महत्वाद् भारवत्वाच्च महाभारतमुच्यते'' इत्युक्तरीत्या महाभारतम् वैशिष्ट्ययपूर्ण निर्णयग्रन्थेषु सर्वोत्कृष्टग्रन्थमित्युच्यते। ''न भारतसमं शास्त्रं'' इति तस्य महती शास्त्रेत्वेव श्रूयते। ''निर्णयः सर्वशास्त्राणां सदृष्तान्तोद्धि भारते'' इत्युक्तरीत्या समस्तशास्त्रीयप्रमेयपुञ्जः भारतादेव निर्णेतुं शक्यम्। एतत् न कौटुम्बिककलहं अधिकृत्य व्यासैः विरचितम्। किन्तु अधापि परिशुद्धजीवनं सुखशान्तिसमाधानेन निर्वर्तयितुं दर्पणायितोऽयं ग्रन्थराजः। सात्विकशक्तेः विजयः, दुष्टशक्तेः पराजयः, असूयादीनाम् प्रतीकानां दुर्योधनादीनां अधोगतिवर्णन परतया, ज्ञानभक्ति विरक्तिनां प्रतीकानां भीमादीनां औन्नत्यवर्णनपरतया महाभारतम् मानवीय मौल्यानां – उत्तुङ्गशिखरे संस्थापितः रचितः एकैकनिर्णयग्रन्थः अत एव अस्य ''जयो नामेतिहासोऽयं'' इति – नामान्तरमास्ति।

प्रकृते तु मानवीयव्यक्तित्वविकसने महाभारतोक्तनीतिबोधकवाक्यानि सर्वकालीनानि, सर्वदेशीयोपयुक्तानि, सर्वजनानुकरणीयानि इति प्रत्येकं न वक्तव्यमस्ति तत्रापि विदुरनीतिः व्यक्तित्वविकसने बहूपयुक्ता इति सर्वैर्मान्या। संसार गाढान्धकार मार्गे दीपायितेयं विदुरनीतिः न केवलं बाह्यचक्षु विद्रोनस्य

धृतराष्ट्रं प्रति उपदेशपरा इयं नीतिः किन्तु अन्तश्चक्षुर्विहीनानाम् अस्मदादीनामपि दिव्य तेजः प्रभा इव देदीप्यते। जीवने प्रतिघटेषु स्खलतां पततां जनानां उद्धर्तुं इयं विदुरनीतिरूपा यष्टिः अस्मदादीना आधारः। विदुरनीतेः अनेकानि व्यख्या नानि सन्ति तेषु श्रीमद्वादिराजतीर्थानां लक्षाभर णाख्यं व्याख्यानमव्यपूर्वतया राराजते। सर्वासु अवस्थासु, बाल्ये, यौवने, वृद्धाच्ये च ततद्योग्य कर्मावबोधने, तत्तदव्यक्तित्वविकसने, विकासने च कुमुदिनीनां चान्द्रीप्रभेव विद्योतते।

एषा महाभारतीय-उद्योगपर्वणि, प्रजागराध्यायेषु सुप्रथिता अस्ति। के ते प्रजागराः? किं किमर्थं प्रति ते प्रजागरीति इति चेत्

विदुरः उवाच-

अभियुक्तं बलवता दुर्बलं हीनसाधनम्।
तस्वं कामिनं चोरमाविशन्ति प्रजागराः॥

यः बलिष्ठैः सह विरोधवान्, बुद्धयादिसाधनसामग्रिहीनः परकीयद्रव्यादि भागमपि स्वयमेवभोक्ता, परवनिताभोगलिप्सावान्, चोरः एते पञ्च प्रजागरा इत्युच्चन्ते। ते अहर्निशं चिन्तातुरा, निद्राविहीना भूत्वा सदा जागरिता वर्तन्तां। अतः एव श्रेयस्कामैः एते दुर्शुणः हातव्याः एव।

तथैव -

ईर्षुर्घृणी न सन्तुषृः क्रोधनो नित्यशङ्कितः।
परभाग्योपजीवी च षडेते नित्यदुःखिताः॥

चरोन्ततिमसदुमानः, निष्करूणि, सदा कोपविप्तः, सदा संदेहयुक्तः, परेषां भाग्यानां अवलम्ब्य उपजीवि चा राते सदा दुःखिताः। अतः पडेते दोषाः स्वात्मव्यक्तित्व विकसने त्याज्या एव।

वेषभूषणमपि व्यक्तित्वोद्धरणे महत्वं पात्रमावहति।

यो नोद्धतं कुरुते जातु वेषम्।
न पौरुषेणापि विकथ्यतेऽन्यान्।

न मूर्छित कटुकान्याह किञ्चित्।
प्रियं सदा तं कुरुते जनो हि।।

वेषभूषमपि मनुष्यस्य गौरवमानयति च। सभ्यभारतीयवेषमादरणीयम्। "कुवस्त्रता शुभ्रतया विराजते" इति नीतिः। विकृतवस्त्रैः स्त्रियश्च सामाजिक स्वास्थ्यं नाशयन्ति इति भाति।

स्वकीयपराक्रमजल्पेन परनिन्दाकरणमपि दोषावहमेव। परं प्रति रोषपूर्णविकृतनिन्दां न कर्तव्यम्। एतानि वाक्यानि स्वजीवने पालितानि चेत् सः सर्वजनादरणीयो भूत्वा प्रियो भवति।

आर्यसम्मतमेव कार्यं कुर्यात् कारयेच्च।

के ते आर्याः इति चेत् वक्ति –

"न वैरमुद्धीपयति प्रशान्तं न दर्पमारोहति शन्तिमेति।
न दुर्गतोऽस्मीति करोत्यकार्यं तमार्यशीलं परमाहुरार्याः।।"

शन्ति–समृद्धिवातावरणे स्थिते यत् किञ्चित् पूर्वतनद्वेषाग्निँ उद्भाव्य यः नोद्दीपयति; यः दर्पं अहंङ्कारं न प्रदर्शयति। सत्यपि भयकारणे मदात् – तदभावप्रदर्शनं दर्पः।

यः तद्धर्पं नारोहति, शान्ति समृद्धिमेति।
अहं दुरवस्थायां अस्मीति मत्वापि यः
अकार्यं न करोति तं पूज्यस्वभावं
श्रोघ्रपुरुषं आर्याः इति आहुः।।
विवाहं विवादं वा समैरेव कुर्यात्। न
अस्मदुत्तमैः माधमैः सह कुर्यात्
यदुक्तम्
ययोरेव सम वित्तं ययोरेव सम बलम्।
तयोर्विवाहो मैत्री च नोत्तमाधमयोः क्वचिता।।
तदेवोक्तं विदुरेणापि –

समैर्विवाहं कुरुते न हीनैः
समैः सख्यं व्यवहारं कथां च।
गुणैर्विशिष्टांश्च पुरो दधाति
विपश्चितस्तस्य नयाः सुनीताः।।

विवाहो मैत्री च समेष्वेव शोभते। गुणविशिष्टान् जनानेव पुरतः कृत्वा तदाध्यदन्ये एव सत्कार्यं कुर्यात्। एवं क्रियमाणे सति तस्य सकला आपदः परिहृताः भवन्ति।

कार्यो कार्यविवेकः सदसद्विवेकोऽपि व्यक्तित्वविकसने मुख्यः। व्यक्तिश्चित्कार्यं कृत्वा यम तेन किं प्रयोजनं, अकरणे का हानिः इति सम्यक् विचार्यैव कार्यं इति उक्तं विदुरेण -

किंनु मे स्यादिदं कृत्वा किंनु मे स्यादकुर्वतः
इति कर्माणि सञ्चिन्त्य कुर्याद्वा पुरुषो न वा।

"बालादपि शुकादपि" इत्युक्तरीत्या सारग्राही पुरुषः छन्मन्त प्रलापेऽपि यदि गुणं विद्यते तत् गृहीशुत्येव, तथैव बालस्य परिजल्पेऽपि यदि गुणं विद्यते तदपि गृह्णात्येव अश्रमन्यः यथा काञ्चनं गृह्णाति तर्थवेत्यर्थः। न कमपि उदासितव्यमिति तात्पर्यम्। --

"अप्युन्मत्तात् प्रलपतो बालाच्च परिजल्पतं
सर्वतः सारमादद्यात् आश्रमभ्य इव का रचना

सर्वाभरणेषु शीलं परं भूषणम्

यथोन्तम् - शीलं प्रधानम् पुरूषे तद्यस्येहप्रणइश्या न तस्य जीवितेनार्थो न धनने न बन्धुभिः।। यदि धनहानिर्भवति तदा तत्पुनः लब्धु शक्यम्। यदि कालं नष्ट किञ्चिन्नष्टमेव। यदि शीलं नष्टं तर्हि सर्वमपि नष्टमेव।

If Money is Lost Nothing is Lost
If Time is Lost Something is Lost
If Character is Lost Everything is Lost

जिता सभा वस्त्रवता
मिष्टाशा गोमता जिता।
अध्वा जितो यानवता
सर्वं शीलवता जितम्।।
यदि श्रेष्ठं वस्त्रं धृतं तेन सभावशी भवति।
यदि क्षीरदध्याज्यं वर्तते तत् सुग्रासं भवति।
यदि यस्य उत्तमयानो वर्तते सः मार्गं सुलभमेवतिक्रमति।
यदि उत्तमशीलमस्ति तर्हि तेन सर्वं जितमेव।।

वाग्भूषणं भूषणम्

राजा धुन्नतस्थनेषु अलङकृतानां पुरुषाणां वाक् संयमो अत्यन्त दुर्लभम्। तदवश्यं सम्पादनीयम्। यमत्कृत वाक्यानि, आनन्दवर्धक वाक्यानि मनुष्याणां भूषणान्येव यथोक्तं विदुरेण-

"वाक् संयमो हि नृपते सुदुष्करमयो मतः। अर्थवच्य विचित्रं च न शक्यं बहुभाषितम्।। यदि दुर्भाषितं चेत् तत् अनर्थायोपपद्यते। अतः मधुरं, मङ्गलकरं, मितं यो वक्ति तस्य व्यक्तित्वं वर्धते एव।

यदि वृक्षं वा वनं वा परशुना हतमपि पुनः तद्रोहते एव। किन्तु यदि वाक्शरैः दुर्भाषितदुरूक्तं चेत् तत् वाक्क्षतं हृदयं न पुनः वेदनां हीयते।

यथोकतं --

रोहते सायँ कैर्विद्धं वनं परशुना हृतम्। वाचा दुरूक्तं बीभत्सं न संरोहति वाक्क्षतम्। वाक्शल्यस्तु न निर्हर्तुं शक्यो हृदिशयो हिसः।।

पण्डित पदव्याख्या

प्रथमतः को नाम पण्डितः को वा मूढः? कथं च तद्गुणाः अस्मासु आनेयाः, सम्भावनीयाः कथं मूढजनमौढ्यं निरसनीयमिति द्रक्ष्यामः।

1. निषेवते प्रशस्तानि निषेवते प्रशस्तानि निन्दितानि न सेवते।
   अनास्तिकः श्रद्धधानः एतत्पण्डितलक्षणम्।

यो नरः प्रशस्तानि – शास्त्रविहितानि कर्माणि एव निषेवते, निन्दितानि – सुजनैर्गर्हितानि कर्माणि न सेवते, यश्च पारमार्थिकोऽस्ति, परलोकः वर्तते, पुण्यपापानि सन्ति इति मन्यमानो मानवः, गुरूदेवादिषु विश्वासयुक्तो हि पण्डितः इत्युच्यते–

तथैव

2. "क्रोधो हर्षश्च द्वी स्तम्भो मान्यमानिता यमर्थात्तापकर्षन्ति सर्व पण्डित उच्यते।।

यं पुरुषं क्रोधः, हर्षः, दर्पः, (परावज्ञानं), ह्री अकार्यकरणे लज्जा, मपन्यमानिता स्वयं मान्यं मानादि–मन्यमानत्वं इत्यादयः यं पुरूषं नामकर्षन्ति सः पण्डितः इत्युच्यते।

पुनश्च वक्ति–

3. क्षिप्रं विजानाति चिरं श्रृणोति
   विज्ञाय चार्थं भजते न कामान्
   नासंपृष्टो व्यपयुङ्क्ते परार्थे
   तत्प्रज्ञानं प्रथमं पण्डितस्य।।

तदर्थस्तु–

यो नरः परप्रयुक्तवाक्याभिप्रायं झटिति विजानति यद्वा परेङ्गितं शीघ्रमेव विजानाति, ज्ञानदर्याय चिरं यः श्रुणोति, असम्पृष्टः यथावदप्रष्टः परार्थे न व्याख्यानं कुरुते, तत् पण्डितस्य प्रथमं लक्षणम्। तल्लक्षणं अस्मद्व्यक्तित्व विकसने अवश्यं सम्पादनीयम्।

तथैव

4. नाप्राव्यमभिवाञ्छन्ति नरा नेच्छन्ति शोचितु।
आपत्सु च न मुह्यन्ति नराः पण्डितबुद्धयः।।

यल्लब्धुमशक्यं तदलभ्यवस्तुपलभ्यने ये जनाः नेच्छन्ति,

यथोक्तं-

अयोग्यमिच्छन् पुरुषः पतत्येव न संशयः इति। किञ्च ये जनाः नष्टं प्रति नानुशोचन्ति, यथोक्तं "गतस्य शोचनं नास्ति" तथैव विपत्काले ये न मुह्यन्ति, ये न किंकर्तव्यमूढतामालम्बन्ते, एतत् त्रयं पण्डितलक्षणम्।।

किञ्च स्वप्रयत्नसाध्यं इदं कर्मेति निर्धार्यैव यः कार्यमारभते, न तु डोंलायमानबुद्धया। तथा कर्मणो अन्तमध्ये नोपरमते, अमूल्यं समयं यो निष्फलं न कुरूते स एव पण्डितः इति विदुरः पुनः तल्लक्षणमभिदधाति-

निश्चित्य यः प्रक्रमते नान्तर्वश्नति कर्मणः।
अवन्धकालो वश्यात्मा स वै पण्डित उच्यते।।

तथैव-

शिष्टयोग्यकर्मकरणे एव अनुरागयुक्तः सन् ऐश्वर्यकराणि कर्माणि कृत्वा, स्वकीय हितोपदेशकर्तारं हितं, पथ्यं प्रति न असूयेर्त्त्यादिकं कुरुते, सोऽपि ज्ञानी एव

आर्यकर्मणि रज्यन्ते भूतिकर्माणि कुर्वते।
हितं च नाभ्यसूयन्ति पण्डिता भरतर्षभ।।

"... तथा मानापमानयोः"

इति गीतोक्तरीत्या यः पुमान् समबुद्धया तिष्ठति सोऽपि ज्ञानी।

न दृष्यत्यात्मसम्माने नावमानेन तप्यते।
गाङ्गो दृढ़ इवाक्षोभ्यो यः स पण्डित उच्चते।

यः केनापि हेतुना अचाल्यमानः सन् गङ्गायाः गंभीर दृढ इव क्षोभहीनो भवति सः ज्ञानी।

सर्वप्राणिनां तत्वं यो जानति, सर्वकर्मणां रचनाप्रकारं यो वेत्ति मनुष्याणां मध्ये यः उपायज्ञः सः ज्ञानीत्युच्यते।

यः उपन्यासवेलायां अकुष्टितवचनः लोकवार्ताभिज्ञः तर्केण यद्विषयंजानाति, तत्कालस्फूर्तिमान प्रतिभायुक्तो नरः पण्डित इत्युच्यते –

यथोकतं – प्रवृन्तवाक् चित्रकथः ऊहवान् प्रतिभावनवान्।
आशुग्रन्थस्य वक्ता च यः स पंण्डित उच्यते।।

यस्य ज्ञानं बुद्धयनुसारं यस्य बुद्धिः शास्त्रानुसारिणी। आर्याणां मर्यादां अनुल्लघ्य वर्तते स चापि पण्डितः

तदुक्तं – श्रुतं प्रज्ञानुगं यस्य प्रज्ञा चैव श्रुतानुगा।
असम्भिन्नार्यमर्यादः पण्डिताख्यां लभेत सः।।

पुनरेवं आह

अर्थं महान्तमासाद्य विद्यामैश्वर्यमेव च।
विचरत्यसमुत्तद्धो यः स पण्डित उच्चते।।

महान्तं प्रयोजनमासाद्य विद्यामैश्वर्यं च लब्ध्वाऽपि यः किञ्चिदपि विचलति, अर्थात् गर्वाहंकारयुक्तो न भवति सः एव विचक्षणः।।

अयमेव अभिप्रायः गीतायां अपि भाति

दुःखेण्वनुद्विग्नमनाः सुखेषुविगतस्पृहः।
वीतरागभयक्रोधः स्थितधीर्मुनिरुच्यते।।

दुःखेषु प्राप्तेषु सत्स्वपि यस्य चितं नोद्विग्नं भवति

सुखेषु सत्सु विषये विगतेच्छो भवति, अशोभने शोभनाध्यासः भयं क्रोधः इत्यादिभ्यो अपगत बुद्धिर्भवति सः तादृशो मुनिः अपरोक्षज्ञानीत्युच्यते।

पुनः आह गीताचार्यः–

यः सर्वत्र नातिशायितस्नेहो भूत्वा, वत्तत् शुभाशुभं प्राप्यापि नभिनन्दति सन्तोषं आप्रोति, न द्वेष्टि नापि द्वेषं कुरुते सः ज्ञानी -

यः सर्वत्रानभिस्नेहः तत्तत्प्राव्यशुभाशुभम्।
नाभिनन्दति न द्वेषि तस्य प्रज्ञा प्रतिष्ठिता।।

एवमादिपण्डितलक्षणान्यभिधाय तानि लक्षणानि यथायोग्यतया अस्मास्वपि आरूढानि कर्तुं प्रयतितव्यम्। मानवानां व्यक्तित्वविकसन विषये एते विदुरोक्तगुणाः अवदुयं संग्राहयाः तत्रोप्सुभिः।

2. **मूढपरव्याख्या**

मूढानां लक्षणमपि ज्ञात्वा तद्विहातुमपि मनुष्येण प्रयतितव्यम्।

यचोक्तम्-

अश्रुतश्च समुन्तद्धो दरिद्रश्च महामनाः
अर्थांश्चाकर्मणा त्रेप्सुर्मूढ इत्युच्यते बुधैः।।

यः ज्ञानिनोऽपि अत्यन्तमुद्धतः सन्, दरिद्रोऽपि अधिकेच्छायुक्ताः, द्यूतादिना अकर्मणा द्रव्यादिकं प्राप्तुमिच्छति सः मूढः इति ज्ञानिभिरुच्यते।

यः स्वप्रयोजनमर्थं परित्यज्य केवलं परार्थमेवानुतिष्ठति मित्रप्रयोजनार्थ मिथ्या वदति, व्यर्थ व्यर्थं कर्माचरति सः मूढः इति उच्चते।

तदुक्तं -

स्वमर्थं यः परित्यज्य परार्थमनुतृषति।
मिथ्या चरति मित्रार्थे यथा मूढः स उच्चते।।

स्वं सर्वतोमुखदृष्टया मित्रान् परित्यज्य स्वमित्रत्वं अनिच्छतो जनान् यः वाञ्छति, यः बलिष्ठं द्वेष्टि सोऽपि मूर्ख एव

यदुक्तं-

अकामान् कामयति यः काममानान् परित्यजेत्।
बलवन्तं च यो द्वेष्टि तमाहुर्मूढचेतसम्।।

तदेव अन्यदुलोके विवृणोति।

अमित्रं कुरुते मित्रं मित्रं द्वेष्टि हिनस्ति च।
कर्म चारभते दुष्टं तमाहुर्मूढचेतसम्।।

इममेव अभिप्रायं भारविर्मन्यते।
"अहो दुरन्ता बलवद्विरोधिता"।। इति।।

यानि स्वकीयकर्तव्य कर्माणि स्वयमकृत्वा भृत्यादि द्वारा प्रवर्तयति, सर्वत्र सर्वविषये अतीव चिकित्सां करोति; शीघ्रतया कर्तव्यानि विलम्बेन वहुकालपर्यन्तं करोति, एतत्त्रयमपि मूढलक्षणम् - उक्तं च भारते-

संसारयति कृत्यानि सर्वत्र विचिकित्सते।
चिरं करोति क्षितार्थे स मूढो भरतर्षभ।।

अन्यच्च-

अनाहूतः प्रविशति अपृष्टो बहु भाषते।
अविश्वस्ते विश्वसिति मूढचेता नराधमः।।

आह्वानं विना न कस्यापि गृहं प्रविशेत्,
'नापृष्टुः कस्यचिद् ब्रूयादित्यादिना अपृष्टुः
बहु जल्पते, विश्वासानर्हेषु विश्वासं कुरूते सोऽपि मूढ एव

स्वयं दोषेणैकेन वर्तमानोऽपि परं तेनैव दोषेण क्षिपति यश्च प्रतीकारं कर्तुमसमर्थोऽपि यस्मै क्रुध्यति सोऽपि मूढः

तदुक्तं -

परं क्षिपति दोषेण वर्तमानः स्वयं तथा
यश्च क्रुध्यत्यनीशानः स च मूढतमो नरः।

किं च स्वशिष्याशासनमकृत्वा, शिष्येतरनरं यः शासितुं प्रवर्तते। अदातारं यो दातारमिति मत्वा बहु सेवते सोऽपि मूढत्वपदवीं गच्छेदेव।

अन्यच्च

एकया द्वे विनिश्चित्य त्रीश्चतुर्भिवशीकुरु।
पञ्च जित्वा विदित्वा षट् सप्तह्वित्वा सुखी भव।

एतदर्थो इत्थं वर्तते। एकया बुध्या द्वे कार्याकार्ये विनिश्चित्य (इदं कार्यं इदमकार्यं चेति सम्यक् विविच्य, त्रीन् - मित्रोदासीनशत्रून् चतुर्भिः साम-दान-भेद-दण्डैः स्ववशं कृत्वा पञ्चेन्द्रियाणि जित्वा, षट् विदित्वा सन्धिविग्रहादीन् ज्ञात्वा, सप्त ह्वित्वा- ''स्त्रियोऽस्या, मृगया, मानं, वाक्पारुष्यं य पञ्चमम्। मह्वच्च दण्डपारुष्यं अर्थदूषणमेवच'' इति एते सप्त त्यक्त्वा सुखी भव

एतत्यागेनापि स्वव्यक्तित्वविकासं सुलभसाध्यम्।

यद्विदुरेणोक्तं अन्यनीतिरपीदृशी वर्तते - सत्यं-क्षमा इत्यादि सद्गुणाः आवश्यकमेव व्यक्तित्वविकसने - तदुक्तं

सत्यं स्वर्गस्य सोपानं पारावारस्य नौरिव

क्षमा हि अशाक्तानां गुणः, शक्तानां भूषणमलंकारो भवति। लोके क्षमा एव वशीकरणम् क्षमया किं न साध्यते। तदेव दृष्टान्ततया विवृणोति

''अतृणे पतितो वह्निः स्वयमेवोपशाम्यते'' इति इत्थं अनेकवाक्यैः क्षमागुणस्य अतिमहतीमुवाच विदुरः धृतराष्ट्रं प्रति तर्थव शान्तिरप्यावश्यकमेव श्रेंयस्कामानाम् शान्तिखड्गः करे यस्य दुर्जनः किंकरिष्यति?

एवमेव व्यक्तित्वविकासमिच्छता जनेन षडेते दोषाः हातव्याः एव

अकालिकनिद्रा, मनोजाड्यता (तन्द्रा), भयं स्वस्य परस्माभ्दयं, परस्य स्वस्मादपि भयं, क्रोधः - द्वेषहेतुकमानसिकदैहिकविकारः, आलस्यं (क्रियाजडत्वं), दीर्घसूत्रता सर्वत्र विलम्बनवृत्तिः इत्येते दोषाः भूतिकामैः मानवैः त्याज्या एव - यदुक्तं

षड्दोषा पुरुषेणेह हातव्या भूतिमिच्छता।
निद्रा, तन्द्रा, भयं, क्रोधः आलस्यं दीर्घसूत्रता।।

इत्थमनेकवाक्यैः विदुरः धृतराष्ट्रप्रत्युक्तनीतिभिः मानवः कथं स्वव्यक्ति विकासमाप्नो-तीति विस्तरेण प्रतिपादयति-

व्यक्तित्वविकासार्थाः नैके विषयाः एवं विदुरनीत्यां सविस्तरं प्रतिपादिताः

प्रायेण विदितचरमेव भवतां महाभारतम् सर्वविषयकतत्वमञ्जूषा इति। "यथोक्तं - "यदिहास्ति तदन्यत्र यत्रेहास्ति न कुत्रचित्" इति। महाभारते उद्योगपर्वणि विशेषतः धृतराष्ट्र-विदुरसंवादात्मके भागे स्वीयव्यक्तित्वविकसनं मानवाः कथं सम्पादयेयुः इति अनेकाध्यायेषु सविस्तरं नीतिबोधकं, रीतिवेदकं, कीर्तिसाधकं, प्रमेयपुञ्जः दरीदृश्यते। एषा एव विदुरनीतिः सुप्रसिद्धतया देदीप्यते च विदुषां चेतसि। तदनुकरणेन व्यक्तित्वविकसनं सम्पादयेयुः।

7

भगवद्गीतायां व्यक्तित्वविकसनसमीक्षा

के. नारायण भट्ट

नौमि नीलाभ्रसङ्काशं पाण्डवानां च रक्षकम्।
व्यक्तित्वविकसनं चात्र समीक्ष्येऽहं यथामति।।

भगवद्गीता-

अथ तदिदानीं भगवद्गीतां विचारयामः। यद्यपि पिङ्गलगीता, हारीतगीता, पराशरगीता, हंसगीतेत्यादयश्च महाभारते श्रूयन्ते। न ताः सर्वाः भगवद्गीतेति लोके प्रथिताः। अतः संदिह्यते का सा भगवद्गीता इति।

या तु भगवद्गीतेति लोके प्रसिद्धा सा श्रीकृष्णेन अर्जुनं प्रत्युपदिष्टविषयिका महाभारतस्य भीष्मपर्वान्तर्गता चोपलभ्यते। अपि च सा युद्धसन्नद्धस्यार्जुनस्य मोहं निरस्य युद्धं प्रतिप्राचोदयदिति "धर्मक्षेत्रे कुरुक्षेत्रे" इत्यारभ्य "नष्टो मोहस्स्मृतिर्लब्धा त्वत्प्रसादान्मयाच्युत। स्थितोऽस्मि गतसन्देहः" इत्यन्तेभ्यः श्लोकसन्दर्भेभ्यः समावेते।

अर्जुनस्य मोहापकर्षितत्वात्, भगवदुपदेशरूपत्वात् लोके परंपरावित्सु विद्वत्सु तन्नाम्नैव प्रथितत्वाच्च भगवदुक्ता सा भगवद्गीता इति निश्चिनुमः। धृतराष्ट्रसञ्जयसंवादरूपैषाष्टा-दशाध्यायात्मिका च विद्यते। सैषा महाभारते

पंचविंशति तमाध्यायादारभ्य द्विचत्वारिंशत्-तमाध्यायपर्यन्तं समाकलिता दृश्यते। श्रीशङ्करभगवत्पादप्रभृत्याचार्यैः भगवद्गीता प्रस्थानत्रय्यामन्यतमत्वेनाङ्गीकृता इत्यवगम्यते। अपि चैषा भारतीयासु सर्वासु भाषासु प्रायशः अनूदिता लभ्यते। तथैव आङ्गलप्रभृतिपाश्चात्यभाषासु च। अत एव भगवद्गीता जनानुरागविषयिणीति जानीमः।

भगवद्गीतां विवृण्वता श्रीशङ्करभगवत्पादाचार्येण "सर्वज्ञो भगवान्गीताख्यैः सप्तभिः श्लोकशतैरुपनिबबन्ध" इत्युक्तत्वात्सप्तशतश्लोकान्वितैषा इत्यवगम्यते। अपि च तेन ज्ञायते यत् श्लोकसंख्या न ततो न्यूनाधिको वा इति। अर्जुनविषादयोगादारभ्य मोक्षसन्यासयोगपर्यन्तेभ्योऽष्टा-दशाध्यायेभ्यः संवलितेयं भगवद्गीता। तत्र व्यक्तित्वविकसनमन्वेषयामः।

व्यक्तित्वम्

'अञ्जू' धातोः 'क्तिन्' प्रत्यययोगेन 'वि' उपसर्गसहितेन च सिध्यति 'व्यक्ति' शब्दः। तस्य स्पष्टतार्थं मन्यते शब्दकौस्तुभकारः। तथा च "तं सन्तः श्रोतुमर्हन्ति सदसद्व्यक्तिहेतवः" इत्यस्मिन्नपरंसन्दर्भे 'व्यक्ति' शब्दः स्पष्टार्थे प्रयुक्तः दृश्यते। "अव्यक्ताद्व्यक्तयः सर्वा" इत्यत्र तु 'चराचरभूतानि' व्यक्तिशब्दार्थ इति भाष्यकाराणामभिप्रायः। "न हि ते भगवन् व्यक्तिम्" इत्यत्र श्लोके 'व्यक्ति' शब्दस्य प्रभवम् अर्थ इति शङ्कराचार्यः। विशिष्टाद्वैतिनां मते तु 'यथार्थस्वरूपमित्यर्थः। अमरकोशे तु "व्यक्तिस्तु पृथगात्मता" इत्युक्तत्वात् व्यक्तिशब्दस्य 'पृथग्वस्तु इत्यर्थः तन्मते इत्यवगम्यते। "व्यक्तेरभेद" इत्यत्र पूर्वोपदर्शितार्थे व्यक्तिशब्दः प्रयुक्त इति तत्सन्दर्भावलोकनेन समावेद्यते। अतः नैय्यायिकानामप्येषः अर्थः सम्मत इति जानीमः। हेमचन्द्रस्तु जनः व्यक्तिशब्दार्थ इत्यभिप्रैति। तेन पृथग्वस्त्वर्थे व्यक्तिपदार्थे तस्यापि सम्मतिरित्य-वगम्यते। अतः सास्प्रतं तमेव पृथग्वस्त्वर्थं व्यक्तिपदार्थत्वेन वयं स्वीकुर्मः।

"तस्य भावस्त्वतलौ" इतीमं सूत्रं व्याख्यास्यन् कौमुदीकारः "प्रकृतिजन्यबोधे प्रकारोभावः" इति विवृणोति। तत्रैव "गोर्भावो कोत्वम्"

इति चोदाहरत्। अस्मिन्नेव सन्दर्भे बालमनोरमाकरः व्याख्यास्यति ''त्वतल्'' प्रत्ययौ यत उत्पत्स्येते तस्मात्प्रकृतिभूतशब्दात् व्यक्तिबोधे जायमाने यज्जात्यादिकं विशेषतया भासते तद्व्यक्तिविशेषणं भावशब्देन विवक्षितमित्यर्थः'' इति। तस्मादत्रापि 'त्व' प्रत्ययः प्रकृतिभूतात् 'व्यक्ति' शब्दादुत्पत्स्यते। अतः व्यक्तिशब्देन व्यक्तिबोधे जायमाने या जातिः विशेषणतया तत्र भासते सा 'त्व' प्रत्ययार्थ इत्यवगम्येते। एवं च सर्वासु व्यक्तिषु सर्वदा वर्तमाना जातिः असाधारण-धर्मः। सैवात्रविशेषणम्। तद्वति व्यक्तिरित्यर्थः। तथा च व्यक्तित्ववति व्यक्तौ व्यक्तित्वधर्मस्य प्रकारविधया भासमानत्वात् इदं यथार्थश्चेत्यर्थः। तच्च प्रमाशब्देन व्याहरन्ति शास्त्रज्ञाः। ''तद्वति तत्प्रकारको यथार्थः'' इत्युक्तत्वात्।

विकसनसमीक्षा

'वि' उपसर्गपूर्वकस्य 'कस' धातोः 'घञ्' प्रत्यययोगेन सिध्यति 'विकास' इत्येषः शब्दः। तस्य विकसनाद्यर्थेषु सत्सु वृध्यर्थेऽप्यन्यतमः। माघे ''यद्वहुर्वहिरिवाप्य विकासम्' इत्यत्र वृध्यर्थ प्रकाशते विकासशब्दः। तथा च वयमप्यत्र वृध्यर्थकं विकास शब्दमङ्गीकृत्य व्यवहारं साधयामः। एवं च भगवद्गीतायां ये मानवस्याभिवृद्धिपरकाः अंशा भवन्ति तानत्र समीक्ष्य सङ्गृह्णीमः।

यद्यपि गीतायां व्यक्तित्वविकसनपरकाः विषयाः भवन्ति बहवः तथापि संयोजनसौकर्यमालक्ष्य तानत्र त्रिधा विभज्यन्ते। ते हि ऐहिकफलकव्यक्तित्वविकसनविषयकः, आमुष्मिकफलकव्यक्तित्व-विकसनविषयकः, ऐहिकामुष्मिकफलकव्यक्तित्वविकसनविषयकश्चेति। तत्रादावुद्देशातिधानमनुसृत्य ऐहिकफलकव्यक्तित्वविकसनविषयकमन्वेषयामः।

अस्मिन्जगति ये भवन्ति ते ऐहिकाः। गीतायामुपलभ्यमानाः इन्द्रियनिग्रहः, कामक्रकोधादिजयः, द्वन्द्वसहिष्णुता चेत्यादयः जीवनोत्कर्षहेतव इति तदध्ययनेनावगम्यते। तस्मादिमे ऐहिकफलक-व्यक्तित्वविकसनोपायाः भवन्तीति जानीमः। तत्रादाविन्द्रियनिग्रहः - चक्षुरादीन्द्रियाणां निरोध इत्यर्थः। ''पराञ्चिखानि

व्यतृणत्स्वयंभूः'' इत्येषा श्रुतिः रूपादिविषयाधीनत्वं इन्द्रियणस्वभाव इति श्रावयति। तानि स्वस्वविषयेभ्यः परावृत्य तेषां ध्येयविषयकत्व सम्पादनमिन्द्रियनिग्रह इत्यर्थः।

यत्नवन्तं मेधाविनमपि प्रमथनशीलानीन्द्रियाणि विषयानुसारिणं पुरुषं विक्षोभयन्तीति ''यततोह्यपि कौन्तेय'' इत्यनेनोक्त्वा मत्परस्त्वं तानि संयम्य समाहितो भवेदिति ''तानि सर्वाणि संयम्य युक्त आसीत् मत्परः'' इत्युपदिशति भगवान् श्रीकृष्णः। तत्रैवाग्रे ''वशे हि यस्येन्द्रियाणि तस्य प्रज्ञा प्रतिष्ठिता'' इत्यनेन निगृहीतेन्द्रियकः स्थिरबुद्धिमाप्नोतीति उपदिष्य हे कौन्तेय त्वमिन्द्रियाणि नियम्य कामं जहीति ''तस्मात् त्वमिन्द्रियाण्यादौ नियम्य भरतर्षभ'' इत्यनेनार्जुनमनुशास्ति। मनुरपि ''शौचमिन्द्रियनिग्रहः'' इति इन्द्रियाणां संयमनं स्तौति। सांप्रतिकेऽपि बहवः इन्द्रियनिग्रहाभावात् स्वोद्देशेन वञ्चिताः दृश्यन्ते क्वचिदत्र निगृहीतेन्द्रियकत्वेन स्वल्पे वयसि बहुतरपटुत्ववन्तश्चोपलभ्यन्ते। शुकादयश्च तथैवासन्निति पुराणाध्ययनेन विजानीमः। एवमुत्तरोत्तरवृद्धिं कामयमानेन पुरुषेणेन्द्रियनिग्रहस्य कर्तव्यत्वात् स व्यक्तित्वविकसनेष्वन्यतम इति निश्चिनुमः।

कामक्रोधादीनां जयः

तत्र कामः – सुखविषयकत्वेनानुभूतं वस्तु पुनः इन्द्रियगोचरं सत् तदवाप्तुमिच्छा कामः। विषयतृष्णा इति नामान्तरम्। कामः यदा प्रतिहन्यते तदा क्रोधत्वेन परिणामो भवति। अतः सः काम जन्यः। आदि पदेन लोभमोहौ गृह्येते। लोभः अत्याशा इति पर्यायः। ''परद्रव्यादित्सा-- इत्युक्तत्वात्। मोहः – अविवेकः यथार्थस्यापवरकः। कामक्रोधलोभमोहाः दोषाः भवन्ति। अतः ''कामक्रोधवियुक्तानां यतीनां यतचेतसाम्'' इत्यत्र कामक्रोधवियुक्ततां यतचेतसां विशेषणं कृतं संगच्छते। ''लोभोपहतचेतसः'' ''मूढोऽयं नाभिजानाति'' इत्यत्र लोभमोहौ दोषत्वेन परिगणितौ दृश्येते। अपि च कामक्रोधलोभाः नरकस्य त्रिविधं द्वारमात्मनाशाकश्चेतयुक्तत्वा तेषां त्यागः विधीयते ''त्रिविधं नरकस्येदम्''

इत्यारभ्य "त्रयं त्यजेत्" इत्यनेन। एते दोषाः अन्तःकरणे सम्भवन्ति। तैः संवलितः जीवः यथार्थं न प्राप्नोति, ते जेतव्याः भवन्ति। अतस्तेषां जयः व्यक्तित्वविकसनेष्वन्यतमः।

द्वन्द्वसहिष्णुता

तितिक्षा इति तस्याः नामान्तरम्। शीतोष्णसुखदुःखे द्वन्द्वपदार्थाविति लोके प्रसिद्धौ। "कौन्तेय शीतोष्णसुखदुःखदाः" इत्यत्र तथैवोक्तत्वात्। श्री शङ्करभगवत्पादास्तु "सुखदुःखहेतू सप्रतिपक्षौ पदार्थौ द्वन्द्वशब्दवाच्यौ" इत्यूचुः। अतः मानापमानौ द्वन्द्वपदार्थाविति नीलकण्ठभाष्योक्तं संगच्छते। एवं च वर्धिष्णुना सुखदुःखादिद्वन्द्वसहिष्णुतानुसर्तव्या। श्रीकृष्णः अर्जुनं "निर्द्वन्द्वो नित्यसत्वस्थो निर्योगक्षेम आत्मवान्" इत्यनेन द्वन्द्वरहितो भवेत्युपदिदेश। इदानीमपि तितिक्षावन्तः साधका तत्र तत्र दृश्यन्ते। स्पल्पमात्रमपि कष्टस्य दुःखस्य च सहिष्णुताभावात् तत्र तत्र जनाः म्रियन्त इति दिने दिने वार्तापत्रिकादिभ्य श्रूयन्ते स्मः। साधनोपायेष्वन्यतमत्वात्तितिक्षापि व्यक्तित्वविकसनपरका इति जानीमः।

श्रद्धाभक्तिलाभः

पूर्वोक्तेन आदिपदेन श्रद्धा, भक्तिः, प्रणिपाताश्च गृह्यन्ते। श्रद्धा नाम आस्तिक्यबुद्धिरित्यर्थः। "यजन्ते श्रद्धयान्विताः" इत्यत्र श्रीशङ्करभगवत्पादैः "श्रद्धया आस्तिक्यबुद्ध्या" इत्युक्तत्वात् "शास्त्रस्य वाक्यस्य सत्यबुध्यावधारणा सा श्रद्धा कथिता" इति विवेकचूडामण्यां तल्लक्षणोक्तत्वाच्च। वेदान्तसारे तु "गुरुवाक्येषु विश्वासः श्रद्धा" इत्युच्यते। अमरकोशे "श्रद्धात्वास्तिक्यकांक्षयोः" इत्युच्यते। तथा च विश्वासोऽपि आस्तिक्यबुध्यात्मिकत्वात् आस्तिक्यबुद्धिं श्रद्धापदार्थत्वेन जानीमः। गीतायां च श्रूयते "श्रद्धावान् लभते ज्ञानम्" "अश्रद्धधानापुरुषः" इति। अनेन ज्ञायते यत् श्रद्धावत्वे ज्ञानावाप्तिस्तदभावे ज्ञानाभाव इति। अतः ज्ञानापेक्षिभिरवश्यमेव श्रद्धा लभ्या भवति। जगति सर्वे भवन्ति ज्ञानापेक्षिणः। तदवगन्तुं श्रद्धायाः सर्वैरनुसर्तव्यत्वात्सा व्यक्तित्वविकसनेष्वन्यतमा।

भक्तिः सा च भगवतः ध्यानम्। "स्नेहपूर्वकमनुध्यानं भक्तिरित्यभिधीयते" "हृषीकेशसेवनं भक्तिरुच्यते" इत्युक्तत्वात्च्चा गीतायां च "भक्त्या युक्तो योगबलेन चैव" सन्दर्भेऽस्मिन्नाचार्यः शङ्करः "भजनं भक्तिरिति विश्लेषयामास। तत्रैव नीलकण्ठभाष्ये "भक्त्या भगवति वासुदेवे आराध्यत्वबुद्ध्या युक्तः" इत्यवोचत्। अतः आराध्यत्वबुद्धिं भक्तिपदार्थमिति जानीमः। सा च ध्यान पदान्तरम्। आराध्यत्वबुध्यभावे ध्येयवस्तु न प्राप्नोति। तत् सत्वे तु ध्येयवस्तु प्राप्नो तीत्येषः प्रायशः सर्वैरनुभववेद्यविषयः। 'जानातीच्छति यतते' इत्येषः प्रवृत्तिक्रमः तमनुद्रढयति। अपि च "भक्त्या लभ्यस्त्वनन्यया" इत्यर्जुनमुपदिशति श्रीकृष्णः। गीतायां भक्तियोगाध्याये भक्तिपदार्थं च विशदीकृतं दृश्यते। ध्येयलब्धौ ध्यानस्यावश्यकत्वात् सा च व्यक्तित्वविकसनेष्वन्यतमा भवति।

प्रणिपातादयः "तद्विद्धि प्रणिपातेन परिप्रश्नेन सेवया। उपदेक्ष्यन्ति ते ज्ञानं ज्ञानिनस्तत्वदर्शिनः" इति हि गीतावचनं श्रूयते। अत्रस्थाः प्रणिपातादयः ज्ञानोपलब्धिविधानानि। भाष्यकारेण "येन विधिना प्राप्यते" इति व्याख्यातत्वात्। तानि प्रणिपातः, परिप्रश्नः, सेवा इति त्रीणि विधानानि भवन्ति। तत्राद्यः प्रणिपातः। "प्रणिपातेन प्रकर्षेण नीचैः पतनं प्रणिपातः दीर्घनमस्कारः तेन" एवं व्याख्यातत्वात् – निष्कपटदीर्घनमस्कारः प्रणिपातपदार्थ इत्यर्थः। द्वितीयः परिप्रश्नः। तत्सन्दर्भे भाष्यकारेण "कथं बन्धः कथं मोक्षः का विद्या का चाविद्येति परिप्रश्नेन" इत्येवं व्याख्यातं दृश्यते। नीलकण्ठटीकायां "परिप्रश्नेन जिज्ञासुतया प्रश्नेन" एवं व्याख्यानं कृतम्। अतः जिज्ञासया यथार्थावगत्यनुकूलः वार्तालापः परिप्रश्नपदार्थः इत्यवगम्यते। तृतीया सेवा। सा गुरुशुश्रूषा परिचर्या वा। यया सुप्रीताः गुरवः तत्त्वमुपदिशेयुः। सांप्रतिके एतानि ज्ञानोपदेशसाधनानि क्वचिदेव दृश्यन्ते। सर्वत्रार्थकरीविद्याव्याप्तत्वात्। तत्प्राप्त्युपायानां पार्थक्येन सत्वाच्च। यदा तु ज्ञानेप्सवः भवन्ति तदा प्रणिपातनाद्युपायान्येवाधुनापि तैरनुसर्तव्यानि भवन्ति। तैर्विना नान्यः पन्थाः। अतः प्रणिपातादयः व्यक्तित्वविकसनोपायाः इति विजानीमः।

प्राणायामः चतुर्थाध्याये श्रूयते प्राणायामः। यथा- ''अपाने जुह्वति प्राणं प्राणेऽपानं तथापरे। प्राणापानगती रुध्वा प्राणायामपरायणाः'' इति। अत्र अपानवृत्तौ प्राणवृत्तिप्रक्षेपेण पूरकाख्यः प्राणायामः उपदिश्यते। तथा प्राणवृत्तौ अपानवृत्तिप्रक्षेपेण रेचकाख्यः, पुनश्च प्राणापानयो र्गतिं रुध्वा कुम्भकाख्यः प्राणायामः अनेन श्लोकेन बुबोध्यते। प्राणायामः आरोग्यप्रवर्धक आयुष्याभिवर्धकश्चेति आयुर्वेदविदां वैद्यानामभिप्रायः। तेन प्राणायामः व्यक्तित्वविकसने हेतुरिति निश्चीयते।

योगः ''शुचौ देशे प्रतिष्ठाप्य स्थिरमासनमात्मनः नात्युक्ष्छ्रितं नातिनीचं चैलाजिनकुशोत्तरम्'' इत्यस्मिन्श्लोके आसनविधानमुपलभ्यते। तद्यथा - संस्कारवति पवित्रीकृते प्रदेशे नात्यन्तमुन्नतं नीचं वा आसनं विदध्यात्। तच्च कुशः अजिनश्चैलेति क्रमेण प्रसारयेत्। तत्र शरीरविन्यास विधानं ''समं कायशिरोग्रीवं धारयन् अचलं स्थिरः'' इत्यादिना निर्दिश्य ''युञ्जन्नेव सदात्मानं योगी नियतमानसः'' इत्यादिना युञ्जानयोग उपदिष्टः। स च गुरूपदेशपूर्वकमनुसर्तव्येति तत्सन्दर्भस्थेन ''तद्विद्धि प्रणिपातेन'' इत्यनेनावगम्यते। चित्तवृत्तिनिरोधविषयकत्वात् सः व्यक्तित्वविकसनसमर्थः आरोग्यप्रदश्च। साम्प्रतं लोके बाहुल्येन योगाभ्यासिनं पश्यामः। सामाजिकानामधिकप्रयोजनवत्वाच्च योगः व्यक्तित्वविकासकेति निश्चिनुमः।

अथेदानीमामुष्मिकफलकव्यक्तित्वविकासकं चिन्तयामः। आमुष्मिकस्य शब्दस्य अमुष्मिन्भवः इति विग्रहः। तेन पारलौकिकः आमुष्मिकपदस्यार्थः। स च यज्ञः। ''यज्ञः कर्मसमुभ्दवः'' इत्युक्तत्वात्। इमं पदसन्दर्भे विवृण्वन्भाष्यकारः ''यज्ञः' अपूर्वं स च यज्ञः कर्मसमुभ्दवः ऋत्विग्यजमानयोश्च व्यापारः कर्म ततः समुभ्दवः'' इत्येवं व्याख्यास्यति। अतः अपूर्वं च तत् वस्तु अलौकिकं कर्मजत्वात्। तथा च तदामुष्मिकमित्यवगम्यते। तेन यज्ञः आमुष्मिकमित्यर्थः। ''दैवमेवापरे यज्ञमित्यारभ्य तृतीयचतुर्थाध्याययोः नानाविधाः यज्ञाः उपदिश्यन्ते। ते यज्ञाः मनुष्याणां भोगसाधकाः सन्ति। अतः पशुपुत्रादि साध्यलिप्सावता पुरुषेण यज्ञा अवश्यमनुष्ठेया इति ''इष्टान् भोगाह्नि वो देवा

दास्यन्ते यज्ञा भविता:'' इत्यारभ्य 'अघायुरिन्द्रियारामो मोघं पार्थ स जीवति इत्यन्तेभ्य श्लोकेभ्यावगम्यते। ते च द्रव्ययज्ञा:, तपोयज्ञ:, योगयज्ञा: इत्यादय:। आमुष्मिकफलबाहुल्यादिमे आमुष्मिकफलकेति गीयन्ते। अन्नमयो यज्ञ: इतिवत्। भोगलिप्सावन्त: सन्ति सामाजिका:। तल्लब्धुं यज्ञ: लौकिकसाधन:। अत: अनुष्ठेया: यज्ञा व्यक्तित्वविकसनेष्वन्यतमा इति निश्चिनुम:।

अथ ऐहिकामुष्मिकफलकव्यक्तित्वविकासकमन्वेष्याम:। यश्च इहलोके परलोके च फलप्रदातुं समर्थ: स: ऐहिकामुष्मिकफलक इति गीयते। गीतायां ''कर्मण्येवाधिकारस्ते मा फलेषु कदाचन'' ''नियतं कुरु कर्म त्वम्'' ''तस्मादसक्त: सततं कार्यं कर्म समाचर'' इत्येतेभ्य: कर्म अवश्यानुष्ठेयत्वेन विधीयते। तच्चाग्निष्टोमादय इति केचित्। शङ्करभगवत्पादास्तु ''कर्मणि एव अधिकारो न ज्ञाननिष्ठायां ते तव तत्र च कर्म कुर्वतो मा फलेषु अधिकार: अस्तु कर्मफलतृष्णा मा भूत्'' इति व्याख्यातवान्। अपि च ''नियतं नित्यं यो यस्मिन् कर्मणि अधिकृत: फलाय च अश्रुतं तत् नियतं कर्म तत् कुरु'' इत्युक्तवांश्च। तेन फलतृष्णारहितकर्मकर्तव्यत्वेन बुबोध्यते इति विज्ञायते। ''यज्ञार्थात् कर्मणोन्यत्र लोकोऽयं कर्मबन्धन:'' ''तस्मादसक्त: सततं कार्यं कर्म समाचर'' इत्यादिना भगवत्प्रीत्यर्थं कर्म अनुष्ठेयम्। तच्च असक्तकर्म इति प्रतिभाति। अग्रे ''संसिद्धिमास्थिताजनकादय'' इत्युक्तत्वात्। तच्च स्वविहितं कर्म, ब्रह्मज्ञेनापि जनकेन प्रजापरिपालनमाचरितत्वात्। स्वयमेव भगवान् कथयति ''लोके किञ्चिदपि मयि अप्राप्तं वस्तु प्राप्तव्यमिति नास्ति। तथापि अहं कर्मणि वर्ते। यद्यहं न वर्ते कर्मणि तदा इतरे जना: मामनुसृत्य कर्मभ्रष्टा: भवेयु:। तेन जगत् नश्येत्। कर्मणा जगत् सन्धारितत्वादिति ''न मे पार्थास्ति कर्तव्य'' ''यद्यदाचरति श्रेष्ठ:'' ''उत्सीदेयुरिमे लोका:'' एतेभ्य: श्लोकसन्दर्भेभ्य:। अत: जगत: सुव्यवस्थामालक्ष्य स्ववर्णाश्रमविहितानि कर्माण्यनुष्ठेयानि भवन्ति। जगत: सन्धारकत्त्वात्तानि व्यक्तित्वविकसनपरकाणीति ज्ञेयानि। अपि च गीतायां ''स्वधर्ममपि चावेक्ष्य नाविकम्पितुमर्हसि'' ''अथ चेत्वमिमं धर्म्यं संग्रामं न करिष्यसि'' श्रेयान्स्वधर्मो विगुण: परधर्मात्स्वनुष्ठितात्''।

स्वधर्मे निधनं श्रेयः परधर्मो भयावहः'' इत्यादिभ्यः धर्मस्यानुष्ठेयत्वेन श्रूयते। तन्न स्वविहितकर्मतः अत्यन्तभिन्नः भवतीत्युक्त्वा ग्रन्थविस्तरभयाच्चात्राधिकं न विश्लेष्यते।

एवं सङ्कलिते ह्यत्र व्यक्तित्वस्य विकासके।
यदि दोषाः संलभेरन् सुधियः क्षन्तुमर्हथ।।

आधारिताः ग्रन्थाः

1. मनुस्मृतिः
2. वेदान्तसारः
3. वैय्याकरणसिद्धान्तकौमुदी
4. भगवद्गीता (गीताप्रेस्)
5. श्रीमद्भगवद्गीतारहस्य (बि.जि.तिळक्)
6. गीताभाष्य (शाङ्कर)
7. गीताभाष्य (आनन्दतीर्थ)
8. गीताभाष्य (नीलकण्ठी)
9. गीताभाष्य (रामानुजीय)
10. महाभारत
11. तर्कसङ्ग्रह
12 न्यायसिद्धान्तमुक्तावलि
13. वैदिकसाहित्यचरित्रे
14. अमरकोशः
15. शब्दकौस्तुभः
16. वाचस्पत्यम्
17. चरकसंहिता
18. पातञ्जलयोगभाष्य
19. मुण्डकोपनिषभ्दाष्य

8

Āyurvedic Approach to Personality Development

Shripad Bhat

An ancient Sanskrit poet has aptly emphasized the need to discriminate what is important and what is not:

> "Sciences are vast, there is so much to be learnt. Since time at our disposal is limited and there are too many obstacles.
>
> That which is of essence should be imbibed like the swan that separates and consumes milk only
>
> From a mixture of milk and water[1]"

"शरीरमाद्यं खलु धर्मसाधनम्।" "The body is the first requisite for proper performance of life's duties". This old Sanskrit saying shows that from historic times man had recognized that a healthy body is the first and foremost requirement which enables us to discharge our duties in life efficiently.

According to Hindu scriptures, man's life in this world should be aimed at the pursuit and attainment of four objectives viz. *Dharma* (righteous living), *artha* (material prosperity), *kāma* (fulfillment of legitimate physical needs) and finally *mokṣa* (liberation). First comes Dharma, to achieve which the first requirement is physical well-being. Thus physical fitness and virtuous living, the two most important aspects of life have been aligned. It goes without saying that man enjoys the good things of life only if he is on top health.

Paradoxically, maintaining good health is very easy and at the same time very difficult ! Inspite of the best care, human life is heir to many ills. Health or fitness is not merely absence of sickness. It is a dynamic state where not only one's body but also mental faculties function at peak level. "A sound mind is a sound body." Mental and physical things go hand in hand and the two contribute to total well-being[2].

A man is identified by his personality. It is a public image of what a person is and how he is perceived by society. We, at times mistake it for physical appearance, dress sense and looks, but a personality can be known by person's character, behavioral traits and attitude towards life. A person with low self-esteem, moral and low effectiveness can be transformed into a successful personality. The wisdom of our ancestors has left for us valuable procedures for physical and mental health and vigorous living. Āyurveda is one of them.

The word 'Āyurveda' is composed of two Sanskrit terms, viz., 'āyus' life and 'veda' knowledge, and taken together it means the "science of life". In limited sense, however, it is always used to imply "the science of medicine". Caraka has defined Āyurveda as:

हिताहितं सुखं दुःखमायुस्तस्य हिताहितम्।
मानं च तच्च यत्रोक्तमायुर्वेदः स उच्यते।। Caraka, sūtra 1.41

"That (science) is designated as Āyurveda where useful and harmful as well as happy and sorrow (states of) life along with what is good and bad for life, its measurement and life itself are described"

Broadly speaking, Āyurveda stands for knowledge of life.

The term 'āyus' in the term 'Āyurveda', stands for the combination of body, sense organs, mind and soul. Caraka says –

शरीरेन्द्रियसत्त्वात्मसंयोगे धारि जीवितम्।
नित्यगश्चानुबन्धश्च पर्यायैरायुरुच्यते।। Caraka, sūtra 1.42

The 'āyus' represents the combination of the body, sense organs, mind and soul and its synonyms are *dhāri* (the one that prevents the body from decay), *jīvita* (which keeps alive), *nityaga* (which serves as a permanent substratum of this body) and *anubandha* (which transmigrates from one body to another).

Components of Personality: There are some components, mentioned in Caraka, Suśruta and Vāgbhaṭa as bhāvas of personality. They are as follows:

1) **Mātṛja** – The foetus is produced out of the mother. Without mother, there is no possibility of conception and birth of viviparous (*jarāyuja*). The organs derived from the maternal source are skin, blood, flesh, fat, umbilicus. Heart, kloman, liver, spleen, kidneys, bladder, rectum, stomach, *palevasaya*, upper and lower part of the anus, small intestine, mesentry and omentum[3].
2) **Pitṛja** – The foetus is produced out of father. Without father, there is no possibility of conception and birth of viviparous creatures. The organs derived from paternal source are hairs of the head and face, nail, small hairs of the body, teeth, bones, veins, ligaments, arteries and semen[4].

3) **Rasaja** – The foetus is produced out of rasa (digestive product of mothers food). Without rasa even the mother will not live. The aspects of individual derived from rasa are manifestation and growth of the body, continuity of the strength, satisfaction, plumpness and enthusiasm[5].

4) **Ātmaja** – The foetus is produced out of the soul. The *antarātman* (soul inside the body) is the same as *garbhātman* (soul in the foetus). This is known as *jīva* or soul. He is eternal. He does not get afflicted by diseases; does not undergo the process of aging; does not succumb to death; does not undergo diminution. He cannot be penetrated. He cannot be cut. He cannot be made get irritated. He is omnipresent, omnipotent, invisible, beginningless, endless and unchangeable. By entering into the uterus it gets combined with the sperm and the ovum thereby reproducing himself in the form of foetus. Thus the foetus takes the designation of soul[6].

5) **Sātmyaja** – The foetus is produced out of the wholesomeness. The aspects of the individual derived from wholesomeness are health, unlazyness, ungreedyness, clarity of senses, excellence of voice and seeds, and excessive sex-vigor[7].

6) **Sattvaja** – Mind is also the connecting link which connect the soul with physical body. (The objects of sense organs of three aspects, viz., *sāttvika*, *rājasa* and *tāmasa*). The aspects of an individual derived from mind are manifested because of its existence. They are likings, conduct, purity, enmity, memory, attachment, detachment, jealousy, valour, fear, anger, drowsiness, enthusiasm, sharpness, softness, seriousness, unstability and such other manifestations[8].

Among these *sātmyaja* could be developed by nurturing, training, etc. The basics of other components may not change but the training regarding physical, mental and behavioral aspects may help to compensate for the ill effects.

Other things playing role in personality – Other factors playing their role in personality are as follows:

1) **Doṣaprakṛti** – Some persons maintain the equilibrium of *vāta*, *pitta* and *kapha* from the very time of conception; some are dominated by *vāta*; some are by *pitta* and some by *kapha*. Those of the first category are not susceptible to diseases and the rest of them are always likely to suffer. The body constitution (*dehaprakṛiti*) of persons is named according to the predominance of dosas[9].

2) **Deśaprakṛti** – Both the land as well as the patient constitute *deśa* or habitat. Nature of the land is examined with a view to ascertaining the specific features of individual patients as well as the medicinal plants in different localities. The following points are to be examined with reference to a patient:

    1. Place of birth, growth and affliction with the disease;
    2. Specific features concerning food, exercise, customs, strength, mental condition, homalogation by habit, dominance of one or the other of the *doṣas*, liking, manifestation of diseases and things which are useful and harmful[10].

3) **Kālaprakṛti** – Kāla stands for both the time in the form of day and night and the status of an individual. The latter is relevant to the disease where as the former for the determination of the wholesomeness in different types of seasons[11].

4) **Sāraprakṛti** – Patients are to be examined with reference to *sāra* or the excellence of their *dhātus*. With a view to determining the specific measure of strength

they are classified into eight categories, depending upon the *sāra* or excellence of their *dhātus*, viz., *tvak* (skin but here *rasadhātu*), *rakta* (blood)[6], *māṁsa* (muscle tissue), *medas* (adipose tissue), *asthi* (bone tissue), *majjā* (marrow), śukra (semen), and sattva (mental faculties[12].

5) **Mānasaprakṛti** – The concept of mind is very important and significant in Āyurveda. In Āyurveda, diseases are classified into two categories, viz., physical and mental. In the former the body is considered to be the seat of disease and in the latter, the mind. In both categories, the mind plays an important role in causing diseases. Psychic factors exercise control over the physiological functions of the body and vice-versa. Therefore, even for the treatment of some physical diseases certain psychic measures are prescribed in Āyurveda[13], to know the mental situation of patient.

Equilibrium of Dhātus – Dhātus having mutually opposite qualities undergo increase and decrease simultaneously. A thing which increases a particular *dhātu*, is also responsible for the decrease of *dhātu* of opposite quality[14].

Maintaining equilibrium of *dhātus* is the significant object of treatment. Therefore, medical therapies when properly administered simultaneously bring both the reduced and increased ones and increasing the reduced ones[15].

It is the equillibrium of *dhātus* which is sought as the result while administering therapies and also while resorting regimens for the maintenance of positive health. Even healthy persons should properly use wholesome food with appropriate *rasas* (tastes) and *guṇas* (attributes) and processed properly with a view to maintain the equilibrium of *dhātus*. After taking the food dominated by particular attributes, it is desirable to neutralize their effects by resorting to such of the regimens as are contradictory to them[16].

Instructions for Maintaining Equilibrium –

For the maintenance of the equilibrium of *dhātus* which provides positive health, one should observe the following instructions:

1. One should properly resort to such actions and take such food as are of contrary disposition to the locality, season and physical constitution of an individual, e.g., one should indulge in sleep while living in a desert; one should resort to exercise during the spring season; an individual with a patty body should resort to exercise and vigil in excess.
2. One should refrain from excessive utilization, wrong utilization and non-utilization of time, intellect and object of senses.
3. One should not suppress manifested urges.
4. One should not refrain from exhibiting strength beyond one's real capacity[17].

Healthy Person – Suśruta, one of the greatest authorities on Āyurveda, has described the signs and symptoms of a healthy person as follows.

समदोषः समाग्निश्च समधातुमलक्रियः।
प्रसन्नात्मेन्द्रियमनाः स्वस्थ इत्याभिधीयते।। Suśruta, 15.41

"The *doṣas* must be in equilibrium and his digestive fire must be in balanced state and his tissues (*dhātus*) and *malas* must work in normal state. The sensory and motor organs, mind and ātman must also be in pleasant state. Such a person is called *swastha* or healthy."

Samadoṣa – The *doṣas* which are present in the body, viz., *vāta, pitta* and *kapha* must be in balanced state in order to keep a person healthy. When the balance of them is imbalanced. It will produce a state of *dosa vaiṣamya* called a disease.

Samāgni – In order to keep an individual healthy, the digestive fire (*koṣṭhāgni*) and *dhātvagni* (tissue enzymes) must be in a proper state. When agni is less in quantity (*mandāgni*) it will cause many diseases. So it is well known fact that the health of an individual depends upon the proper strength of his digestive power.

Samadhātumalakriyāḥ – According to Āyurveda, there are seven *dhatus*, viz., *rasa*, *rakta*, *māṁsa*, *asthā*, *majjā*, *śukra* and *malas*. These should function properly and so also the *malas* of the body.

Prasannātmendriyamanaḥ – In the Āyurveda, the functions of sensory and motor organs and mind have given special importance. When these are not in equilibrium and not discharging their functions properly, it would lead to a state called disease. Even though they are functioning properly, the bodily activities must not vitiate the above. The mental health is more important than the physical health[18].

Two aspects of prevention of illness – There are two prevention aspects, viz. curative aspects as well as prevention aspects. In curative aspects a patient should follow the instructions regarding medicine, consuming good food and walk as exercise for pleasure and good health. Prevention aspect consists of *svasthavṛtta* and *sadvṛtta* for the improvement of physical, mental and behavioral health.

Svasthavṛtta – *Svasthavṛtta* is a word composed of three words viz., *sva*, *stha* and *vṛtta*. These three represents three doṣas, viz., *vāta pitta* and *kapha* in the body with their working in full co-operation and coordination along with one another. According to Monier Williams Sanskrit Dictionary, '*sva*' – natural, self abiding, being one's own natural state, doing well, healthy in body and mind. Usually '*sva*' represents possesses or attention. In the Āyurveda, Āyu or a life is always and almost beneficial producing happiness and healthyness in the body. '*Sthaḥ* .' denotes the stability of maintenance and it means one who stands. In the Āyurveda, '*svastha*' is a person who enjoys normal health. '*Vṛtta*' represents the existence of deliberate communication. It means acting or playing one's part. In the Āyurveda, it is he who acts well and distributes his belongings and his any duty bounds. Sometimes who leaves no stone unturned for carrying out what is proved to be beneficial from the point of view of food and behavior and the rules and regimens one has to follow. It may prove to be beneficial and happy[19]. Thus, *svasthavṛtta* is deemed to help, to attain an individual to secure health. Health and happiness always go hand in hand, one cannot go without them. It is the science of *svasthavṛtta* which is aimed at giving happiness and healthy and prosperous life in order to attain *dharma*, *artha*, *kāma* and *mokṣa*.

Dinacaryā and Ṛtucaryā – One should also observe daily regimen from morning to evening and also the seasonal regimen observing in different seasons. He must also be knowing the treatment for the diseases produced due to the obstruction of natural urges like *mala* (faeces), *mūtra* (urine), *kapha* (cough), *svāsa śvayathu* (sneezing)[20]. He must also know how to prevent epidemic diseases and also how to control them. He must also know the rules and regulations regarding the right conduct (*sadācāra*) to keep his mind in a peaceful state. If one goes through these facts he will definitely have an idea how health can be achieved through following the principles of Āyurveda.

Sadvṛtta (Good Conduct) – Ayurveda shows righteous way to a person to behave well in the society. It says,

सुखार्थाः सर्वभूतानां मताः सर्वाः प्रवृत्तयः।
सुखं च न विना धर्मात्तस्माद्धर्मपरोभवेत्।। A hr.2.20

All activities are meant for the happiness of living beings; such happiness is based on dharma (righteousness, good moral conduct) and therefore every person should follow the same.

Again, it says, friends should be served with affection where-as others should be kept at a distance[21]. Those who have no means of livelihood, who are suffering from diseases and who are afflicted with grief should be helped at the greater extent[22].

उपकारप्रधानः स्यादपकारपरेऽप्यरौ।
सम्पद्विपत्स्वेकमना, हेतावीष्यत्फले न तु।। A hr.2.25

One should be very helpful even to his enemies even though they are not helpful. One should maintain a balanced mind during the period of wealth and disaster. One should be envious of the cause but not be jealous of the effect.

Again Ahr. says, one should speak appropriate to the occasion, with words which are good, in brief, not contradictory and which is pleasing. One should start conversing with a pleasant face; should be virtuous, kind and soft, should not be comfortable and happy alone; should neither believe nor suspect everyone; should not reveal that someone is his enemy and that he is an enemy of someone else; should not make public the insults he had and the dissatisfaction towards the master. Observing the nature of people, one should deal with them in such a manner by which he should be pleased[23].

Besides, Ahr. gives stress on pleasant looking. It says that one should cut his hair, nails, keep his feet and orifices of waste materials clean, take bath daily, put on scents and good dress which is not superfluous but is pleasant look at[24].

Thus, *sadvṛtta* (good conduct) has definite role to play in developing mental activities of a person by which one may develop his personality developmental skills.

Concluding Remarks – Thus, Āyurveda plays an important role in the development of personality. It is the individuals totality of characteristics like, intelligence, looks, character which distinguishes a person from others. Personality comes into play in each and every activity, thought and behavior of an individual. Therefore to attain good personality, one should develop individuality which consists of mental, physical and behavioral aspects. Thus, as we have seen, Āyurveda, although considered as old, contributed a lot to the modern concept personality.

References

1) The legendary swan was supposed to be capable of sucking the essence of milk from a mixture in which water is larger in quantity and the essence of milk, less. Sharma S.P., *Personality Development*, pp 13-14.

2) Ibid pp 41-42

3) मातृजश्चायं गर्भः। न हि मातुर्विना गर्भोत्पत्तिः स्यात्, न च जन्म जरायुजानाम्। त्वक् च लोहितं च मांसं च मेदश्च नाभिश्च हृदयं च क्लोम च यकृच्च प्लीहा च वृक्कौ च वस्तिश्च पुरीषाधानं चामाशयश्च पक्काशयश्चो त्तरगुदं चाधरगुदं च क्षुद्रान्त्रं च स्थूलान्त्रं च वपा च वपादहनं चेति मातृजानि। Caraka, *Śārīra* 3.6

4) पितृजश्चायं गर्भः। न हि पितुः ऋते गर्भोत्पत्तिः स्यात्, न च जन्म जरायुजानाम्। केशश्मश्रुनखलोमदन्तास्थिसिरास्नायुघमन्यः शुक्रं चेति घमन्यः। Caraka, *Śārīra* 3.7

5) रसजश्चायं गर्भः। न हि रसाहते मातुः प्राणयात्रापि स्यात्, ... यानि खल्वस्य गर्भस्य रसजानि, यानि चास्य रसतः संभवतः संभवन्ति, तान्यथा - शरीरस्यभिनिर्वृत्तिरभिवृद्धिः प्राणानुबम्घस्तृप्तिः पुष्टिरुत्साहश्चेति। Caraka, *Śārīra* 3.12

6) आत्मजश्चायं गर्भः। गर्भात्मा ह्यन्तरात्मा यः, तं जीव इत्याचक्षते। शाश्वतमरुजमजरममरमभेद्यमच्छेद्यमलोढ्यं विश्वरूपविश्वकर्माणमव्यक्तमनादिमनिघनमक्षरमपि। स गर्भाशयमनुप्रविश्य शुक्रशोणिताभ्यां संयोगमेत्य गर्भत्वेन जनयत्यात्मनात्मानम्, आत्मसंज्ञा।। हि गर्भे। Caraka, *Śārīra* 3.8

7) सात्म्यजश्चायं गर्भः। ..... यानि खल्वस्य गर्भस्य सात्म्यजानि, यानि चास्य सात्म्यतः संभवतः संभवन्ति तान्यथा - आरोग्यमनालस्य मलोलुपत्वमिन्द्रियप्रसादः स्वरवर्णबीजसंपत् प्रहर्षभूयस्त्वं चेति। Caraka, *Śārīra* 3.11

8) अस्ति खलु सत्त्वमौपपादुकम्: यदिन्द्रियाणामभिग्राहकं च मन इत्याभिघीयते तत्त्रिविधमाख्यायते - शुद्धं राजसं, तामसमिति। ..... यानि खल्वस्य गर्भस्य सत्त्वजानि, यान्यस्य सत्त्वतः संभवतः संभवन्ति तान्यथा - भक्तिः शीलं शौचं द्वेषः स्मृतिर्मोहस्त्यागो मात्सर्यं शौर्यं भयं क्रोधस्तन्द्रोत्साहतैक्ष्णयं मार्दवं गाम्भीर्यमनवस्थितत्त्वमित्येवमादयश्चान्ये, ... Caraka, *Śārīra* 3.13

9) समपित्तानिलकफाः केचिद् गर्भादिमानवाः।
दृश्यन्ते वातलाः केचिद् पित्तलश्लेश्मलास्तथा।। Caraka, sutra 7.39
तेषामनातुराः पूर्वे वातलाद्याः सदातुराः।
दोषानुशयित ह्येषां देहप्रकृतिरुच्यते।। Ibid 7.40

10) तत्र भूमिपरीक्षा आतुरपरिज्ञानहेतोर्वा स्यादौषधपरिज्ञानहेतोर्वा। तत्र तावदियमातुरपरिज्ञानहेतोः। तद्यथा-अयं कस्मिन् भूमिदेशे मनुष्याणामिदमाहारजातम्, इदं विचारजातम्, इदमाचारजातम्, एतावच्च वलम्, एवं विधं सत्त्वम्, एवं विधं सात्म्यम्, एवं विंधो दोषा, भक्तिरियम्, इमे व्याधयः, हितमिदम्, अहितमिदमिति प्रायो ग्रहणेन। Caraka, Vimāna 8.93

11) कालो हि नित्यगश्चावस्यिकश्च; तत्रवस्थिको विकारमपेक्षते; नित्यगस्तु ऋतुसापेक्षः। Caraka, Vimāna 1.6

12) सारतश्चेति साराण्यष्टौ पुरुषणां बलमानविशेषज्ञानार्थमुपदिश्यन्ते।
तद्यथा त्वग्रक्तमांसमेदोऽस्थिमज्जशुक्रसत्त्वानीति। Caraka, Vimāna 8.12

13) Dash Vaidya Bhagwan, Fundamentals of Ayurvedic Medicine, p.45

14) यौगपद्येन तु विरोधिनां धातूनां वृद्धिह्रासौ भवतः। यद्धि यस्य धातोर्वृद्धिकरं तत्ततो विपरीतगुणस्य धातोः प्रत्यवायकरं सम्पद्यते। Caraka, *Śārīra* 4.5

15) तदेव तस्माद्भेषजं सम्यगवचार्यमाणं युगपन्न्यूनातिरिक्तानां धातूनां साम्यकरं भवति, अधिकमपकर्षति न्यूनमाप्याययति। Caraka, *Śārīra* 4.6

16) एतदेव हि भैषज्यप्रयोगे फलमिष्टं स्वस्थवृत्तानुष्ठाने च यावद्धातूनां साम्यं स्यात्। स्वस्था अपि धातूनां साम्यानुग्रहार्थमेव कुशला रसगुणानाहारविकारांश्च पर्यायेणेच्छन्त्युपयोक्तुं सात्म्यसमाज्ञातान्। एकप्रकारभूयिष्ठांश्चोपयुञ्जानास्तद्विपरीतकरसमाज्ञातया चेष्टया सममिच्छन्ति कर्तुम्। Caraka, *Śārīra* 4.7

17) देशकालात्मगुणविपरीतानां हि कर्मणामाहारविकाराणां च क्रियोपयोगः सम्यक्, सर्वातियोगसंधारणम्, असन्धारणमुदीर्णानां च गतिमतां, साहसानां च वर्जनम्, स्वस्थवृत्तमेतावाद्धातूनां साम्यनुग्रहार्थमुपदिश्यते। Caraka, *Śārīra* 4.8

18) Devaraj T. L., *Ayurveda for Health and Family Welfare*, pp 13-15.

19) Ibid

20) Ibid Ahr. 2.26

21) भक्त्या कल्याणमित्राणि सेवेतेतरदूरगः। Ahr. 2.21[a]

22) अवृत्तिव्याधिशोकार्ताननुवर्तेत शक्तितः।। Ibid 23[a]

23) काले हितं मितं ब्रूयादविसंवादि पेशलम्।
पूर्वाभिलाषी सुमुखः सुशीलः करुणामृदुः।। Ahr. 2.26
नैकः सुखी, न सर्वत्र विश्रब्धो न च शङ्कितः।
न कञ्चिदात्मनः शत्रुं नात्मानं कस्यचिद्रिपुम्।। Ahr. 2.27
प्रकाशयेन्नापमानं न च निःस्नेहतां प्रभोः
जनस्याशयमालक्ष्य यो यथा परितुष्यति।। Ahr. 2.28

24) नीचरोमनखश्मश्रुनिर्मलाङ्घ्रमलायनः।
स्नानशीलः सुसुरभिः सुवेषोऽनुल्बणोज्जवलः।। Ahr. 2.31

Bibliography

A. Original Works

1. **Carakasaṁhitā** by Agniveśa, with Dīpikā commentary of Cakrapāṇidatta, Ed. by Vaidya Jaidevji Trikamji Acharya, Chowkhamba Prakashan, Varanasi, Reprint 2009.
2. Ibid, Text with translation and critical exposition, Vol. 1 Ed. by R.K. Sharma and Vaidya Bhagawan Dash, Chaukhamba Sanskrit Series, Varanasi, Fifth Edition 1997.
3. Ibid, Text with translation and critical exposition, Vol. 2, Ed. by R.K. Sharma and Vaidya Bhagawan Dash, Chaukhamba Sanskrit Series, Varanasi, Reprint 2003.
4. **Suśrutasaṁhitā** of suśruta, with Nibandhana Commentary, Ed. by Yadavji Trikamji Acharya, Chaukhamba Surabharati Prakashan, Varanasi, 1994.

B. Modern Works :-

1. Devaraj T.L. *Ayurveda for Health and Family Welfare* UBS Publishers Distributors Ltd. New Delhi, 1997.
2. Dash Bhagwan, *Fundamentals of Ayurvedic Medicine*, Konark Publishers Ltd. Delhi, Seventh Edition, 1989.
3. Murthy K.R. Shrikantha, *Vāgbhata's Aṣṭāṅgahṛdayam*, with text, translation, notes, appendix and indices, Vol. 1, Chaukhamba Krishnadas Academy, Varanasi, Reprint 2003.

9

Personality Development through Aṣṭānga Yoga

Ashwini S. Patil

Every human being does have different perception, attitude and meaning for the broad terminology "Personality", as we, human beings, are said to be social animals and the only animal having a powerful tool called the 'mind'. Its capacity is simply unlimited. Because of this tool, we are ruling the entire universe. Brain also plays a significant role in developing, enriching and boosting our personality as a whole. Personality is a broad topic to discuss. Its definition is not fixed, but instead encompasses a lot of aspects including the mental, physical, and behavioral patterns exhibited by an individual. However, it creates a massive impact when it comes to the way an individual perceives him/herself or by the society in which ṣhe is a part of. Therefore, Personality development is a big focus in helping people boost their level of self-esteem and gain confidence while there are many different theories of Personality. The first step is to understand exactly what is meant by the term Personality. A brief definition would be that, Personality is made up of the characteristic patterns of thoughts, feelings and behaviors that make a person unique. In addition to this, Personality arises from within the individual and remains fairly consistent throughout life. Personality development is developing a personality cult so as to create a strong positive impression about self with the targeted group, or in general. The term 'personality' is derived from the Latin word persona, meaning the mask which the actors wore on the Greek and Roman stage to distinguish their roles and amplify their voices. Why should the mask or outward appearance be used to designate something so essentially inward as Personality? Precisely because it is a convenient symbol with which to mark off the individuality of or difference between one man and another. The three principal raw materials of personality - physique, intelligence and temperament - are determined both by heredity and by conditions subsequent to birth.

Human personality is a very complex topic by itself. Often personality development is acknowledged mostly in professional fields. Companies conduct training programs on communication skills, leadership skills, and creativity and so on. They collectively call these trainings as Personality Development. Unfortunately they talk about only one side of the coin and should consider some Yoga parameter. No doubt that these traits are important but they are just external. These programs miss the more important factor body and mind. There are hundreds of books available which tell how to win or how to be happy but how many really get benefited just by reading the books? Books tell us to think positive but the poor individuals do not know how. Just by thinking that I will think positive we cannot be positive. It requires practice and fine tuning of body and mind. Unless we have proper foundation of body and mind we simply cannot build any superior personality infrastructure.

Yoga is one of the ṣaḍ darśanās. It has been explained thoroughly in Upanishads.. Yoga has to do with examining ones internal states of consciousness, and clearing out the clouded mind, so that the jewel of the center of consciousness, the Self, can be experienced in its unalloyed purity. Yoga is defined from the Sanskrit word 'yuj' meaning union (with the Divine). The real goal of Yoga is to help it's practitioner in realizing true happiness, freedom, or enlightenment. However, Yoga has a number of secondary goals, such as physical health, mental harmony, and emotional balance. In its most integrated form, Yoga seeks to unlock our full human potential. My topic is how Aṣṭanga yoga helps to develop one's personality. In short, its discussed how in general yoga helps for personality development. Astanga yoga, is a part of yoga philosophy and describes the ways of practice to attain the supreme divine. Aṣṭanga yoga is also called as Raja yoga. Yoga Sutras by Patanjali were written to explain the process and systematic analysis of practical methods for awakening and expanding the higher faculties of mind, intellect, quality of consciousness. It explores the true potential of human mind beyond the limits of time and space, a sure way eventually going beyond the mind. This is an ancient but basic text on Yoga as written by Sage Patanjali 400 years B.C. It is interesting journey in understanding these Sutras and to know the basic principles of science of yoga. The total 196 Sutras are divided in 4 chapters also named as pādās, Samādhi pada, sādhana pada, vibhuti pada and kaivalya pāda. Aśtānga is a union of two Sanskrit words, 'aṣṭa' and 'aṅga'. Aṣṭa means eight and anga means limbs. It is the yoga of eight limbs. Aṣṭānga Yoga is mainly concentrated to physical postures or asanas, which help in maintaining mental peace and equilibrium between body and mind, which ultimately merge the individual consciousness into the universal consciousness. With these practices, the bliss and realization of God is achieved which in turn helps us for the entire development of personality.

Different Types of Yoga

There are various types of yoga. It should be remembered that all of them lead to the same goal, unification with the Divine. The yoga paths can be broadly classified into

Bhaktiyoga: Path of Devotion
Karma yoga: Path of Selfless Action
Dhyāna yoga: Path of Transcendental Knowledge
Aṣṭanga yoga: Path of Patanjali (eight step path)

Yoga to Improve Personality

In general if seen how yoga helps for personality development it can be said that, one of the main benefits that can be derived from yoga and the execution of its basic postures is the fusion of mind, body, and spirit. According to our study mind is the main part for personality development as our thoughts build our personality. Given the different dimensions involved within the human personality, one person can help to nourish their personality by focusing not just on the conscious level of human personality, but on the subconscious as well. There are different methods of yoga employed for different dimensions representing the body as defined by yoga philosophy.

- **Yoga postures:** The purpose of executing yoga poses is to relax our body and attain flexibility. Execution of poses is also vital in maintaining and affecting the flow of energy such that we can manipulate them to enter towards specific areas of the body. Hence, people often utilize yoga to relieve of several form of body pains such as back aches, digestive problems, and many others.

- **Concentration and breathing:** This stage in yoga is important to improve mental personality. For its practical application, the ability to increase concentration and focus makes us more productive at work and also increase vitality in whatever we do.
- **Meditation:** This will help us improve intellectual personality as our ability to keep our mind clear off of any form of unwanted thoughts or ideas makes us more capable of focusing on thoughts that will benefit us. Moreover, we are more likely to make wiser decisions as we can look at things in an objective manner and free off any biases.
- **Deep meditation:** This is another distinctive component in yoga wherein meditation goes a step beyond - specifically deep meditation or Samādhi. This is a vital force to attain the ultimate level of blissful self. This enables us to value and appreciate forces in the world that are beyond the physical and superficial, leading us up to the final aim in practicing yoga. In yoga belief concerning personality development, it introduces vedāntic concept that is aimed at achieving perfection of the soul and inner knowledge to attain self-realization and manifest optimum level of self-confidence. To make this objective much easier, yoga experts have broken down different aspects of human personality development into five different dimensions. Each dimension will utilize a specific approach that will build the formula for a well-integrated personality.

The Yogic View of Personality

As per Yoga the human body consists of five sheaths or layers. They are:

- Conscious physical sheath (Annamaya Koṣa)
- Subconscious physical sheath (Prāṇamaya Koṣa)
- Mental sheath (Manomaya Kośa)
- Intellectual Sheath (Vijñānmaya Kośa)
- Blissful sheath (Ānandamaya Kośa)

The Ānandamaya Kośa is related to our conscious physical deeps including walking, talking, viewing and other such functions. These are the functions that we perform using our physical body deliberately.

The Prāṇamaya Kośa deals with physical activities that we do in subconscious state. Digestion, movement of the heart and lungs fall in this category. We never do any deliberate efforts for these actions; still the body knows how to perform them.

The Manomaya Kośa deals with mind, emotions and thoughts. All our gross thinking and emotions fall in this category.

Intellect is that faculty that decides what is good and what is bad. It is the ability for rational thought or inference or discrimination.

The Vijñānmaya Kośa helps us to identify true from false. We can choose the correct path in this "māyā" filled world with the help of nourished Vijñānmaya Kosha.

Ānandamaya Kośa or bliss is a pure state of happiness and joy which is beyond any material pleasure. Samadhi or deep meditation gives such a joy. The Ānandamaya Kośa is the innermost sheath wrapped by other sheaths in succession. If we observe carefully we will realize that each sheath affects certain part of our personality. Accordingly we can classify our personality as follows:

- Conscious physical personality
- Subconscious physical personality
- Mental personality
- Intellectual personality
- Spiritual personality

How Yoga can nourish these personalities?

The conscious as well as subconscious physical personality can be greatly improved by Yoga postures. Yoga postures stretch your body and induce relaxation. They affect the vital force or Prāna and cause it to flow in specific parts of the body. They are excellent remedy for back aches, digestion problems and heart problems. The modern life forces us to sit at a place without much physical activities. Yoga postures can strengthen the joints and various parts of the body. The mental personality is greatly affected through Prānayama and concentration via Yoga. Our mind remains focused at our work and in home enabling us to do the things with full dedication and interest. It naturally results in better personal and professional gains. Yoga meditation enriches the intellectual personality. Our mind becomes calm and clear. We can think with more care and affection for others. Māya cannot delude us anymore. Our decisions prove to be correct. Finally, the deep Yoga meditation or Samādhi brings us the ultimate bliss. The joy that is impossible to achieve through worldly enjoyments. This is the final aim for any Yogi. In summary practicing Yoga regularly nourishes all these five personalities and makes our life joyous, happy and healthy.

As said previously, yoga sutrās has 4 pādās. Aṣṭānga yoga is described in 3rd and 4th pāda. As the name indicates as sādhana pāda, it gives importance for practice. Practice makes man perfect. The path to practice and the destination when practiced sincerely is also described.

2nd chapter Ist shloka

Says the three kriyās of yoga which are to be practiced to attain highest personality development.

How can a yogi attain highest personality development (samādhi) is described in 1st pāda. The man whose mind is disturbed and how he can attain the Divine is described in 2nd pāda. Man's personality depends on his mind as he is a combination of body, mind and soul. Behaviour of man depicts one's mind. Human mind is caught in avidyā. According to yoga philosophy, a man's personality is developed fully when he attains samadhi and looses avidyā.

Patañjali starts the book with the 1st Sutra

अथ योगानुशासनं ।। (Patanjala yoga sutra 1 chap – 1 sutra)

Atha - now, Yoga - science of Yoga, Anushasanam - Discipline or set of instructions Now, (start with) the discipline of yoga.

If we are given a book, then the first question in your mind will be "What is this book?". Knowing the question of the reader or starter in yoga, Patanjali answers this question in first sutra. He says, now I am explaining the discipline / instructions of science of yoga. There are 3 words in the 1st sutra, Atha, Yoga and Anuśāsanam. It is a very old tradition in Indian scriptures to use word Atha in the beginning of every text or every important process. Hence Patanjali wants to mention that he is starting the explanation of Yoga. The literary meaning of Atha is "Now" or "Hereafter". Patanjali expects that the reader has studied many philosophies and now he is starting to study the philosophy of Yoga.

योगश्चित्तवृत्तिनिरोध: (Pātanjala yoga sutra, 1 chap, 2 sutra)

Yoga = Union
Chitta = Mind
Vṛtti = Functioning / Modifications
Nirodhaḥ = Block with Efforts / restraint

"Yoga is to block the modifications of the mind."

This is the 2nd verse, and Patanjali defines Yoga for the yoga practitioners, let us understand the meaning of each word. The first word Yoga. Yoga has number of meanings but the basic is join or process leading to joining. It is derived from a Sanskrit word Yuj which means to join. Now as per Indian stream of thought, it is the highest join between individual soul or Atmaṅ And universal consciousness or Paramatmaṅ Paramatman is the divine reality and atman is part of this divine but separated from it and confined to Body & Mind. The process of unification of atman with paramatman is Yoga. The second word is Chitta? which is derived from word chit? which means to experience, Chitta is past tense meaning "Experienced" so it can be regarded as store of experiences and that is mind, it stores the experiences in form of memories, thoughts, emotions on conscious, subconscious and unconscious mind. More specifically it can be taken as subconscious mind as most of the experiences are stored there. Vritti is derived from Sanskrit word Vrut which means to function, so Vritti is functioning or modifications. Nirodhah is the 4th word, it is taken from rodha which means to block, and nirodha is to block with planned efforts and controlled actions. Thus Patanjali explains the central theme of yoga in this sutra, and to understand the process leading to this goal needs to be studied.

After knowing the meaning of this sutra, next question will be; ?what will happen when the functioning or modifications of mind is blocked?, and Patanjali answers this in next sutra.

तदा द्रष्टुः स्वरूपे अवस्थानम्।। (Pātanjala yoga sutra, chap 1, 3 sutra)

Tadā - then
Draṣṭā - Seer
Swarūpe - True state of self (Real nature of Soul)
Avasthanam - restored or established

"Then the seer is established in his real or true (original) state or nature."

In the earlier sutra Patanjali has explained that Yoga is blocking the functions of the mind. Now if the functioning is blocked or totally controlled the Chitta or mind will also stop interacting with seer or Atman and Atman / soul will be free of the body- mind complex. Otherwise the Atman is confined by this Body - Mind complex and has no way to unfold its true nature or original state. This is like a person who does not have any job or responsibility and peacefully resting in his house without any attachments. This state is the aim or ultimate goal of Yoga. Patanjali says that the practitioner of Yoga can achieve the ultimate goal of Yoga through "control of Vrittis" or control of modifications / functions of the mind. Patanjali talks about a final state of achievement as "Kaivalya". But now the question is how to control these functions of the mind or Vrittis which normally stimulates the Chitta or Mind to act on the Atman, the real self. This question of how to tackle with the Vrittis is tackled by Patanjali in the remaining sutras. Patanjali is explaining different ways to achieve this goal. One way may not be suitable to all Yoga Sādhakās, hence he mentions many ways but in the sutras, he has mostly focused on Ashtanga Yoga. "The Atman or purusha is assimilated with the functioning /modifications of mind in other state." Patanjali explains the final stage of seer or Atman and before starting the explanation of the detailed technique for attaining the same. He explains the present state of the seer or Atman. The seer or 'Purusha' or 'Atman' is to be released from all other ties and he is helped to merge with its real state that is 'Swaroop'. 'Purusha' or 'Atman' has lost his own identity & is always assimilated with the Vrittis or modifications of the mind that is functioning of mind. While majority of people think that yoga is just a form of exercise that enhances flexibility, if you go back to its roots, yoga is actually a set of spiritual practices aimed at helping a spiritual aspirant attain self-realization. Of the different types of yoga, Astanga yoga or eight-limbed yoga provides the most comprehensive blue-print for rapidly realizing one's true divine self. But what is Aśtānga yoga?

यमनियमासनप्राणायामप्रत्याहारधारणाध्यानसमाधियोष्टावंगानि

* Yama and Niyama

अहिंसा-अस्तेय-ब्रह्मचर्य-अपरिग्रहा यमा:शौच-संतोष-तप: स्वाध्याय ईश्वर प्रणिधानानि नियमा:

Taken together, yama and niyama are the first two limbs of Aśtānga yoga. They are a set of guidelines for human conduct in relation with oneself and others. The object of following these guidelines is not for the sake of following a rule, but to attain mental equilibrium.

* Āsana

तत्र स्थिरसुखमासनम्

The third limb of Aśtānga Yoga is āsana. An āsana is a posture that is based on the posture of animals. It is the most well-known part of yoga, but it is often misunderstood as well. Āsanas are not normal exercises, they are special exercises which have specific effects on the endocrine glands, joints, muscles, ligaments and nerves. Thousands of years ago yogis used to observe the animals of the forest. They noticed that each animal had certain qualities and that the animals often assumed different poses. By imitating these poses they began to notice important effects on the human body. For example, the peacock is a bird with a powerful digestive system capable of digesting even a poisonous snake. The ancient sages developed a posture for humans, which imitated the peacock, which strengthens the human digestive system.

* Prāṇāyama

तस्मिन् सति श्वासप्रश्वासयोर्गतिविच्छेद: प्राणायाम:

Prānayama is also known as the control of vital energy. It is a well-known practice of yoga. Prānayama is a special process of breathing which controls the mind and the pulsing life energy at the center of our chest called the Prānendriya. It helps meditation greatly by readjusting the balance of vital energy in the body.

* Pratyāhāra

स्वविषयासंप्रयोगे चित्तस्य स्वरुपानुकार इवेंद्रियाणांम् प्रत्याहार:

Pratyāhāra means to withdraw the mind from its attachment to external objects. We may have heard of yogis who were so deep in meditation, they couldn't even feel pins being stuck into their bodies. Those yogis are the people who have perfected pratyāhāra.

* Dhārana

देशबंध: चित्तस्य धारणा

Dhārana means the concentration of the mind at a specific point. In the basic lesson of Tantric meditation, a spiritual aspirant brings his or her mind to a specific chakra which is his or her spiritual and psychic nucleus. This point (called the Ista chakra) varies from person to person. When the mind is well concentrated on the point, then the process of repeating the mantra begins. If the concentration is lost, the aspirant must again bring his or her mind back to the point of concentration.

* Dhyāna

तत्र प्रत्ययैकतानता ध्यानम्

This is the process whereby the mind is first brought to a particular chakra and then is directed in an unbroken flow towards the Universal Consciousness. This flow continues until the mind becomes completely absorbed in the Universal Consciousness. This process is difficult and in the past was only given to a disciple by his guru, after the disciple has practiced all the preceding steps of Aśtānga yoga, particularly Dhārana.

* Samādhi

स्वरूपशून्यमिव समाधिः

Unlike the seven other limbs of Aśtānga yoga, Samādhi is not a particular method or practice, rather it is the result of practicing the other parts of Aṣṭānga yoga. It is the absorption of the mind in Universal Consciousness. In a state of samadhi, the mind ceases to function, and a person experiences waves of extreme happiness.

Aṣṭānga Yoga Poses: Aṣṭānga yoga is practiced to keep ourselves physically fit and mentally sound. It can easily channelise our hyperactive mind and infinite energy of body. Our body is detoxified, building strength, bringing flexibility and stamina. There are about seventy five postures which are to be practiced. These postures are named standing poses, seated poses, inversions and backbends etc. All these poses are equally beneficial for adults and children along with precautions.

Nervous System Purification: Also known as 'Nāḍi Shodana' in yoga which makes our nervous system quite strong, fully cleansed. Energy channels (Chakras) of our body are opened. Flexibility in the body, mental peace and ecstasy is possible by aśtānga yoga practice. It not only makes us mentally strong but our muscular body is also strengthened.

Power Poses: This yoga is also called yoga of power poses because it helps us to train the muscles. We can start with easy poses like sun salutation, standing and sitting in progressive manner to have benefits for our mind and body. The sun salutation poses can strengthen our deltoids, triceps and pectoral muscles. This makes our muscles to increase in the size and our endurance strength is positively affected. The flexibility of the body is maintained and physical fitness is stored.

Concentration and Coordination: There are many benefits of this yoga and it helps in sharpening our concentration and coordination with the help of focusing and breathing. Blood circulation is purified and metabolism is improved with the help of these positions. Our memory is improved with strong concentration.

Multiple Techniques: Aṣṭānga yoga is more popular for using multiple techniques than any other yoga. It includes the postures, breathing, concentration and meditation, therefore it is also called 'yoga of techniques'. This yoga is dynamic and other yogās are static in the forms. We get benefits in multiple forms i.e. physical, mental, emotional and intellectual. Aśtānga yoga is extremely popular amongst the young people who want more vigorous āsanās with the same benefits. Our suffering in lives is caused by emotional system of our body. All our bodily diseases are cured properly with the help of aṣṭānga yoga. It is always better to learn this kind of yoga from an expert so that all benefits may be attained without any harm.

Yoga is perhaps the only form of activity which massages all the internal glands and organs of the body in a thorough manner. Yoga acts in a healthy manner on the various body parts. This stimulation and massage of the organs in turn benefits the mass by keeping away diseases. Yoga ensures the optimum blood supply to various parts of the body, by gently stretching muscles and joints as well as massaging the various organs. Regular yoga practice brings about mental clarity and calmness, increases body awareness and also relieves chronic stress patterns, relaxes the mind, centers attention and also sharpens concentration. Yoga strives to increase self-awareness on both physical and psychological level. Studies have also shown that Yoga effects in increased brain activity with better performance and doctors even suggest that yoga can enhance cognitive performance. Yogic theory and practice in India has been followed since ages. The knowledge attained through Yoga is not merely that of the practical kind relating to techniques, but of a spiritual type pertaining to grasping something about the nature of the self at rest. Yoga is a complete system that includes practices for body, mind and spirit such as ethics, meditation and physical postures. Classical yoga is practical and is applied to daily life. It is total control of personality complexes which reflects after practicing yoga regularly and consciously. Yoga strongly believes in balanced state of mind. In this state, work performed can be of high quality. The science of yoga is for better and healthy living. It is education of total personality development and the most important aspect of Yoga is the sense of confidence that it generates. This is so because the Yogi views whatever is there in the universe, is a miniature form within every being. Yoga, an ancient Indian concept, represents the way of life which endows perfect health comprising physical, mental, ethical and spiritual development. In Sanskrit this word means 'to unite'. Indeed the practice of yoga leads to the integration of the soul with the Supreme Being. This Hindu discipline is also put into practice to lead a healthy life. In fact, physical education, for the first time, was correlated to health, hygiene, ethics, meditation and even a higher purpose of life by the ancient Yogis of India. Principally, however, yoga does not conceive man only physically. On the contrary it lays greater emphasis on the significance of soul and mind as these characterise man's personality. The human body is made of a physical body, a mind and a spirit, and the three parts are so dependent on each other that any disturbance in one part affects the whole system. Yoga, thus, has a holistic approach as it regards man as a whole being with body, mind and soul.

10

Personality Development Through Education: Past and Present

Archana G. Murgod

The unique feature of ancient Indian culture rests on the foundations, which were laid down by the ancient sages, who relentlessly sought for the integral knowledge and perfection of the highest principle. As a result, even after the lapse of many centuries, Indian culture has been sustained with promising continuity and benefits.

Life takes inspirations from the past. The past history of any country is the inspiration of the country's present or future. Our ancestors have defined life and our moral duties, based on spiritual aspects and not on material ones. They not only thought of development of India but also the development of the whole human race as such. For them, the whole universe was family itself. Thus, the proclamation "वसुधैव कुटुम्बकम्" holds all significant.

In the journey of one's life, personality development plays an important role. The personality is almost, certainly a complex phenomenon. It is, simultaneously, the most fascinating import, this is because everybody hungers for attention, for self-insight and for inner peace, and hence everybody is concerned with understanding the word– 'personality'. The parent wants to understand the personality of his child; the teacher of his student; the executive of his employee; and all of us want to understand our own personality, and study of personality seems to promise these gains.

No two persons are exactly the same, not even identical twins. Some people are anxious, some are risk-taking; some are phlegmatic; some highly-strung; some are confident, some shy; and some are quiet and some are loquacious. This issue of difference is fundamental to the study of personality.

To speak of a word as person is neither male nor female, neither young nor old. The only way to revitalize such frayed concept is to trace its history. The word 'personality' is derived from the latin word *Persona,* which means the theatrical mask, first used in Greek drama and adopted about hundred years before Christ by Roman players. These are the persons that project and display, but also include the inner parts of psychological experience which are collectively called the 'self'.[1]

In the writings of Cicero (106-43 B.C.), at least four distinct meaning of persona are found:[2]

a) As one appears to others (but not as one really);
b) The part some one (e.g. a philosopher) plays in life;
c) An assemblage of personal qualities that fit a man for his work.
d) Distinction and dignity (as in a style of writing).

The first meaning, of course, has the original significance of the mask; the second suggests real status; not the mere pretence; the third meaning signifies the inner psychic qualities of the player himself; and the final meaning connotes the importance and prestige which later were conveyed by the derivative term personage.

Scientifically personality may be defined thus: "The individual's social stimulus value depends on his responses; and these are determined by the cognitive, emotional and motivational systems that make up the personality." According to traditional Indian scholars of the past, "The harmonious growth of the physical, mental, intellectual, social and spiritual aspects constitute the real personality."

Personality is one of the most abstract words in our language; its connotative significance is very broad but its denotative significance negligible. Scarcely any word is more versatile.

Keeping this connotative aspect of personality, it may be said that the very concept of personality development is no doubt the very complex one. It has been keenly observed and taken care of, by the Indians of *Vedic* ages. Hence it is pertinent that the entire vedic literature including *Purāṇas*, *Rāmāyaṇa* and *Mahābhāratha* and other texts of classical age remarkably emphasize the concept of personality development. In this context it should be made clear that the very phrase personality development means "*Vyaktitva Vikasanam* or *ātmoddhāraå*". As a matter of fact, entire ancient Indian literature aims at showing the path of '*ātmoddhārå*' or personality development. Being one of the essentials of personality development education plays a very important role. In this way, howsoever wide is the scope of personality development in the context of ancient Sanskrit literature, an attempt is put forward to integrate all folds of personality development of student through education.

It is beyond doubt that the gems of personality development are unevenly scattered here and there in all the *Vedas*, *Upaniṣads*, *Brahmasūtras*, Epics and so on. And yet, all these texts emphasize that the *Puruṣārthas* play an important role in reaching the culmination of personality development. The *Puruṣārthas* explained very systematically in the *Dharmaśāstras* are briefly dealt with here.

Puruṣārthas

An individual is a representative of his society and both the society and individual have an equal bearing upon each other. Both of them can co-ordinate their course of action, once the individuals constituting the society are able to determine their fundamental values of life. The concept of value is significant as it forms the very basis of a social structure.

The wisest man of Greece, Socrates said, "The noblest of all investigations is the study of what man should be and what he should pursue." Indian thought which has had a hoary antiquity, from the earliest times, focused its attention and directed the search-light of its reasoning and analysis to the subject of the meaning and purpose of man's life on earth. The sages, seers, prophets and poets of India were profoundly interested in this study of what man should be and what man should pursue.

With this background they comprehend the scope of this topic by the significant Sanskrit compound '*Puruṣārthas*'. It means and connotes the aims and purposes of life or the fundamental aspirations of man. The term *Puruṣārtha* not only denotes what the objectives of life should be, but it also comprehends what the objectives of life are as the result of the psychological tendencies of individual. These *Puruṣārthas* are said to be fourfold. They are –

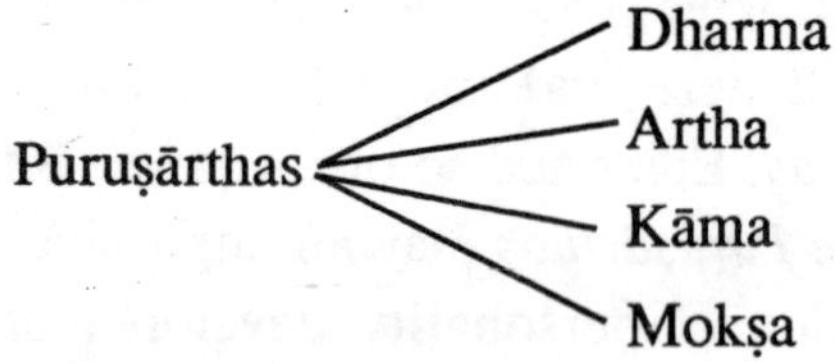

All the aims and aspirations of man are comprised in these four *Puruṣārthas* which are to be pursued consiously. This significant concept of development upholds the legitimacy of man's desire for economic security i.e. *Artha*, and sensuous aesthetic satisfaction i.e. *Kāma* and spiritual welfare i.e. *Mokṣa*. But rightousness i.e. *Dharma* is claimed to be the most important factor of all the above. On the basis of *Dharma* alone, the remaining goals are to be fulfilled.

Even the order of the *Puruṣārthas* has its significance. *Dharma* plays the ruling principle of life while *Mokṣa* is the ultimate goal. In between are *Artha* and *Kāma*, which are natural aspirations of every man in life. They refer to acquiring the means for material prosperity and to enjoy the innocent pleasures of life. *Dharma* being placed first as the ruling principle, both *Artha* and *Kāma* must be subject to *Dharma*. There must be no acquisition of wealth which violates the principles of *Dharma*. Similarly, also no enjoyment is to be desired which is opposed to *Dharma*. As *Artha* enables man to enjoy the comforts and pleasures of life, it is placed before *Kāma*, and it is one of the fundamental ideas in relation to these *Puruṣārthas* that *Dharma* is the legitimate source of rather *Artha* and *Kāma*. All these three must be pursued with the ultimate goal of *Mokṣa* everpresent to the mind.

The most central and core concept of Hindu philosophy is known as *Dharma*. All the other principles and values flow from this beautiful fountain of *Dharma*. The etimological derivation of the word *Dharma* is from the root 'धृ' – 'to hold', 'to maintain', 'to restrain' etc. Mahabharatha proclaims: 'धर्मो धारयति प्रजा:' *Dharma* restrains creatures.

Dharma is a very difficult concept which can not be very precisely defined or explained. This word is variously rendered as "statue, ordinance-law; usage, customary observance, duty; one's own obligation; duty or self-initiated action (ethical, social, spiritual); right, justice, righteousness, good conduct, virtue, morality, religion, religious merit; good, attribute, quality, feature (both in concrete and abstract); also personification of many human beings, deities, abstract phenomena etc.

The solidarity, integrity and prosperity of any nation is invariably dependent on the prevelant educational system. Hence the issue demands our serious attention. For an ordered, gradual and holistic development of human personality and to secure a progressive balance and harmony of growth, the ancient educational thinkers developed this unique concept of '*Puruṣārthas*'.

Importance of Education in Ancient India

Education was considered essentially a process of illumination. And knowledge is the third eye which gives an insight into all affairs and teaches how to act in life.[3]

ज्ञानं तृतीयं मनुजस्य नेत्रं समस्ततत्वार्थविलोकदत्तम्।
तेजोनपेक्ष विगतान्तरायं प्रवृत्तिमत्सर्वजगत्त्रयेऽपि।।
(सुभाषितरत्नभाण्डागार)[4]

This point has also been noted by the scholars like R.N. Aralikatti[4a], Altekar A.S.[4b], Bhatt Rameshwar[4c], Pandey Umeshachandra[4d].

A person who does not possess the light of the education is described as blind. It is education which removes all doubts and is a gateway to the world of abstract thoughts.

अनेकसंशयोच्छेदी परोक्षार्थस्य दर्शकम्।
सर्वस्य लोचनं शास्त्रं यस्य नास्त्यंध एव सः।।
(सुभाषितरत्नभाण्डागार)[5]

Education is veritable desire yielding tree. It increases by enhancing our reputation.

श्रियः प्रदुग्धे विपदो रुणद्धि यशांसि सूते मलिनं प्रमर्ष्टि।
संस्कारशौचेन नरं पुनीते शुद्धा हि बुद्धिः किल कामधेनुः।।
(सुभाषितरत्नभाण्डागार) [6]

Education nourishes us like a mother, directs us to the proper path like a father and gives us delight and comfort like a wife.

मातेव रक्षति पितेव हिते नियुङ्क्ते।
कान्तेव चापि रमयत्यपनीय खेदम्।। (सुभाषितरत्नभाण्डागार)[7]

The direct aim of ancient Indian education was to make the student fit to become a useful and pious member of society.[8] Inculcating the civic and social duties among the students was also a part of ancient Indian educational system. The students were not to lead a self-centred life. They were constantly reminded of their obligations to the society.

The most important idea governing the ancient system of education was that of perfection, for developing the mind and soul of man. Ancient Indian education aimed at helping the individual to grow in the power and force of certain large universal qualities which in their harmony build a higher type of manhood. It also focussed on building a desciplined and value-based culture. Human values such as trust, respect, honesty, dignity and courtesy are the building blocks of any free, advanced society.[9]

Another unique feature of this system is that it aims at creating a mind that is both scientific and spiritual. One that is enquiring, precise, rational, and sceptical but at the same time has sense of beauty, wonder, aesthetics, sensitivity, humility, and an awareness of the limitations of the intellect.[10] It also aims at developing a mind, which is flexible and not dogmatic, open to change and not irrationally attached to an opinion or belief should. In this system of education both scientific and spiritual quests are the complementary quests.[11]

Qualities and Duties of Teacher

A 'Guru' is one who kindles light in his student and destroys the darkness that covers his knowledge and a 'śiṣya' is one who gets his transmission and partaking of light, i.e., the knowledge. Therefore, it goes without saying that the process of imparting and receiving knowledge involves active participation from both the end. It is never a monologue but a dialogue; it is not mechanical but lively; it is not monotonous but vibrant and vivid. Hence the गुरु is invoked in the following verse.

अज्ञानतिमिरान्धस्य ज्ञानाञ्जनशलाकया।
चक्षुरुन्मीलितं येन तस्मै श्रीगुरवे नमः।।

'I salute the Guru who opens the eyes of one who is blind with the cataract of ignorance by applying the collyrium of jñāna or knowledge.'

A teacher should impart his learning only to those students who are intellectually well-qualified and morally sound. Such of the students who are grateful, free from prejudices, intelligent, averse to fault finding and of high moral characters alone should be accepted for imparting learning.

The teachers' instructions were not limited to classroom teachings, but he must know minutely what is beneficial to the society and to an individual as well, what is the standard of moral behaviour for the society. Being included in the *śiṣṭas* (codes of moral laws), he must be competent enough to interpret law. He is generally described as *Dharmajña* and *Śuciả* and therefore was eligible to teach *śaucācāras*.[12]

A remarkable point mentioned in Rāmāyaṇa is that, the father and mother are responsible only for the physical being of a child, but the preceptor grants him wisdom; therefore he is higher than parents. For every one that is born, there are three masters such as the father, mother and spiritual teacher, who deserve great honour.

पुरुषस्येह जातस्य भवन्ति गुरवः सदा।
आचार्यश्चैव काकुत्स्थ पिता माता च राघव।।
पिता ह्येनं जनयति पुरुषं पुरुषर्षभ।
प्रज्ञां ददाति चाचार्यस्तस्मात् स गुरुरुच्यते।।
(रामायणम्, II.111.2-3)

Here, one point is to be noted in this Guru-Śiṣya relation. The teacher is the all knower, he allows his student to ask any doubt and no problem goes unanswered. He reshapes the entire personality of the student not just by instructing him but by inspiring the student.

Qualities and Duties of Student

Generally the students were admitted into the Gurukulas after they had been invested with the sacred thread at the age of eight (Upanayanam). The period of vedic study, generally, was 12 years and for other studies, it varied from 9 years to 18 years to 36 years or till a student masters his lore.

षट्त्रिशदांब्दिकं चर्यं गुरौ त्रैवेदिकं व्रतम्।
तदर्धिकं पादिकं वा ग्रहणान्तिकमेव वा। (मनुस्मृति, III-1)
नैष्ठिको ब्रह्मचारी तु वसेदाचार्यसन्निधौ।।
(याज्ञवल्क्य स्मृति, 1-49)

A student has to follow his course of study of Vedas and Śāstras along with the code of conduct which alone would lead to successful completion of his education in Gurukula.

तस्माद्वेदव्रतानीह चरेत् स्वाध्यायसिद्धये।
शौचाचारमशेषे तु शिक्षयेद्गुरुसन्निधौ।।
(लघुहारीतस्मृति, III.4.10-15)

एवमन्वहमभ्यासी ब्रह्मचारी व्रतं चरेत्।
हितोपवादः प्रियवाक् सम्यग्गुर्वर्यसाधके।। (व्यासस्कृति I-35)
अनेन विधिनाधीतो वेदमन्त्रो द्विजं नयेत्।
शास्त्रानुग्रहसामर्थ्यमर्षीणां च सलोकताम्।। (व्यासस्मृति I-36)
कुर्यादध्ययनं चैव ब्रह्मचारी यथाविधि।
विधिं त्यक्त्वा प्रकुर्वाणो न स्वाध्यायफलं लभेत्।
(लघुहारीतस्मृति III-2)

The student not only had to observe a strict discipline and routine but also render service to his teacher.

The *Rāmāyaṇa* declares "heavenly bliss, wealth, agricultural products, knowledge, progeny and happiness are all obtained by mere service to the preceptors; and there is nothing that cannot be obtained from it."

स्वर्गो धनं वा धान्यं वा विद्या पुत्राः सुखानि च।
गुरुवृत्त्यनुरोधेन न किञ्चिदपि दुर्लभम् (Rāmāyaṇa II 30.36)

Ancient Indian System of Education

Now let us have a peep into the ancient Indian system of education, i.e., गृरुग्रहवास.

The hermitages of sages (*āśramas* or *gurukulas*) were the centres of learning where various disciplines were taught to the choice of the seekers. Acquiring knowledge from the preceptors was not only in accordance with the vedic injunction that, one must study the branches of that Veda to which he belongs स्वाध्यायोऽध्येतव्य:, but also it was everybody's strong desire to acquire and preserve the knowledge that had come down traditionally, कामं खलु सर्वस्यापि कुलविद्या बहुमता।[13] The rulers of the day were to provide required material to maintain these hermitages such as sufficient grazing grounds for cows, playgrounds for students, gardens to grow flowers, orchards for yielding fruits, groves, trees for abundant shade and fuel, huts for worship of fire and to perform sacrifices, moist place by the side of flowing rivers where corn will grow uncultivated. The hermitages, to be free from the distractions of the day to day life, were situated far from the townships. These hermitages with the serene atmosphere and the vedic chantings, uninterrupted glow of sacrificial fires, were the harmoneous abodes not only of human beings but also of wild animals, birds and beasts. The trees and creepers were always rich in fruits and flowers. The doors of hermitages were kept open and warm reception was accorded to the visitors and the students had not to pay. It was thought that knowledge is so sacred that no man ought to sell it.

Plain living and high thinking was the motto of the asramists, the life was exceedingly simple and peaceful. All the inhabitants used to reside in the huts made of reeds and leaves and dressed in bark garments. Their means of subsistence consisted of corn, wild fruits and milk of cows. They had the beds made of Kuśa grass or the the skin of deers. The earthern lamp were fed with ingudi oil for lights at night.[14] Day's activities was to commence well before the dawn since the intellect is well known to receive fresh vigour during the last quarter of the night.[15]

Without the personal life of the teacher, there would be no education. One should live from his very boyhood with one whose character is a blazing fire and should have before him a living example of the highest teaching. In India the imparting of knowledge has always been through the men of renunciation.

Teaching Techniques

Our ancient teachers had already discovered different methods of successful teaching. Mainly they are –

1) प्रयोगमूल (Practical) 2) दृष्टान्तमूल (Illustrative)

3) संकेतमूल (Symbolic) 4) क्रममूल (Graded)

5) प्रश्नोत्तरमूल (Question and Answer)

The practical and illustrative methods of teaching are well exemplified in *Chāndogya Upaniṣad* (6.1.1, 6.13.2-3) (6.10.1, 6.14.2) (1.2.12) whereas the symbolic method of teaching is introduced in *Muṇḍakopaniṣad* (1.2.13, 6.1). The graded method can be observed in *Taittariyopaniṣad* (valli-2) and also in *Kāṭhopaniṣad* (II.12, II.2.12). The method of question and answer can be seen in *Kenopaniṣad* (IV.6).

Although memorization was very important method for vedic study, critical reflection and development of creative intellect was the hall mark of this period. Metaphysics made remarkable progress as evidenced by the Upanishadic, Buddhistic and Jain works. The beginning of all later system of philosophy can be traced to this dharmashastra period. Philosophy and grammer were developed, and literary activity in legal literature (*Dharmaśāstra*) commenced. Speculations in the realm of political thought were fruitful. Kauāilya wrote his *Arthaśāstra*. Similarly, Varāhamihira wrote Astronomy and Bhāskarācārya wrote Mathemetics and Caraka and Suśruta wrote books on medicine and surgery. Similarly, branches of learning like mining and metellargy were also developed.[16]

Memorization, recitation, recapitulation formed the methods of vedic studies. Chinese traveller (675 A.D.) refers to the wonderful feats of memory of these vedic scholars since everything had to be at the tip of his tongue. For the study of *śāstra* and other subjects, exposition was an accepted method for explaining the concepts in subjects, like philosophy, logic, law, grammer. It was accompanied by extensive lectures, discussing exhaustively the opponent's views and establishing one's own stand. Chinese pilgrim again praise Indian teachers for their unsurpassed ability in explaining difficult passages and offering illuminating suggestions on doubtful points.[17]

Another aspect of the Indian education system was that it was very practical. Due to the constant presence of the disciple with his Guru, the disciple used to get exposure to real social life. Attending to the household chores of his Guru's home, was the duty of every disciple. He not only got knowledge of the household things but also got training in following the principles like sacrifice, service and hard work. The disciple also learnt modesty and discipline. Many things, which today have become a major problem, were taken care of, automatically because of this kind of education system.

This goes to prove the point that the ancient Indian education system was not only theoretical but had a very practical and real-life training approach.

Personality Development through *Yoga*

The success in maintaining such a disciplined and hard life style lies in practice of *Yoga* for disciplining the mind and body which results in the wholesome personality development of student. The great sage Pātañjali in his authoritative treatise "*Yoga sūtra*" builds his entire eight-fold path of *Yoga* (अष्टाङ्ग योग). They are –

यमनियमासनप्राणायामप्रत्याहारधारणाध्यानसमाधयोऽष्टावङ्गानि।।
(योगसूत्र-29)

Without the practice of the first two principles i.e. *Yama* and *Niyama*, which lay the firm foundation for building character, there cannot be an integrated personality.[18] The next three *aṅgās* viz., *Āsana*, *Prāṇāyāma* and *Pratyāhāra* would enable the student to gain concentration of mind and physical fitness. Likely, the first five *aṅgās* being the means of outer development (बहिरंगसाधना) of personality, the last three viz., *Dhāraṇā, Dhyāna* and *Samādhi* directly help to achieve the salvation (अन्तरङ्ग साधना).

Since, one can successfully carryout his journey to achieve other *aṅgās* only by observing *Yama* and *Niyama*, now let us have a brief introduction to these boards. The word Yama can be broadly translated as 'Self-Restraints'.

अहिंसासत्यास्तेयब्रह्मचर्यापरिग्रहाः यमाः। (योगसूत्र-30)

These five-fold self-restraints are shown in the following diagram:

यम (Self-restraints)

अहिंसा	सत्य	आस्तेय	ब्रह्मचर्य	अपरिग्रह
(Non-violence)	(Truthfulness)	(Nonstealing)	(Celibacy)	(Non-grabbing)

And the word *Niyama* refers to 'Internal - Restraints' and they are also five in number as shown below:

शौचसन्तोषतप:स्वाध्यायेश्वरप्रणिधानानि नियमाः (योगसूत्र-32)

नियम (Internal Restraints)

शौच	सन्तोष	तपस्	स्वाध्याय	ईश्वरप्रणिधान
(Cleanliness)	(Contentment)	(Hard work)	(Self-study)	(Surrender to God)

Will-power

The essence of personality development also depends on strengthening of will-power. The divine core of one's personality is covered, as it were, by five dimensions (पञ्चकोशः) shown below:

पञ्चकोशाः (Five dimensions)
- अन्नमयकोश (Physical dimension)
- प्राणमयकोश (Energy dimension)
- मनोमयकोश (Mental dimension)
- विज्ञानमयकोश (Intellectual dimension)
- आनन्दमयकोश (Blissful dimension)

1) Physical dimension consisting of our body and senses.
2) Energy dimension which performs digestion of food, circulation of blood, respiration and other activities in the body.
3) Mental dimension characterized by activities of the mind, like, thinking, feeling and emotions etc.

4) Intellectual dimension characterized by the determinative faculty in a person. This is also the seat of discrimination and will power.

5) Blissful dimension experienced as bliss during deep sleep.

Each succeeding dimension is subtler than the preceding one and pervades it.

Personality development implies progressive identification with higher dimensions of personality. Thus a person identified only with the physical dimension and without exercising his higher mental faculties, lives not far different from animals, whose pleasure and pain are restricted to the sensory system.[19]

The convocation address found in *Taittirīya Upaniṣad* throws significant light on the qualities required to be developed by the students even today.

सत्यं वद। धर्मं चर। स्वाध्यायान्मा प्रमदः। आचार्याय प्रियं धनमाहृत्य प्रजातन्तुं मा व्यवच्छेत्सीः। सत्यान्न प्रमदितव्यम्। धर्मान्न प्रमदितव्यम्। कुशलान्न प्रमदितव्यम्। देवपितृकार्याभ्यां न प्रमदितव्यम्। मातृदेवो भव। पितृदेवो भव। आचार्यदेवो भव। अतिथिदेवो भव। यान्यनवद्यानि कर्माणि तानि सेवितव्यानि। नो इतराणि यान्यस्माकं सुचरितानि। तानि त्वयोपास्यानि। नो इतराणि। ये के चास्मच्छ्रेयांसो ब्राह्मणाः तेषां त्वयाऽऽसने न प्रश्वसितव्यम्। श्रद्धया देयम्। अश्रद्धयाऽदेयम्। श्रिया देयम्। ह्रिया देयम्। भिया देयम्। संविदा देयम्। अथ यदि ते कर्मविचिकित्सा वा वृत्तविचिकित्सा वा स्यात्। ये तत्र ब्राह्मणाः संमर्शिनः। युक्ता आयुक्ताः। अलूक्षा धर्मकामाः स्युः। यथा ते तेषु वर्तेरन्। तथा तेषु वर्तेथाः। एष आदेशः। एष उपदेशः। एषा वेदोपनिषत्। एतदनुशासनम्। एवमुपासितव्यम्। एवमुचैतदुपास्यम्। (तैत्तिरीयोपनिषत्–शिक्षावल्लि, I.xi.1-4)

"Speak the truth. Practice righteousness, make no mistake about study. There should be no inadvertence about truth. There should be no deviation from righteous activity. There should be no error about protection of yourself. Do not neglect propitious activities. Do not be careless about learning and teaching. There should be no error in the duties towards the Gods and men. Let your mother be a Goddess unto you. Let your father be a God unto you. The works that are not blameworthy are to be resorted to, but not the others. The offering should be with sympathy. Then, if you have any doubt with regard to duties or customs, you should behave in such matters just as the wise men do, who may happen to be there and who are not directed by others, who are not cruel, and who are desirous of merit. This is the injunction. This is the instruction. This is the secret of the scriptures."

This convocation address outlines some of the domestic and social duties in very clear terms which can be concluded as– students are: to honour father, mother, teacher and guest as gods; to honour superiors; to give in proper manner and spirit, in joy and humility, in fear and compassion. Lastly, the pupil is also asked not to neglect his health and possessions. This convocation address is very important in understanding the role of ancient Indian education in building a value-based culture. It tried to inculcate in the students the following qualities:

- Self discipline based on the sense of duties and responsibilities of an individual.
- Character and honesty based on moral law.
- Social consciousness based on the humanity.

In this regard it has to be admitted that ancient Indian system of education played a major role in making students realize their duties and responsibilities and emphasized on the necessity of discipline for an orderly Social Life. Character and discipline cannot be imparted to an individual by preaching or through speeches. He can be made to act in conformity with the required standard of behaviour and through personal example. These qualities are acquired by emutation in addition to education.

It is only by generating these qualities in individuals the ancient Indian educational system prompted the students to utilize their educational attainments and capacities for the benefit of society restricting their own selfish desires and prevented them from acting in a manner harmful and detrimental to the common good.

Mere knowledge of what is virtue and what is not, does not make a man virtuous. This aspect is forcefully brought forth in the character of Duryodhana in the epic Mahābhārata. He says:

जानामि धर्मं न च मे प्रवृत्तिः। जानाम्यधर्मं न च मे निवृत्तिः।

I know what righteous conduct is, but I have no inclination to act accordingly. I know what unrighteous conduct is, but I can not abstain from doing it."

A very useful observation has been made by Swami Vivekananda in this context:

"The character of any man is but the aggregate of his tendencies, the sum total of the bent of his mind. We are what our thoughts have made us. Thoughts live; they travel far. Every work what we do, every movement of the body, every thought that we think, leaves an impression on mind stuff. What we are every moment is determined by the sum total of these impressions on mind. Every man's character is determined by the sum total of these impressions. If good impressions prevail, the character becomes good, if bad, it becomes bad. When a large number of these impressions are left on the mind they coalesce and become a habit. The only remedy for bad habit is counter habits; all the bad habits that have left their impressions are to be controlled by good habits."

Many rites and rituals were developed in order to infuse piety and religiousness in the students. The rituals that a student had to perform at the beginning of his educational career, the religious observations that he had to observe during the educational course, the daily prayers that he offered morning and evening, the religious festivals that were celebrated very often in the school or the preceptors house – all these tended to foster piety and religiousity in the mind of the young learner.[20] Ancient education system aimed at character formation through proper development of moral feelings to make the students really learned, pure in their life, thoughts and habits.[21]

The ancient Indian thinkers felt that a healthy society was not possible without educated individuals. They framed educational set up carefully and wisely aiming at the harmonious development of the multiple dimensions of the human personality. This is a universally applicable educational framework highlighting the purpose of human life and interconnectedness at all levels of existence as a basis of human values. In this system understanding oneself (self-knowledge) is as important as understanding the world. According to them without a deep understanding of one's relationship with nature, with ideas, with fellow human beings, with society, and deep respect for all life, one is not really educated.[22]

Teaching of values, ideal life led by teachers, and examples of extraordinary personalities cited from the epics, poetry, literature and history, all these helped to mould the character of students.[23]

Ancient Indian educational system also aimed at the development of personality by eulogosing the feeling of self-respect, by encouraging the sense of self-confidence, by inculcating the virtue of self-restraint and fostering the powers of discrimination and judgement. In ancient times the student used to listen and understand the mysteries and complexities of life and this world, in a very beautiful, quiet and peaceful atmosphere. He used to be with the teacher to understand all this. His life was pure. Students knowledge was not restricted to books, but he was also exposed to practical knowledge and true experience of life.

It is a strange, Indian tradition that a disciple stays with his Guru to attain knowledge. This tradition is rarely found in any other part of the world. All virtues of the Guru are naturally imbibed in the student because of his continuous presence with the teacher. This was very important for the development of the personality of the taught.

"To sum up, we may say that the qualities of an ideal teacher and those of students, plain living and high thinking, intellectual freedom, individual attention to the students, residential system of education i.e., Gurukula system, monitorial system as a substitute for training course, location of educational institute away from the din and dust of city life and maddening crowds, are some of the features which are worthy of emulation even today since they have relevance even in modern times with suitable modifications whenever necessary."[24]

Education at Present

It is seen that the present generation is flowing towards the havoc of west culture. Everyone is struggling hard to earn more and more money and hence greed, selfishness, delusion, enmity, indignation acquiring the places of happiness, love, morality, brotherhood and peace. People are becoming more and more self-centred and this mindset is strongly influencing on the present education system too. Now the goal of education has remained just for the sake of examination.

The present scenario of the relationship between student and teacher is known to all of us. Most of the teachers have reduced themselves as simple transmitters of information and the students have become storehouses of information. We can see today's children are not inculcating the knowledge to serve for the mankind, but just to fulfill the unending desires of worldly pleasures.

Even the educational institutes have become commercial places, where the knowledge is bought and sold to even an unworthy person. The schools were treated as temple then, but now they are just money-minting machines.

The disturbed and busy life-style of parents, the influence of radio, televisions, newspapers, mobiles, unhealthy food habits, etc., are turning off the students from their main goal of life. Though they are beneficial to collect information but most have become slaves after them. As a result they fail to regulate their lives in accordance with the principles of social co-operation.

The lack of interest in learning as well as teaching can be observed now a days. In ancient era through being highly knowledgesome the Preceptor used to keep studing for his lifetime. श्रवण-मनन-निदिध्यासन was practiced. But now once a person gets permanently appointed, then seldom feels the need of extra studies.

Such points increase the gap between the teacher and taught. Infact now a new concept is introduced world wide, "Learning without a Preceptor." But this system would help very few people who are highly intelligent, to larger number of people there is need of Preceptor, at least at the initial stage to clear the obstacles faced in the path of acquiring knowledge, by this constant guidance.

Current system of education may seem to be effective for the growth of our nation, but it is temporary remedy. Through fastening the life style it is forcing people to lead a tensionful life whereas our ancient system of education goals at the betterment of the whole world, it promotes both individual and social development of nation by making the people to lead a healthy, peaceful and a happy life. The present education should be the combination of western technology and rich Indian system of education, which would destroy all-consuming darkness and bless the humanity with evershining light.

There are few good educational institutes and ideal teachers even in present days. But they are very few and they remain unnoticed and a very small number of fortunate people can only be benefited by them.

Now there is a great need of such a teacher who has to generate that energy in oneself and handles it in one's work of educating the students. A teacher has not only to instruct but also to inspire the students; and equip them with ideas and values which will fit them to enter the stream of national life as worthy citizens.

The students are to be educated on the need to recognize the equality of men and women in our democracy, to discard all caste exclusiveness and pride, untouchability, and communal distinctions and antagonisms and to strengthen, the dignity of the individual and the unity of nation, as our constitution proclaims.

The students must be educated to become the instruments to develop an integrated nation out of our diversities. They must be made acquainted with the noble humanistic sentiments of our constitution and impressed with the passion to translate them into socio-political realities. They should be bestowed with a high character-energy, a pure national awareness, a firm democratic loyalty a dedicated social responsibility.

In the foregoing discussion, it has been seen that the ideal relationship between the student and the teacher as found in the ancient system of education and the current, also the authenticity of ancient Indian education system. If those disciplines are strictly followed even today which is not impossible, all students irrespective of any cast and creed can develop their overall personality and by successfully fulfilling the *purusharthas* can lead a worthy and satisfactory life. And if once again, the disciplines of ancient time are whole-heartedly accepted then the student becomes most eligible person to look the welfare and from then, the happiness and the well-being of the nation.

References

1. H. Rheinfelder, "*Das wort 'Persona'*" Zsch of Roman Philol. 1928 Beiheft 77-pp 22 ff.
2. Q, Gordon W. Allport, "*Personality – A Psychological Interpretation*", p.26
3. Q, V.N. Jha, *Dharmaśāstra and Social Awareness*, Sri Satguru Publication, 1996, p.125
4. *Ibid.*, p.130

4a. R.N. Aralikatti, "*Vedanta Education apropos caste system*", B.R. Sharma Felicitation Volume, 1989

4b. A.S. Altekar, *Education in Ancient India,* Manohar Prakashana, Varanasi, 1978

4c. Rameswar Bhatt (Ed.), *Manusmṛti,* Chaukhamba Sanskrit Prakashana, Delhi, 1990

4d. Pandey, Umeshchandra K., *Yājñavalkyasmṛti* (Hindi Translation), Chaukhamba Sanskrit Series, Varanasi, 1967

5. *Subhāṣita Ratna Bhaṇḍāgāra* – Vidyapraśaṁsā, verse 2, p.29.

6. *Subhāṣita Ratna Bhaṇḍāgāra* – Vidyapraśaṁsā, verse 12, p.30.

7. *Ibid.*, verse 14, p.30, *Bhojaprabandha*, 5.

8. Rangachar S., *Early Indian Thought*, Mysore, Geetha Book House, 1964

9. Markandan N., "*The value and purpose of education*", Contribution towards an Agenda for India, Indian Institute of Advanced Study, Shimla, 2005.

10. James Moffett, *Spiritual Awakening through Education* (San Francisco : Jossey Bass), 1994.

11. J. Krishnamurti, *Education and the significance of life*, Harper San Francisco (Reprint) .... 2000 On Education, Krishnamurti Foundation India, (Reprint), 1981.

12. V.N. Jha, '*Dharmaśāstra and Social Awareness*', Sri Sadguru publications, A Division of Indian Books Centre, Delhi-India, 1996, p.137.

13. Kālidāsa, *Mālavikāgnimitram* - 1

14. Kālidāsa, *Abhijñāna Śākuntalā* IV-14.

15. Kālidāsa, *Raghuvaṁśam* XVII-1.

16. V.N.Jha (ed.), "*Dharmaśāstra and Social Awareness*", Sri Satguru Publication, 1996, p.126.

17. V.N.Jha (ed.), "*Dharmaśāstra and Social Awareness*", Sri Satguru Publication, 1996, p.127.

18. B.K. Iyengar, *The Tree of Yoga*, Harper Collins Publications, New Delhi, (Ninth impression), 2005.

19. Swami Vivekananda, '*Personality Development*' Advaita Ashram Kolkata, November 2009, pp.17-18.
20. Rajbali Pandey, *Hindu Samskaras*, Motilal Banarsidass, New Delhi, 1994.
21. Biswanath Ghosh, *Ethics in Management and Indian Ethos*, Vikas Publishing House, New Delhi, 2005.
22. Ramachandra Rao, S.K. 1992, *Original Ancient thought*, Bangalore University, Bangalore.
23. Altekar, A.S. 1943, *Education in Ancient India*, Motilal Banarsidass, New Delhi.
24. V.N. Jha, "*Dharmaśāstra and Social Awareness*", Sri Satguru Publications, 1996, p.130.

11

Buddha and His Concept of Human Values

B.L. Nadoni

India during its long and profound period of philosophical activity, in its early creative phase produced the six systems of philosophy based on and sanctioend by the authority of the Vedas. They constitute the six systems of Vedic philosophy i.e., Nyāya, Vaiśeṣika, Sāṅkhya, Yoga, Mīmāṁsā and Vedānta. Besides these, it has produced two prophetic religions, Buddhism and Jainism, based on the spiritual experience of Gautama Buddha and Mahāvīra. Buddhism is today a world religion. Though it was born in India, it has crossed its borders and is today accepted by one-fifth of humanity. It has influenced the thought, art, literature and ways of life of vast sections in Asia including Sri Lanka, Burma, Cambodia, Thailand, Vietnam, Laos, Nepal, Sikkim, Tibet, Mangolia, China, Korea and Japan.

The age in which Buddha was born, was a time of great spiritual unrest and remarkable intellectual fermament. It gave birth to a galaxy of spiritual leaders of mankind. Hindu tradition looks upon the Buddha as one of the ten incarnations of the Lord, in spite of the traditional Vedanta outlook on the Buddha as one who is the heterodox and beyond the pale of the Vedas. Though Buddha was acclaimed as the incarnation of the Lord, his teaching was criticised by all the scholars of Vedanta because he did not accept the authority of the Vedas.

"In Gautama Buddha, we have a master-mind from the east, second to none so far as the influence on the thought and life of the human race is concerned and sacred to all the founder of a religious tradition whose hold is hardly less wide and deep than any other. He belongs to the history of the world's thought, to the general inheritance of all cultivated men; for judged by intellectual integrity, moral earnestness and spiritual insight, he is undoubtedly one of the greatest figures in history. Buddha was born in 563 BC to a feudal lord Śuddhodana and his full name was Siddhārtha. Śākhya was the name of the clan to which he belonged. He was surrounded by women, pomp and joy. He grew to manhood, surrounded by scenes of luxury and sensuous enjoyment. Once when as usual he went out, the servants ran in advance to keep the road clear of all the scenes of the sorrows in life, e.g., sickness, death, poverty etc.

One day, Siddhārtha started on a glorious journey which gave the world the gospel of universal compassion. When he went out in his chariot, he saw four sights, an old man, a sick man, a corpse and a mendicant. These different sights taught the lessons about the mortality of things into his life, their impermanence and the fact of pain and sorrow that is found in human life. Siddhārtha had an alert mind, eager spirit, an inquiring temper and a quivering and quick sensibility from which it was impossible to hide anything. The last sight of a mendicant who was serene, cheerful without any comfort inspired Gautama to question him. The mendicant explained his mission "I am an ascetic who, in sheer fear of birth and death, have left home to gain liberation."

The enlightened Gautama became Buddha and did not fall a victim to the temptation of keeping the wisdom exclusively to himself. He shared it with all by an active ministry of four decades. He spread the gospel with his dialogue, in simple dialect, and above all by his abundant compassion. The success and the influence of Buddhism was in no small measure due to his magnetic personality. "He was the pioneering lover of mankind and philosophic genius rolled into a single vigorous and radiant personality."

The Buddha's personality and philosophy had a tremendous influence on the intellectuals as on ordinary men. Even the agnostics loved and revered him. The humanism of Buddha has touched the imagination of ailing humanity and has held their loyalty firmly.

The philosophy of Gautama Buddha is very simple and is an original formulation of his enlightenment. It is not a philosophy of pure rationalism as it is often hastily misunderstood by the moderns. He discovered the solution to human misery through his plenary spiritual experience and formulation the intuition in intellectual terms. He accepted a faculty transcendent to human reason, though he believed that it could be explained and made intelligible in terms of human reasoning.

He formulated the four noble truths. They are the facts of human sorrow. Human existence is full of pain and sorrow. "Birth is sorrow, death is sorrow, to be conjoined to things is sorrow... Not to get what one wants, is sorrow. Even though there are some so-called pleasures in life, when the balance-sheet is drawn it is in favour of pain. This is the conclusion drawn by the author of the Yoga Sūtra also. He says: "All is pain to the reflective minds." The author of the Gītā describes saṁsāra as "the sorrowful impermanent abode of pain." All the systems of Indian philosophy accept the fact that human exixtence as it is, is not a state of unmixed joy. Lowes Dickinson puts it : "Too few of us get many of the good things of life, we just get it for a while, many are denied even the minimum of subsistence goods." Buddha's discovery that all is sorrow is not without its truth.

The eight-fold path is a therapy and a treatment. Right knowledge is the realisation of the truth of the four noble truths disclosed by Buddha. It is not a mere casual gathering of information. The truth must be borne as a firm conviction. Character and trial proceed more often out of conviction than the consistency of an argument. Right knowledge is necessary. As a preliminary step to this right knowledge, the Buddha often refers to the need of the company of good men who inspire hope in him and sustain our drooping faith. It is like the taming of a wild elephant by yoking it to the one that is already tamed. Faith grows by association with spiritual men and it generates conviction. By conversing with the spiritual minds, observing their ways, serving them, we imbibe their spirit by osmosis. Atmosphere is more than a creed.

Right aspiration is the deliberate resolve to pursue the chosen path to crack the ego. It is dedication to the ideal with the strength of our entire being. It is not enough if our intellects are sharp and discriminating. We must also have strenuous resolute will to seek the goal. The aspirant accepts his strife and is prepared to make all the renunciations necessary. It is aspiration that makes the individual put into practice the necessary methods to attain it.

Right aspiration is the determination to deliver oneself from "body-identified self." First, one must see clearly what is wrong. Next, resolve and decide to be cured. Then you must act, speak and pursue that kind of livelihood which helps us to break the ego. In short, the first thing prescribed for the aspirant is simple ethical life. One should learn to think and speak with care and truthfulness, abide by basic moral laws, earn one's living by ways that are not objectionable and deterious to one or to others and never slaken the effort to reach to the goal.

Right speech is abstention from falsehood, back-biting, harsh language and frivolous inane utterance. Right action is unselfish action. Under the head of right behaviour, the Buddha gives his celebrated five commands known as the Panca Śīla : (a) do not kill, (b) do not steal, (c) do not tell lies, (d) do not be unchaste and (e) do not drink intoxicants. Under the head of right livelihood, Buddha ruled out certain professions, e.g., that of a butcher, brewer, armament manufacturer etc. Buddha believed in self effort and perseverance. Buddhistic ethics has a severe form of self-culture and self-control. It stood for the middle path and eschewed the extremes of self-indulgence and self-mortification. He advocated careful and calculated moderation. Its repression produced neurosis, so does reckless and uninhibited action. We must strike the middle path. Buddhist ethics is an attempt to get rid of egoism in all its forms.

Buddha believed in the Law of Karma and in rebirth. He found one life too short for an individual to work out his salvation. It may appear strange that the Law of Karma could work in the absence of an enduring self. If there can be action without an agent, there can be transmigration without a soul. "When a person dies his character lifes after him and by its force brings into existence a being who though possessing a four/five different form is entirely influenced by it."

In the 'Abhidhamma' philosophy we come across a good psychological date of ethics, conduct or external behaviour of men in the form of an outward expression of their internal character. The analytical study of the internal personality of a man has been made with a view to know his 'Cit' and 'Cetasika' powers and how far they are helpful to bring about Salvation by ending the miseries of life. Remove the cause and the effect will be no more, is the doctrine of Buddhism. Remove those tendencies which give birth to action and the cycle of births and deaths will cease to exist in the absence of any saṁskāras. The tendencies which give birth to action, whether good or bad, have been enumerated six. They are :

1) Lobha (Covetousness)
2) Dvēṣa (Antipathy)
3) Mōha (Infatuation)
4) Alobha (non-covetousness) - Tendency of doing good to others
5) Adveṣa (non-antipathy) - Tendency of thinking good of others
6) Amoha (non-infactuation) - Tendency of Prajñā.

The first three are the roots of all bad actions and so are called 'Akuśala mūlas'; the last three are the roots of all good actions and so are called 'Kuśala-dharmas'. These should be understood as positive qualities and not the negative.

For the purpose of obtaining enlightenment the 'Ārya Aṣṭāṅgika Mārga' has been prescribed in Buddhism. It is the path of eightfold moral practice. This is the fourth noble truth, leading to the end of misery. This eightfold path with its subspecies, described as four Smṛtiprasthāna, four Samyakpradhānas, four Ṛddhipādas, five Indriyas, five balas and seven budhyaṅgas - known as 'Bodhipakṣīya dharmas', have been dealt with in detail in Mahāparinibbāṇa sutta (Digha No.

2/3). This method for liberation as preached by Buddha is a method of psychological analysis and so deals with the treatment accordingly. So useful is this path that Buddha says, "to obtain the enlightenment, this is the only way, not the other. Going on this path, you will destroy misery.[1]" As the Ganges goes towards east, so the follower of the aṣṭāṅgika mārga goes towards Nirvāṇa."[2]

This path is briefly described here as under:

1) Right belief (Samyak Dṛṣṭi) - Our actions depend on our thinking, so wrong acts will spring from wrong belief. So to remove wrong views, right knowledge is required. So in this step, the knowledge of four noble truths is prescribed.

2) Right Resolves (Samyak Saṅkalpa) - It is produced from right vision. "It is the longing for renunciation; the hope to live in love with all ; the aspiration of true humanity.[3]

3) Right speech (Samyak Vāk) - The resolve should be put into practice, which can find its expression in right speech, right action and right living. So good thoughts expressed in speech are called right speech. "To abstain from falsehood, to abstain from harsh language, and to abstain from frivolous talk is called right speech."[4]

4) Right Action (Samyak Karmānta) - It is unselfish action. Thus action should be aiming at purifying the heart. Buddha does not believe in superstitions as homage to agni or bathing in river for washing off the sins. It insists on purity of motive and humility in life. Abstaining from taking life, showing kindness to others, helping the needy, respect to the deserving, such actions are called right actions.

5) Right living (Samyak ājīva) - Right mode of living is adopted, fair means are used and one is to abstain from

the forbidden modes such as lying, deceet, fraud and chicanery. Here the actions aim at removing the causes of sorrows.

6) Right Effort (Samyak Vyāyāma) - Here the passions are controlled with a view to preventing the rise of bad qualities. Efforts are made to suppress the rising of evils, and to eradicate those which have arisen. Reinforcement of the good is stimulated and efforts are made to perfect those goods which have already come into existence. "Though my flesh and blood may dry up and be reduced to only a skeleton but till that which can be achieved by efforts, power and endeavour, it is not achieved by me, I will not take rest".[5] Such an effort should be there. All efforts should be made to inculcate the good and expel the evil. Buddha recommended five methods to expel the evil:

    i) Good ideas should be attended to.
    ii) The danger of the consequences which will arise by letting the bad idea develop into action, should be faced.
    iii) Attention from bad idea should be turned away.
    iv) Its antecedents should be analysed in order to nullify the consequent impulse.
    v) The mind should be coerced with the aid of bodily tension. These are in fact the efforts which have been discussed in four Pradhānas,[6] mentioned as under:
        i) Saṁyama Prayatna - Not to inculcate any such desire which may give birth to the undesirable deeds. For it, the mind is controlled with hard labour.
        ii) Prahāṇa Prayatna - Vigorous effort is made to expel the evil already arisen.

iii) Bhāvana Prayatna - Forceful effort is made to reinforce the good not obtained yet.

iv) Anurakṣaṇa Prayatna- Effort is made to preserve the good already arisen and also to bring an increase in it.

v) Right Thinking (Samyak Smṛti) - Body and spirit are to be looked in such a way as to remain ardent, self-possessed and mindful of each and every activity related to body. One is fully conscious of whatever is done by him. While breathing he is mindful of the fact that he is breathing. This is possible only when both hankering and objection have been overcome. This right thinking aims at overcoming the various false visions and thus seeing the truth. Senses are so cultured that they are able to discriminate all forms of Sense-consciousness and estimate their real worth.

8) Right concentration (Samyak Samādhi) - It is a steady endeavour to bring the mind into concentration on truth. Here egoism is eliminated. The four Smṛtiprasthānas cause the meditation to take place and the four Samyak Prayatnas nourish the material to be pondered upon.

The eight steps can be grouped under three parts - Prajñā, comprising of the first three steps, means the knowledge of truth; Sila comprising of the next two steps, stands for 'morality', good conduct, as the observance of Ahiṁsā etc.; dāna, though being active as against Śīla may be included in it. Śīla is the synthesis of our thought and Karmas, while Samādhi representing the last three steps, is the state of synthesis of desire, knowledge and resolve.

This Eight-fold is powerful enough to break the chain of causation, the root of all miseries. Right faith works against ignorance by making one understand the four noble truths viz., misery, its cause, its cessation, and the path leading to cessation. In this way the other steps of the Path, such as right resolve, right speech, right action, right effort, right thinking, and right concentration control dispostion, consciousness, six sense organs, contact sansation, thirst and attachment (grasping), and becoming and birth respectively and thus destroy the miseries of life.[7]

Every society requires some moral rules or principles for peace and harmony in the society. In this regard, the Buddha pointed out some moral principles of general interest, which are the basic foundation of humanism. Here without going into detail, we may take into consideration the five precepts (Panca Sila). They are as follows :

1. Abstinence from killing does not merely imply the avoidance of murder but that of all forms of injury to others. It involves the recognition that all have equal right to live. It inculcates the generating factors of humanism like friendliness, love, kindness and compassion.
2. Refraining from taking what is not given suggests respect for other's property and rights. It creates joy and the feeling of humanity.
3. Abstinence from excessive or unlawful indulgence in sense pleasures is intended to promote social and moral stability.
4. Refraining from falsehood encourage mutual trust and understanding between individual and groups.
5. Abstinence from intoxicants fosters an atmosphere of social harmony without which we cannot survive.

These five-precepts are called Pancasila, which keeps everything in order in individual life. In the larger sense, the same precepts can be extended to wider sphere of politics and economics and made to guide the foreign policies of nation. It has a great role in creating and maintaining peace, pleasure, tranquility, happiness, harmony and humanism in the society.

Buddha lays special emphasis on some more humanistic virtues through which the seed of humanism develop fully and the society becomes saturated with peace and harmony. They are: Metta, Karuna, Mudita and Upekkha. They play an important role in social and humanistic philosophy of the Buddha. Description of all in detail is not possible in this limited framework. However, a brief description of them is presented here.

Metta is universal love and friendliness where there is Metta,there cannot be any room for ill will and hatred. In Metta-Sutta, the Buddha says that first as a mother protects her only son even at the cost of her life, even so one should cultivate boundless loving-kindness towards all living beings.

Karuṇa is compassion. It is a feel for helping those who are in trouble. Where there is compassion, there cannot be indifference towards the suffering of others.

Mudita is not only sympathy but also sympathetic joy, which tends to destroy its direct enemy that is jealousy. It is an act of feeling of happiness or pleasure to see the happiness and pleasure of others. Where is Mudita, there cannot be any room for jealousy and unhealthy states.

Upekkha is equanimity. The etymological meaning of the term Upekkha is looking impartially. It is necessary especially for laymen who have to live in ill balanced or fluctuating circumstances in the world. It maintains the balance of mind.

Now-a-days anti-humanistic feelings of powerful destructive vices are seen among the people such as anger, ill-will, cruelty, jealousy etc. They are obstacles to humanism. Therefore, they need to be uprooted from the human. It is possible through the cultivation of the four sublime virtues termed as Brahmavihara that anger, and ill-will are eradicated by loving-kindness (Metta) cruelty by compassion and jealousy by Mudita.

These four sublime virtues are called illimitable (appamanna) because they find no barrier or limit and should be extended towards all beings without exception. They are pillars of individual happiness, social amity and universal peace. Their cultivation would lead to the establishment of perfection humanism in the nation and the world.

Buddha said to follow the middle way, a golden mean that will give us higher knowledge and ultimately Enlightenment. This middle way will give us the knowledge of the four noble truth which are the true about suffering, the true about cause of suffering, the true about cessation of suffereing, the noble path that shows us the way of suffering. This is the last kernel of the Buddhist code of ethics.

The teaching of Buddha is a realistic system of ethics such as the ethics of non-violence, loving kindness, compassion and harmony amongst people, a penetrative analysis of life, a profound philosophy and practical method of mental culture and training, leading to perfect wisdom. Buddhism lays great stresses on development of moral and spiritual character for a happy, peaceful and contented society. Buddhism is designed to attain universal peace. It is a human discovery based on a very scientific procedure living to leading the ultimate level of perfection of human consciousness. It can make a great contribution to the modern world in guiding its search for the meaning of life.

References

1. एसो न मरगो नत्यञ्जो दस्सनस्स विसुद्धिया ---- एतं हि तुम्हे पटिपन्ना दुक्खस्सन्तं करिस्सथ। धम्मपद 20; 3
2. Pathama Pāda in sutta (Sam. Ni).
3. Sutta Vibhaṅga.
4. Aṅguttara, 10, Buddha Vācana, pp. 32-33
5. See Nīdāna Kathā.
6. चूलवेदल्ल-सुतन्ना (मज्भिम) 5-4
7. Cf. Anāgārika Govind; The psychological attitude of early Buddhist Philosophy, p.102.

12

Vātsyāyana's Ethics for Personality Development

V.K. Hampiholi

The term and the concept of Personality Development belong to Western Psychology. In the West the study of Psychology begins with Socrates. He studied Psychology as a branch of Philosophy as the term psycho was denoting two meanings. i.e. Mind and Soul. Plato recognized the difference between the body and the mind and came to the conclusion that mind is the root cause for behaviour. He did not pay attention to the abstract Soul and emphasized on the body. Aristotle considered mind is base for all the activities of the body. Thus once again the study of Psychology neglected the soul. Afterwards the great psychologists like Wilhelm Wundt and Edward Tichener belonging to school of Structuralism, William James and Edvard L Tharndike of Functionalism, John B. Watson and Ivan Pavlov of Behaviourism, Max Werteimer, Kurt Koffka and Wolfgang Kohler of Gestalt School and Freud, Alfred Adler, Karen Harney of Psycho-analysis school studied deeply about mind and behaviour. They observed the condition and the activities of the mind in conscious, preconscious, subconscious and unconscious stages. But all studies became futile as they failed to describe the mind properly and objectively. Hence afterwards the school of humanism became more popular. The psychologists of this school opined the study of self or soul is necessary not only to understand the behaviour but also to study personality development. The Self theory of Rogers and the Self Actualization theory of Abraham Maslow brought the psychology near to philosophy once again.

Personality development according to Indian philosophy is attaining salvation. It is called *Mokṣa, Mukti, Nirvāṅa* or *Apavarga.* Our ancients considered *Mokṣa* as the highest goal of life. The characteristics of Universal Man described by the School of Humanism resembles to the characteristics of *Muktātmā* or *Sthitaprajña* or *Yogi* or *Jnānī* in Indian Culture. Our ancestors recognized *Dharma, Artha* and *Kāma* are other three goals of life and these will help a person to attain *Mokṣa.* Hence we find many texts on these. These texts are full of injunctions and prohibitions and they will guide a man to attain *Mokṣa.*

The western psychologists have explained the concept of personality on the basis of physical-mental-emotional-moral-creative-cultural-social-natural and environmental development. They gave much and more importance to extrinsic qualities. In India along with these extrinsic qualities, intrinsic qualities gained more importance in the concept of personality development. Therefore ethics has more value not only in our culture but also in Personality Development. Ethics consists of morality and moral principles approved by the society. Rāvaṅa was physically strong and attractive; mentally stable; economically sound; and socially popular. But he was not respected as he had no ethics.

In India ethics was and is a part of *Dharma*. They are inseparable in our tradition. According to Encyclopedia of Humanities and Social Sciences (Vol. XIV. p.523) Ethics is a branch of philosophy and it concerns with conduct and character. It assists to distinguish right from wrong and good from bad. In India, the texts on *Dharma* play that role. Hence all the texts on Dharma have respect. *Dharma, Artha* and *Kāma* are goals for one extent and at another extent they are means to attain *Mokṣa*. One should practice all the three without contradicting each other. Practicing *Kāma*, without contradicting *Dharma* and *Artha* is advised by Vātsyāyana in his popular book i.e. Kāmasûtra. There we find the role of ethics in enjoying the pleasures and the role of enjoyment in personality development.

The Kāmasûtra begins with the salutations to *Dharma, Artha* and *Kāma*.[1] Vātsyāyana displays the importance of ethics by paying respect to *Dharma* in the beginning itself. Further he says- "a man should practise *trivarga* without conflicting each other. The life span of man is a hundred years. One should learn arts and sciences and be capable of earning one's own bread. In the second quarter one should enjoy *Kāma* and one should think about salvation during old-age."[2] According to Vātsyāyana one should enjoy *Kāma* in *gṛhasthāśrama* which is also accepted by *Dharma*. It clearly indicates that sexual enjoyment is not approved before marriage. Vātsyāyana allows copulation only after the marriage and that too only between married couple. Here Vātsyāyana upholds the ethics.

There is a close relation between *Dharma* and *Kāma* (religion and desire) in India and in Indian culture. Geoffrey Parrinder aptly points out – "Nowhere have close relationships of religion and sex been displayed more clearly than in India and, with divine and human models of sexual activity, sacramental views of sex were abundantly illustrated."[3] Sex is natural instinct and no one can suppress it. It should be practiced according to rules and regulations framed by the society. Vātsyāyana considers sex like a food.[4] It is well known fact that food is necessary for the development. Therefore the texts on *Dharma* have framed rules and regulations regarding place, time, and method of food taking and described quality and quantity of the food. These are based on medical science. In the same way Vātsyāyana frames rules and regulations to enjoy sexual enjoyment on the basis of ethics and social science. He opines that one should enjoy the enjoyments without contradicting *Dharma* and *Artha*. According to our ancestors Dharma means ethics and ethics means code of conduct. Thus Vātsyāyana shows the importance of ethics in enjoying the pleasures. Further he assures that the person who practices *Trivarga* properly will enjoy happiness in this world and in the higher world after death.[5] The person who follows the dictums of *Dharma* properly will attain salvation. In this matter Vātsyāyana considers *Dharma* is superior among *trivarga*[6] and it will assist in personality development.

Here Vātsyāyana illustrates the King Dāndakya, Indra, Kīcaka, Rāvana and others who were ruined with their family and relatives on account of their immoral behaviours.

Vātsyāyana states that a man should study and earn money and then he should enter in to *gṛhasthāśrama*. His intention is that one should be economically sound either by employment or by commerce or by ancestral property. One should have well equipped house.[7] Vātsyāyana further adds that one should marry a virgin girl of his own class according to *Śāstra*. Such marriages will bring good progeny and good fame because it is not opposed to the customs of the society.[8] Vātsyāyana remarks that marriage with a virgin and *savarṅā* brings happiness because it is accepted by the society and social ethics. Marriage is considered as a sacrament in our culture and it is a social ceremony. Married men and women had respect and responsibility in the society. And such respect and responsibility help in the process of personality development. There are many duties and responsibilities for *grahastha* and *gṛhiṇī*. Among them sexual pleasure and getting progeny are important. It helps their physical, psychological and social development. Hence Vātsyāyana lauds *savarṇa* marriage. Vātsyāyana censures inter-class marriage and prohibits sexual relation with wife of others.[9] Such marriages and relations will not bring fame as they are not approved by the society as they are unethical. It should be noted that codes of morals are framed by the society and for the society. Hence J. Jolly remarks that ethics is a science that denotes the right or the wrong of human conduct in relation with individual and society.[10]

The second *adhikaraṇa* deals with pre and post acts of copulation. The advice given to the couples in this chapter strengthens the love and affection of husband and wife. Vātsyāyana warns that one should not follow his advice blindly and one should not use all techniques which are described in the text. His intention is that those techniques should be used at the proper time in proper countries and proper places.[11] Some techniques are prohibitive in some region and they are necessary in another region. In such matter, Vātsyāyana states that one should follow the custom of his country and his own inclination.[12] Vātsyāyana's instructions are based on social ethics. He mentions the Kings of Chola, Kuntala and Pandya who used wrong techniques and killed their female partner.

The third *adhikaraṇa* deals with marriage and types of marriage. The objectives of marriage according to Vātsyāyana are acquisition of *Dharma* and *Artha*, offspring, affinity, increase of relatives and untarnished love.[13]All these help a person in the process of personality development. Vātsyāyana states that marriage and friendship should be done among equals. The social status, economic condition, the culture and the customs of both families should be equal.[14] The matrimonial relations held between such families will bring happiness in conjugal life as it is based on social ethics and it will help in personality development.

Vātsyāyana remarks – "roughness and impetuosity are the characteristics of manhood and tenderness, sensibility and weakness are distinguishing qualities of womanhood.[15] Hence Vātsyāyana suggests- "Women are delicate like flowers. They aspire for tender beginnings. Man should not behave with his wife crudely. He should not force her. He should win her heart with decent and moderate behaviour. Otherwise she will hate her husband or will become hater of male sex."[16]. Vātsyāyana upholds the ethical values like kindness, love, patience, decency and so on. All these qualities are helpful in the development of personality.

Vātsyāyana instructs newly married couple to maintain celibacy at least for three days after the marriage. This instruction is according to *Dharmaśāstra*. The *Dharmaśāstra* mentions eight forms of marriage.[17] Among them, *Dharmaśāstra* approves six types and allows remaining two. It is according to social ethics. Marriage is a social sacrament and it helps in the process of personality development. Vātsyāyana upholds this and states – "the fruit of marriage is love; the *gāndharva* form of marriage respected because it fulfils the object of the marriage. It brings happiness, causes less trouble and it is result of previous love."[18] Vātsyāyana prefers to *gāndharva* form as it represents the ethical values like love, affection, co-operation, coordination and equality than complex rituals done in the other forms of marriage.

The fourth *adhikaraṅa* deals with the duties and the conduct of wife and husband. Vātsyāyana narrates the conduct of a wife when her husband is out of station. His narration represents the ethics of those days and it appears that they are necessary even today. The wife who is devoted to her husband and doing everything for his welfare will acquire *dharma, artha* and *kāma* will obtain a high position and generally her husband devoted to her.[19] Vātsyāyana appreciates monogamy and upholds it. But he mentions the polygamy as it was prevailed in the society. He opines that a man can marry another girl if his first wife is a fool, a barren, or has a bad character or gives birth to only daughters. Even in continence of the man was also a cause for polygamy.[20] Vātsyāyana advises a man who has many wives – he should act fairly towards them all; he should neither disregard nor pass over their faults; he should not reveal the love, passion, physical blemishes and confidential reproaches of one wife to another; he should not allow any of them of speaking to him about their rivals.[21] In the same way Vātsyāyana advises a woman about her role when she has a co-wife. All these advice help to lead a happy and peaceful life. He is of the opinion that all the wives of a person should live together harmoniously and they should not quarrel each other. The happiness of the family and harmony among the members of the family will certainly influence on personality development.

The fifth *adhikaraṅa* deals with the wives of the other men. The author describes the causes and effects of adultery. Further he expresses the characteristics of the women who are easily gained over, the women who are not easily seduced and the plans to seduce so on. Vātsyāyana considers adultery as illegal and illicit. But Vātsyāyana knew that though adultery is illegal, immoral, illicit and unethical, it was there, it is there and it will be there in the society. Because all men are not like Śrī Rāma and all women are not like Sītā. At the of this chapter Vātsyāyana concludes – A clever man, learning from *śāstras* the ways of winning over the wives of other people, is never deceived in case of his own wives.[22] It will help in guarding their own wives. Vātsyāyana upholds ethics and condemns adultery as it destroys *dharma* and *artha*.

The sixth *adhikaraṅa* deals with prostitution and prostitutes. Vātsyāyana is aware of that prostitution is against *dharma śāstra* and it is unethical. But he deals this matter as he was a practical man. A society without prostitution or prostitutes is a utopia. Fickle mind desires more and more. There are some men and women whose passion will not be quenched by a single partner. Such people will destroy social ethics and their behaviour creates unrest in the society. And it decreases the morality in the society. Therefore the whole chapter advises to be away from prostitutes and upholds ethics.

Thus the whole text written by Vātsyāyana instructs to enjoy the pleasures as per the dictum of *dharmaśāstra*. He opines that one should enjoy the pleasures as a master of sense-organs and not as a slave of senses. Vātsyāyana gave importance to *indriyajaya* and *indriyanigraha*. Manu and Yājnavalkya considered *indriyanigraha* as an important part of *dharma*.[23]

Indian culture respects those who have controlled their sense organs. This is the unique land where the persons are called *vīra* who conquers others and *mahāvīra* who conquers their own sense organs. Therefore, Vardhamāna Mahāvīra, Buddha, Shankara, Rāmānuja, Madhva, Gurunānak, Dayānanda Sarasvati, Ramakrishna Paramahamsa, Swamy Vivekananda, Mahatma Gandhi and so on, were and are respected in our country. All these persons are ever living examples for personality developed persons as their ethical back-ground is pure and fault-less.

Vātsyāyana's ethics for personality development is more relevant at present. Today man has all the comforts but he is not comfortable. He is running after the sensual pleasures. His desires and demands are increasing day by day. He is enjoying pleasures without any restriction. His sense organs are becoming weak and his mind is not yet satisfied. He is not loyal to his life-partner. His personality is demoralizing day by day. His sexual relations are not safe. Hence AIDS (Acquired Immune Deficiency Syndrome) is spreading rapidly in India. More than five million HIV infected persons are there in India at present. The government is taking various steps to prevent this disease by enlightening the mass through advertisements for safer sex. In fact these advertisements are provoking the youngsters to indulge in sexual activities. Hence the numbers of HIV patients are increasing. Therefore today the advice of Vātsyāyana is more relevant. His concept of ethics only can destroy the problem of AIDS and STDs.

The man or woman who is not in a position to enjoy the physical pleasure on account of such diseases has neither physical fitness nor mental peace. Such people will neither grow nor develop. Hence the personality of these people will not develop and these people become burden for society. Therefore Vātsyāyana's concept of ethics which is based on dharma is the need of today not only for personality development of individual but also to build a strong society or a country.

Bibliography

1 Kāmasūtra of Vātsyāyana – Ed. Devadhara Shastri, Chaukhamba Sanskrit Sansthana, Varanasi 1982

2 Kāmasūtra of Vātsyāyana – Trans. Richard F. Burton

3 Manusmṛti – Ishvarashastri Samaja Pustakaalaya Dharwad1994

4 Kāma Without Dharma – Shaji George Kochuthara, Journal of Dharma 34, 1 (January – March 2009) p 65-95

5 Vātsyāyana's Ethics for Modern Man- Dr.V.K.Hampiholi, Ethics for Modern Man Ed. by K.B.Archak, Sundeep Prakashana Delhi, 2007

References

1. धर्मार्थकामेभ्यो नमः। 1.1.1
2. शतायुर्वै पुरुषो विभज्य कालमन्योन्यानुबद्धं परस्परस्यानुपघातकं त्रिवर्गं सेवेत्। 1.2.1
3. Geoffrey Parrinder, Sex in the World's Religions, Oxford University Press, New York 1980. p.5
4. शरीरस्थितिहेतुत्वात् आहारसधर्माणो हि कामाः। फलभूताश्च धर्मार्थयोः। 1.2.37
5. एवमर्थं च कामं च धर्मं चोपाचरन्नरः। इहामुत्र च निःशल्यमत्यन्तं सुखमश्नुते।। 1.2.39
6. एषां समवाये पूर्वः पूर्वो गरीयान्। 1.2.14
7. गृहीतविद्यः प्रतिग्रहजयक्रयनिर्वेशाधिगतैः अर्थैः अन्वयागतैः उभयैर्वा गार्हस्थ्यमधिगम्य नागरकवृत्तं वर्तेत्। 1.4.1
8. कामश्चतुर्षु वर्णेषु सवर्णतः शास्त्रतश्चानन्यपूर्वायां प्रयुज्यमानः पुत्रीयो यशस्यो लौकिकश्च भवति। 1.5.1
9. तद्विपरीत उत्तमवर्णासु परपरिगृहीतासु च। 1.5.2
10. Encyclopedia of Ethics and Religion Vol. IV p.414
11. न सर्वदा न सर्वासु प्रयोगाः सांप्रयोगिकाः। स्थाने देशे च काले च योग एषां विधीयते।। 2.7.35
12. शिष्टविप्रतिपत्तेः स्मृतिवाक्यस्य च सावकाशत्वाद्देशस्थितेरात्मनश्च वृत्तिप्रत्ययानुरूपं प्रवर्तेत। 2.9.34
13. धर्मोऽर्थः पुत्राः सम्बन्धः पक्षवृद्धिरनुपस्कृता रतिश्च। 3.1.1
14. समस्याद्याः सहक्रीडा विवाहाः संगतानि च। समानैरेव कार्याणि नोत्तमैर्नापि वाधमैः।। 3.1.20

15. पारुष्यं रभसत्वं च पौरुषं तेज उच्यते। अशक्तिरार्तिर्व्यावृत्तिरबलत्वं च योषितः।। 2.7.22

16. कुसुमधर्माणो हि योषितः सुकुमारोपक्रमाः। तास्त्वनधिगतविश्वासैः प्रसभमुपक्रम्यमाणाः सम्प्रयोगद्वषिण्यो भवन्ति। 3.2.6

    सा प्रीतियोगमप्राप्ता तेनोद्वेगेन दषिता। पुरषद्वेषिणी वा स्याद्विद्विष्टा वा ततोऽन्यगा।। 3.2.34

17. ब्राह्मो दैवस्तथैवार्षः प्राजापत्यस्तथाऽसुरः। गान्धर्वो राक्षसश्चैव पैशाश्चाष्टमोऽधमः।। मनु. 3.21

18. सुखत्वादबहुक्लेशादपि चावरणादिह। अनुरागात्मकत्वाच्च गान्धर्वः प्रवरो मतः।। 3.5.30

19. धर्ममर्थं तथा कामं लभन्ते स्थानमेव च। निःसपत्नं च भर्तारं नार्यः सद्वृत्तमाश्रिता।। 4.1.48

20. जाड्यदौःशील्यदौर्भाग्येभ्यः प्रजानुत्पत्तेराभीक्ष्ण्येन दारिकोत्पत्तेर्नायकचापलाद्वा सपत्न्यधिवेदनम्। 4.2.1

21. पुरुषस्तु बहून् दारान् समाहृत्य समो भवेत्। न चावज्ञां चरेदासु व्यलीकान्न सहेत च।। 4.2.67

    एकस्यां या रतिक्रीडा वैकृतं वा शरीरजम्। विस्रम्भाद्वाप्युपालम्भस्तमन्यासु न कीर्तयेत्।। 4.2.68

22. संदृश्य शास्त्रतो योगान्पारदारिकलक्षितान्। न याति च्छलनां कश्चित्स्वरान् प्रति शास्त्रवित्।। 5.6.46

23. अहिंसासत्यमक्रोधो शौचमिन्द्रियनिग्रहः। मनु 10.63

    अहिंसासत्यमस्तेयं शौचमिन्द्रियनिग्रहः। याज्ञ. 1.122

13

Ways of Personality Development in Sanskrit Literature

M.N. Joshi

संगच्छध्वं संवदध्वं सं वो मनांसि जानताम्।

Meet together. Discuss together.
One must know the other person's view.

Every man is his own ancestor, and every man his own heir.
He devises his own future, and he inherits his own past.
– [H. F. Hedge]

Human personality is affected by culture through the process of a culturalization. This word "Personology" was coined by Mr. Henary A. Murray. Its means Study of personality. The book by name Personality was written by G. W. Allport. In Latin, Personality means mask. Honesty, hostility, submissiveness, sociability can be termed as personality. Webster's Unabridged Dictionary contains 18000 adjectives to explain the term Personality. Majority of the definitions of personality emphasize on Integration of individual characteristics and it refers to the whole individual. Mr. Whitrkar defined personality as – "a unique organization of characteristics that determine the individual's typical or recurrent pattern of behavior." The sum total of all the ways of acting thinking and feeling that are typical for a person and those that make a person somewhat different from others is called Personality. Always it is Dynamic. We need to develop a good and sound personality to – become good and successful professional, good communicator, evolve as a responsible citizen. Heredity and Environment are the result of Personality development. It starts early in the life. Mr. Breckenridge opines that – Core of the personality pattern is the individual's concept of himself, as a person related to the world in which he lives. Long ago the same statement was given by Srikrishna in the Bhagavadgeeta. We can even today remember the statement in Gita -

तत्रैकाग्रं मनः कृत्वा यतचित्तेन्द्रियक्रियः। (VI. 12)

Concentration of the mind is essential to make any progress with proper understanding. 'Practice yoga by disciplining your sensory organs and purifying your heart', says Krishna to Arjuna. It is applicable to one and all, although addressed to Arjuna. No one can be inactive in this world. *Satva, Rajas, Tamas* are the inalienable characteristics of the mind and man has to be involved in some vocation or the other as long as he remains in this world. In that case, can anybody remain silent and not expose such an attitude which is a hindrance to any decent occupation ? One has to call a spade a spade. Otherwise, the words *durjana* and *sajjana* lose their meaning. All such canons of religion recommend punishment to evil-doers. It is possible for any *duṣṭa* to become a *Siṣṭa*. So fairness in the discharge of one's duties is always hailed by every religious law-book.

All this is the outcome of that determination of the mind to seek success at all costs. The teacher warns the student to be aware of all consequences before determining to do any action and keep the head cool. The Vedas direct the disciples to undertake any responsibility after weighing the pros and cons and follow a path without hurting the family or society in general by their actions. The welfare of the community, as mentioned in the Vedas, is not upset by such a course of collective action through co-operation and co-existence in the land.

Sanskrit is the most ancient language in the world known to man. It was spoken by the Ancient Indian people for centuries before its script was found out. Naturally the Vedic hymns that flowed out from the mouths of the Seers were considered to be inspired utterances. The Vedic people's civilization which is reflected in the Vedic hymns is also known to be the most ancient in the world; and it is very interesting to note that in the hymns some references are made to even more ancient seers and situations. From the history of their civilization we can get a clear picture of the life of the Ancient Indian people, their religion and education, their polity and society, their economy and industry, their arts and crafts.

Sanskrit literature became vast and varied in course of time and the ideas and ideals described in the Vedic hymns were analyzed and amplified, were sorted and systematized, were clarified and codified by great thinkers in it. Here it is proposed to note their educational ideals as can be gathered from the various references in Sanskrit books. It is hoped that this kind of review may give us some clue when we are at the cross- roads on the question of national education and Nature and ways of Personality development. Vedic hymns are many. The oldest literature available for mankind is in poetic style. Indian Philosophy is based on the Vedas.

The Indians were sufficiently practical, never neglected their health and exhibited a realistic approach to life, Kautilya's

Arthasastra is a work on politics for guidance in all times. In ancient Indian education social values were adequately recognized. The principles of *Advaita* Vedanta namely, the individual souls are so many sparks of the universal spirit and the like have explained them so clearly. According to this philosophy, therefore, the relationship of universal brotherhood among all human beings is fundamentally established; no laws are required for that. All laws of morality and social amity are derived from this inner unity. This brotherhood in Indian philosophy is not restricted to the people in India only: it embraces the whole human race, as can be seen from the common prayer sung by the ancient prophets, this can be seen in the *Bhṛguvalli* of *Taittiriya Upanishad* -

ऊँ सह नाववतु। सह नौ भुनक्तु।
सह वीर्यं करवावहै। तेजस्विनावधीतमस्तु।
मा विद्विषावहै। ऊँ शांति: शांति: शांति:।।

'Om, May all prosper. Let the Creator protect both the teacher and the taught. Let us both discharge our rightful duties. Let our studies be full of light and dynamism. Let us have no ill-will towards each other. Om, Peace ! Peace ! Peace !, This proves that the teacher's voice was heard patiently in shifting the truth from falsehood. The Vedic system of education aimed at establishing a society without any natural ill-will. It was for this reason that there was great respect for a teacher in the ancient educational system. The teacher was at the top in that society. The teacher lived a simple and contented life only to pass on the values from generation to generation. Now-a-days, money has become the standard for measuring respect or recognition. The Vedas are full of *mantras* regarding organising society free from malice or jealousy. It was for this reason that the teachers commanded respect. An imposing building with all latest equipments cannot be equated with a teacher of noble character. An ideal teacher would discharge the educational and social responsibilities. He would look after the physical, emotional and intellectual fitness of a student. He would look after the growth of skill and character of the student. No person other than a teacher can inspire a student to possess these qualities. A combination of these made a perfect teacher who commanded respect in society. He alone is a person to be the guiding light. He is, therefore, equated with *Brahma, Vishnu* and *Mahesha* -

गुरुर्ब्रह्मा गुरुर्विष्णुः गुरुर्देवो महेश्वरः।
गुरुः साक्षात् परब्रह्म तस्मै श्रीगुरवे नमः।

This is a befitting compliment paid to an ideal teacher in the past. India is a sacred land where even quadruped animals like cows never entertained evil thoughts. How can a teacher ask his students to disobey such sanctions. This land adores him. "Who can consent to an evil-person to become a virtuous person, people of virtue to enjoy peace and a person enjoying peace be liberated from bondage and these liberated inspire others also to seek liberation from bondage."

दुर्जनः सज्जनो भूयात् सज्जनः शांतिमाप्नुयात्।
शान्तो मुच्येत बंधेभ्यो मुक्तश्चान्यान् विमोचयेत्।।

Noble-minded souls spread noble thoughts and with a broad outlook pray for the welfare of mankind without any distinction -

Western thinkers like Rousseau pray to Nature to inspire our fellow beings to 'Look at Nature which has no bounds. Rise up casting off parochial considerations. Everything in Nature is free from blemish. Everything is good as it comes from the hands of the author of Nature, but every thing degenerates in the hands of man'.

There was nothing wanting in the system of education in Bharata. Normally in the *Gurukula* system, there was a happy blending of theoretical and practical education for a wholesome development of the student. Education meant cultivating any cultural, moral, physical, character development and vocational aspect in that system. This was the daily routine in that system. As the atmosphere was congenial for such a blending, students imbibed those qualities also. Students as also teachers, in such a *Gurukula* system would be intelligent, learned and become noble citizens of society. Their contribution would enrich every social value. Society also could develop in such a healthy atmosphere. Governments of the day repeatedly state that the student is the central focus of Education. We always agree on that point. No one is capable of lighting the lamp that would dispel the enveloping darkness from the scene. So, the present day society is in a fix and is suffering. All are scared of such a situation existing in modern society.

English writers on education have said: "Man is born as animal and education transforms him into a human being."Of course, here the word 'education' means, good education, education of the right type given by well-qualified teachers in favorable surroundings. It is also said that education is a panacea against all individual and social evils. This is half the truth; because bad education or lop-sided education cannot be a remedy against any social malady. Only good education can mould individual minds properly and improve social life considerably. Our Sanskrit authors have said the same thing. The word Saakshara has a very good connotation, including the development of inborn powers and also improvement of individual tendencies in conformity with the ideals of social and national life. Our ancients have laid great stress on *Samskara* to be given to the individual on sixteen different occasions during his life-time; when the person receives blessings from family-deities, priests, relatives and well-wishers. They are sure to have a good effect psychologically, socially and spiritually. Some modern scientists in America have made experiments and proved that prayers, recitation of hymns and repetition of God's name produce healthy effects not only psychological, but also physical and chemical. "Well begun is half done" is a significant saying that supports this *Samskara* theory.

Modern educationists take into account two factors of education, namely, nature and nurture, otherwise called endowment and environment. The first of these is the heredity of the child, that is, whatever good or bad tendencies he has inherited from his parents and forefathers; and the second includes all that is done at home, at school and in the society to train him up in thinking, doing and collecting knowledge. Our ancients mention a third factor of education, namely, self-hood, which is the capital collected by the child in his previous births. They believed in rebirth and took into consideration whatever the child brings with him in this life as the fruit of his *Prarabdhakarma*. This has not been experimentally proved; but it has been a fairly correct conclusion arrived at after careful observation of the achievements of children of the same parents brought up under the same environment.

"A child becomes good-natured through his mother's merit, intelligent through his father's merit, religious through his family-merit and fortunate by his own merit." Here one's own merit is the product of one's own deeds in the past births; and the first three can be included in heredity.

The *Aacharya or Teacher* was a model of humanity before the students, who were inspired by his example to work towards a high goal of life. Naturally, cultivation of virtue and acquisition of learning were their chief pursuits. Bodily pleasures were not thought of, though regular efforts were made to maintain health, to sustain growth and to gain strength; because the body was considered to be a boat, with the help of which the ocean of this worldly existence was to be successfully crossed. That was the high spiritual ideal before the students whose character-formation was the ultimate aim of education. The divine qualities that constitute character have been clearly mentioned in the *Bhagavadgita*.

During these days we see inter-state jealousies. Selfishness and jealousy breed wars. Mutual intolerance is the root cause of inter-national rivalry. One can only count on one's fingers really selfless and generous persons, states or nations. Society is formed by individuals of varying temperaments. The general good is the uniting force beginning from an individual. Rotten fruits spoil the other usable frutis. So, one has to guard against destabilizing society. One has to exercise great caution and see that society survives in spite of all weaknesses on the part of individuals. Discrimination between the good and the bad is very necessary. Otherwise, society dismembers by the tricks of sinners who are thriving as saintly persons wearing the robes of saints. Anger can be considered as a deadly disease, say elders, because an angry person loses his personality. *Somevvara III* is of the opinion that anger spoils the mind, separates the dear and near ones, deprives one of all his belongings and desires in solace or comfort one's own religious beliefs. So shun anger at all costs.

क्रोधो नाशयते बुद्धिमात्मानं च कुलं धनम्।
धर्मनाशो भवेत् कोपात् तस्मात् तं परिवर्जयेत्।। (I - 7.57)[6]

The meaning is very clear. 'Along with this, men of fame do not boast of their achievements. This is another feather in their cap : undue self-praise is as good as death. So one should not speak highly of his/her accomplishments.' Every person has to live in society. Society is a co-operative enterprise. So one has to conduct oneself properly in a company. A Poet says-

ऋतं वाच्यं प्रियं वाच्यं न वाच्यं हितमप्रियम्।
प्रियं च नानृतं वाच्यमेष धर्मः सनातनः।। (I -10.64)[7]

'One has to speak the truth. It must be pleasant to hear. Even a pleasing truth should not be spoken in an unpleasant manner. Desist from speaking untruth, however pleasant it may be. 'This is true *dharma* handed down to posterity. People treading a righteous path have made this statement. One can see this in the literary output of men of letters. If each member in a society conducts himself/herself properly, the entire society can enjoy peace and progress. But such persons are very rare. Social service in the real sense is possible only by a negligible number of persons. Persons belonging to this order enjoy respect in society only if they lead a life of their self respect and proper behaviour. What should therefore, a person do? The *Bhagavdgītā* says –

उद्धरेदात्मनात्मानं नात्मानमवसादयेत्।
आत्मैव ह्यात्मनो बंधुरात्मैव रिपुरात्मनः।। 5 ।। (आध्याय 6)

Let a man raise himself by his own self, Let him not debase himself. For he is himself his friend, himself his foe. They consider it a proper step in worldly life and derive satisfaction of discharging their rightful duties and through self-control, attain the ultimate reality. (*Kaṭhopaniṣat*. II. 14)

उत्तिष्ठत जाग्रत प्राप्य वरान् निबोधत।
क्षुरस्य धारा निशिता दुरत्यया दुर्गं पथस्तत् कवयो वदन्ति।।

'Arise, awake and get advice from all-knowing *Guru*. Men, knowing all things, are of the view that this is a razor-edged path and it is no smooth-walking.' Every person in this world can be freed from ignorance through the help of a strong-willed G*uru*. If the soul has to get up from sleep or slumber of ignorance, the help of a *Guru or Teacher* ?is essential. Our activities in the world should be transparent and backed by spiritual content. No sinful action will be committed then. (मुंडकोपनिषत् .III- 1.6)

सत्यमेव जयते नानृतं सत्येन वन्था विततो देवयानः।
येनाक्रमंत्यृपयो ह्याप्तकामा यत्र तत्सत्यस्य परमं निधानम्।

'Truth alone triumphs. Untruth can never. Beloved Rishis always upheld Truth - *Satya* - as the highest goal. The path they tread is the only righteous path.'

ऊँ भद्रं कर्णेभिः श्रुणुयाम देवाः भद्रं पश्येमाक्षभिर्यजत्राः।
स्थिरैरङ्गैस्तुष्टुवांसस्तनूभिर्व्यशेम देवहितं यदायुः।।
(प्रश्नोपनिषत्–1.1)

'Let us hear something pleasant for the ear. Let us see something appealing to our eyes. The body should always be kept strong and healthy. Then only life can be considered fit to serve God.' *Riṣis* in the above mentioned verse have the welfare of the universe and brotherhood of man when they pray for the well-being of the world without any distinction. These form the meaning of noble sentiments of the *Riṣis*. All this includes different definitions of modern Personality.

Like – Personality development is the development of the organized pattern of behaviors and attitudes that makes a person distinctive. Personality development occurs by the ongoing interaction of temperament, character, and environment.

Growth of habitual patterns of behavior in childhood and adolescence.

An improvement in all spheres of an individual in Life, be it with friends, in office or any environment

Personality development is the development of the organized pattern of behaviors and attitudes that makes a person distinctive. Personality development occurs by the ongoing interaction of temperament, character, and environment.

Growth of habitual patterns of behavior in childhood and adolescence.

An improvement in all spheres of an individual in Life, be it with friends, in office or any environments

This spiritualistic philosophy (as formulated by our ancient prophets) seems to be quite acceptable in modern times. It rises above all sectarian religions and embraces the whole humanity. The word 'spirit' gets its meaning from the Greek root that means "breathing". Thus philosophy can apply to all those that breathe and this shows the usefulness of deep breathing in the process of God-realisation, as explained by our ancient sages and saints. The universal spirit pervades the whole world and keeps it in working order. Its sparks are in the hearts of all men and keep them alive and supply them the necessary energy for work. Thus all men are brothers to each other, being children of the same God or Universal spirit. In the modern times of democratic life this principle of Universal brother-hood should be greatly conducive to peace and happiness in the national and also in international matters. This idea of oneness or unity is sure to result in good morality; but difference or duality generally leads to enmity. When men are conscious of mutual oneness, they will certainly behave peacefully with each other. Then they care more for spiritual goods than for material goods, their need will not grow into greed; and then struggle will be rare in practical life. Consequently the atmosphere will be more favorable to peace and happiness. It is not expected that people will all be saints or *yogins* by observing the principles of our spiritualistic philosophy in life and education; but their conduct in practical dealings will surely be conducive to peace, as they will become more introspective. Nor is it expected that the observance of this philosophy will solve all problems of modern life (like the struggle between capital and labour) as if by the touch of a magic wand; but the general attitude of sympathy (that will be created by it) can help to a considerable extent their peaceful solutions. This philosophy of ours stands for one world, one mankind and one God; and it can inspire men to deal with men as human beings. As regards the contents of education in "Gurukulas", the main objective was attainment of "Moksha", which in spiritual terms, is described as self-realisation.

So, education was meant to lead the student to self-realisation.

"सा विद्या या विमुक्तये"-

All this is the outcome of that determination of the mind to seek success at all costs. The *Guru or teacher* warns the student to be aware of all consequences before determining to do any action and keep the head cool. The Vedas direct the disciples to undertake any responsibility after weighing the pros and cons and follow a path without hurting the family or society in general by their actions.

Mahābhārata tells –

धारणद्धर्म इत्याहुर्धर्मो धारयते प्रजा: (Karna Parva 69, 59)

"That which supports, that which holds together the peoples for the universe, that is Dharma".

Dharma is not merely a set of beliefs having no necessary connection with the daily life of humanity, but it is the very principles of healthy and beneficent life. We can say this is perfect personality. "Therefore to know those principles and act upon them is to be a true Man (or follower of *Vaidika* Dharma), and to tread the sure road to happiness, individual as well as general. The etymological meaning of "religion" is also the same, "that which binds together". Hence *Vaidika* Dharma means "the Religion of Perfect knowledge or perfect man".

श्रुतिस्तु वेदो विज्ञेयो धर्मशास्त्रं तु वै स्मृतिः।
ते सर्वार्थेष्वमिमांस्ये ताभ्यां धर्मो हि निर्बभौ।। (II -10)

Of the authority of the Shruti and Smriti, Manu says:

"The Veda is known as Śruti, the Dharma shastras as Smriti; these should not be doubted (but carefully consulted and considered) in all maters, for from them Dharma arose". Of these Smṛtis, the two of Manu and Yajnavalkya are universally accepted at the present time as of chief authority all over Indian, and Yajnavalkya is chiefly consulted in all matters of Hindu law. The other Smṛtis are drawn upon when it is necessary to supplement these.

References

1. Vaidika Sahitya Charitre - N. S. Anantarangachar, Prasaranga, Mysore University, 1975, Mysore.
2. सुभाषित सप्तशती। मंगलदेवशास्त्री सस्ता साहित्य मंडल प्रकाशन 1972, मुंबई।
3. सार्थ सुभाषितानि। विष्णु विनायक परांजपे केशव भिकाजी ढवळे। 1931 गिरगांव, मुंबई।

4. Sanskrit Sahitya Itihasa - Translation S. Ramachandra Shastri, Bangalore, University, 1980, Bangalore.
5. संस्कृतमहाकवियों के सम्बन्ध में प्रचलित लोकोक्तियाँ। आचार्य श्री रामचन्द्र झा। 1963 आरा विहार
6. The Kiratarjuniya of Bharavi - M. R. Kale, Motilal Banarasidas, 1977, Delhi.
7. Manasollasa of King Bhulokamall Somesvara, Vol. I, II and III. Oriental Institute, 1976, 39, 61, Baroda.

14

Śukanāsa's Advice on Ethical Behaviour

Umesh. G. Shastri

Bāṇa is the supreme master of Sanskrit prose, and the emperor Harsha had conferred upon him the title वश्यवाणी कविचक्रवर्तिन् i.e. Sovereign lord of poets, who is the master of language. Any person who reads his two famous works हर्षचरितम् and कादम्बरी will be easily convinced that, he fully deserved it. No doubt, Bāṇa is a great learned man, well versed in every branch of learning. He himself has drawn our attention regarding his poetic style in हर्षचरितम्

नवोऽर्थो जातिरग्राम्या श्लेषः स्पष्टः स्फुटो रसः।
विकटाक्षरबन्धश्च कृत्स्नमेकत्र दुर्लभम्।।

But, Bāṇa is successful in incorporating all these qualities in his famous work Kadambari.

Govardhanacharya considered Bāṇa as the incarnation of Goddess Saraswati – प्रागल्भ्यमधिकमवाप्तुं वाणी बाणो बभूवेति। Another worshipper of Bana has praised him like this-

रुचिरस्वरवर्णपदा रसभाववती जगन्मनो हरति।
सा किं तरुणी? नहि नहि वाणी बाणस्य मधुरशीलस्य।।

Thus, style of Bāṇa is very attractive, but looking at his lengthy compounds and lengthy sentences Weber has put forth the following criticism against the poet: "Bana's prose is an Indian wood, where all progress is rendered impossible by the undergrowth until the traveller cuts out a path for himself, and where, even then, he has to reckon with malicious wild beasts in the shape of unknown words that affright him". But Keith says, "it is fair to remember that, बाण is by no means without sense of propriety". We find regularity, uniformity, precision and balance in the use of words, which are considered to be four main characteristics of a good prose.

The address of Śukanāsa to Chandrapīḍa on the occasion of the young prince's coronation as 'Yuvarāja' may be cited as a best example of precepts on ethical behaviour. The advice is a masterly review of the dangers to which not only Chandrāpīḍa, but every youth is necessarily exposed to.

The new Lexicon Webster's Dictionary defines ethics as moral philosophy or moral science, i.e. that branch of philosophy which studies the principles of right or wrong in human conduct. In other words, the moral principles which determine the rightness or wrongness of our acts or activities. In a way, ethical behaviour is nothing but the 'Code of conduct' and its practice.

Advice of Śukanāsa to Chandrāpīḍa is a master piece of its kind and in it Bāṇa displays his great and varied knowledge of the world as well as of court life. Śukanāsa's advice (on ethical behaviour) is one of the grandest passages in Kādambari. It fully bears testimony to Bāṇa's rich imagery and facility of expression as well as to his considerable experience of the world.

There are many general statements in this advice, which are of universal application. He mainly deals with the possible evils arising from youth-hood and wealth. The fact that the advice is imparted to Chandrāpīḍa, who is already आरुढविनय brings a great charm to it. Sukanasa appreciates the good qualities of Chandrapida and thereby conquers his mind and intellect. He follows the path of कान्तासम्मित, so that his advice is more effective. Chandrapida having acquired fresh youth. Sukanasa naturally begins with the youth-hood. But youth-hood is not the only अनर्थ, there are three more, गर्भेश्वरत्वम्, (unlimited wealth by birth) अप्रतिमरुपत्वम् (extra-ordinary beauty) and अमानुष शक्तित्वम् (extra-ordinary power). All these are not naturally bad, but if not used rightly with precautions, they lead to अनर्थपरम्परा a series of adversities. That is why Hitopadeśakāra has rightly pointed out that –

> यौवनं धनसम्पत्तिः प्रभुत्त्वमविवेकिता।
> एकैकमप्यनर्थाय किमु यत्र चतुष्टयम्?।।

Śukanāsa says, the darkness due to youth can not be removed even by the sun, diamond or the lamp; so deep it is! In early youth the mind loses its purity, the eyes of the young become inflamed, in short, nature carries a man, in his young age, at its own, will like a dry leaf borne on the wind. Even in काव्यादर्श, Daṇḍin expresses similar views –

> अरत्नालोकसंहार्यमवार्यसूर्यरश्मिभिः।
> दृष्टिरोधकरं यूनां यौवनप्रभवं तमः।।

Mind of the youth become so much egoistic (or 'malina') that they do not care to hear even the advice of their Guru, which is a bath without water, वृद्धत्वम् without जरा (old age without its adversities) and it burns within and dispels the inner darkness. It is a wakefulness, which causes no disgust. Such an advice is particularly needed by the kings or rulers, because, proud kings treat their advisers with the indifference of the drowsy elephant and make the elderly persons repent. Thus, Sukanasa has drawn our attention towards the importance of Gurupadesha particularly to our younger generation.

Then, Sukanāsa advices on the possible evil effects of लक्ष्मी in detail. She has acquired passion वक्रता, चंचलता, मोहनशक्ति, मद and अतिनैष्ठुर्यम् with her very birth. Nothing else in this world is more regardless of familiarity than this vile woman. Even though protected with care, she vanishes. She neither respects familiarity nor cares for nobility of birth, beauty, vigour, good character, literary attainments, performance of religious duties, charitableness, truthfulness and such other good qualities. Like the sketch of a 'Gandharvanagara' she vanishes even as we look on her. She does not remain confined to one place, but goes from one person to another moving in a circle. This rotatory motion is due to her by the whirling waters of the sea churned by the Mandara Mountain. Probably, Laxmi has run a thorn of the lotus plant into her foot and does not, therefore set it firmly any where. She is चंचला, तमोबहुला, and अचिरद्युतिकारिणी. Sukanasa compares her to a दुष्टपिशाची. She never cares for a person with qualities like liberality and nobility; she does not care for a humble, truthful and a man with self-respect. Laxmi and Saraswati are poetically described as jealous of each other, the fact being that a rich man is not always a learned man. She herself is an abode of contradictions. Though she is अमृतसहोदरा, she is कटुविपाका; though विग्रहवती, अप्रत्यक्षदर्शना; though पुरुषोत्तमरता she is खलजनप्रिया.

No one is there who was not deceived, after the embrace by her. And especially kings, favoured by her become distressed. At the very moment of their coronation, their courtesy, forgiveness, truthfulness, good words and deeds etc., are washed off. There are some other rulers who are deceived by praise, fit for super-human beings. These persons are very clever in fulfilling their selfish desires and they are after wealth. Sukanasa calls them as आस्थाननलिनीबकऽ. They represent even faults as virtues. Thus, they represent द्यूत, परदाराभिगमन, मृगया, पान, प्रमत्तता, अजितभृत्यता, परिभवसहत्वं, स्वच्छन्दता, तरलता etc., as विनोद, वैदग्ध्य, श्रम, विलास, शौर्य, सुखोपसेव्यत्व क्षमा, प्रभुत्व, उत्साह etc., respectively and thus pleases the king. Therefore, Śukanāsa gives precautions about such deceivers. It is necessary for an administrator to conduct himself in such a way that, he is not laughed at by people, nor condemned by the elders, or lamented upon by the learned. He should not be deceived by विटऽ, कुशलऽ, भुजङ्गऽ, सेवकवृकऽ, धूर्तऽ, वनिताऽ, लक्ष्मी, मद, मदन विषयऽ, राग and सुख. Again and again one should remember that –

विद्वांसमपि, सचेतनमपि, महासत्त्वमपि, अभिजातमपि, धीरमपि, प्रयत्नवन्तमपि, पुरुषमियं दुर्विनीता खलीकरोति लक्ष्मी। Thus, the advice ends. Bāṇa seems to be so much carried away by his enthusiasm to depict the evils of wealth that he tells only a little about the evils of youth and forgets about अप्रतिमरुपत्व and अमानुषशक्तित्व. Perhaps, Bāṇa does this intentionally, because already he has proved his ability in this regard.

There is a similar episode in दशकुमारचरितम् of Dandin, wherein the elderly minister Vasurakshita advises the prince Anantavarman. Though, Śukanāsa's advice is meant for the prince, this advice is applicable to all, who are entering the prime youth-hood. Thus, Śakanāsa has dealt with possible adversities of youth hood, importance of Gurupadesha and evil effects of Laxmi in detail. If a man is aware of these maxims, and brings them into practice definitely he will be successful in his life.

No doubt, values emphasized by Bana in Sukanasopadesh are in accordance with established ancient Indian tradition and vision. He expects the tradition to be continued by us. But dishearteningly, in the present scenario of LPG (Liberalization, Privatization and Globalization) one has a serious doubt, whether the present Indian politics agrees with political ideals of Bāṇa, at least to their minimum level. According to Bāṇa qualities required by a politician or a person, who is in highly responsible position are आरुढविनयत्व, विदितवेदितव्यत्व, अधीतसर्वशास्त्रत्व and समारोपित संस्कारत्व.

Unfortunately, modern materialistic world is after money and luxuries of life. Especially our younger generation is attracted by the western culture and some of our youths blindly follow them. Western land is a land of सुखोपभोग, where as, भारतवर्ष is known for its कर्म and योग. Our ideal is 'तेन त्यक्तेन भुञ्जीथाः, मा गृधः कस्यस्विध्दनम्'। Therefore Śukanāsa has shown the right path to be followed in connection with लक्ष्मी or wealth. Intoxication generated by लक्ष्मी can not be removed, or persons who are after money will never be happy and contented in their life. We come across several cases in our news-channels or media about the plight of persons, who are after wealth. Realization of Yayāti at the end of his life is quite remembering –

न जातु कामः कामानामुपभोगेन शाम्यति।
हविषा कृष्णवर्त्मेव भूय एवाभिवर्धते।।

Precautions to be taken at the time of youth-hood and possible evils of लक्ष्मी, as advised by Śukanāsa is a pathway to success.

Bibliography

1. J.M. Ashar, Kādambarī of Banabhatta
2. Jha Bandhu, Kādambarī - Sukanasopadesh - (Chowkamba)
3. P.V. Kane (ed.) Kādambarī
4. M.R. Kale (ed.) Kādambarī
5. Nerurkar and Devasthali (ed.) Kādambarī
6. K.B. Archak (ed.) Ethics for Modern Man in Sanskrit Literature

15

Bhavabhuti's Ethics for Personality Development

V. Girishchandra

Drama is considered as the best poetic creation. It is considered as the mirror of life and society. Most of the Sanskrit Dramas deal with the problems of society and ethics of personal development or individual responsibility. Drama is the only literary composition where people of different levels of society get an opportunity to be represented. Their happiness and sorrow, joy and suffering, aspiration and frustrations are revealed and projected effectively in dramas.

Sanskrit dramas are many in number. Dramas of Bhasa, Śūdraka, Kālidāsa, Bhavabhūthi, Viśākadata, Śrīharṣa are very famous.

The sum total of ideals, characteristics and qualities as reflected in the activities and behaviour of a person is called his personality. It plays a significant role in shaping individual prosperity and social upliftment. The success of life depends upon one's good personality which is related to both physical beauty and mental power based on intelligence, knowledge and human good qualities.

To mould the personality of anybody in the society there stands the best instrument. Having known the importance of this instrument the ancient poets revealed their skill.

अपारे काव्यसंसारे कविरेकः प्रजापतिः।
यथास्मै रोचते विश्वं तथेदं परिवर्तते।। - Ānandavardhana

Hence they are given a driving seat in writing of works. Thus some of the ancient Alankarikas have honoured the poets – "In the vast world of Kavyas the poet is the Supreme Being, the creator. As he feels, tastes and pleases he changes the world."

Personality should be built up with spirituality. The real faith in religion or God can help the growth of spirituality. It constitutes the foundation of Indian culture.

Bhavabhuti represents the grandeur of Indian culture in its full richness and his works being the preservations of values fondly cherished by Indian culture. The validity of spiritual ideals reflects as personality. There are four spiritual values (पुरुषार्थाः) – धर्मः – अर्थः – कामः and मोक्षः of Rāma the hero of उत्तरामचरितम् represents the मोक्षः. It should be the ultimate aim of human being. This can be achieved only by observing the values of spiritual personality like Rāma. Bhavabhuti revealed the same in the personality of Rāma as heroic spirituality.

However taking into consideration the utility and necessity of good personality, the Sanskrit play writers like भास, कालिदास, शूद्रक, भवभूति, विशाखदत्त, श्रीहर्षादयः have visualised the various facets of personality in the form of human good qualities, which have been reflected in the characters of their Dramas.

However Bhavabhuti, a known writer of Sanskrit Dramas stands for his own spirituality in bringing the ethics of personality development. Hence he is appreciated as भवभूतिर्विशिष्यते। (Bhavabhuthi excels all). Vividly he has expressed his ideas, ideals and communicated messages about personality through his great Dramas like – महावीरचरितम्, उत्तररामचरितम् and मालतीमाधवम्, which are the products of his matured intelligence. He has thrown the light on the personality through noble characters (patras). Some facets of personality in the vision of Bhavabhuthi on the basis of some important characters are really worthwhile for all ages. His mental state at crucial moments is indefinable and incomprehensible.

Further, Bhavabhuti has shown the inner beauty of personality. In order to indicate the politeness of the hero रामायणम्, he considers Sri Rama as रामो विग्रहवान् धर्मः। He appreciates the character of Sri Rama for whom the subjects were as his breath, and the country as his body. Thus the noble personality of Sri Rama has occupied the unique place in the hearts of compassionates.

Being the supreme ruler of the earth Rāma fears about the criticism of a common man who is a washer man. Again he has sent his beloved wife Sita to the exile who was a pregnant. There Bhavabhuthi pointed out a big question क्व रजकः? क्व रामः? Where he gave prominence of human witness rather than the Divine witness (अग्निसाक्षिः) such was the personality of Rāma the hero of उत्तररामचरितम्। Thus Bhavabhūthi is appreciated as

भवभूतेः सम्बन्धाभ्दूधरभूरेव भारती भाति
एतत्कृतकारुण्ये किमन्यथा रोदिति ग्रावा।। आर्यासप्तशती - 36

According to Bhavabhuti, the greatness of personality lies in selfless sacrifice which is found in the character of Sri Ramachandra. The Author Bhavabhuthi has pointed out the sacrifice of Sri Rama in उत्तररामचरितम् and appreciates Rāma as an incarnation of धर्मः. Similarly the character of Sita for her tolerance and utter love about her beloved husband Sri Rama as क्षमया धरित्री areal daughter of Earth goddess. She sacrificed her true love and life for the good cause of her good husband.

Man is measured by his personality. Bhavabhuthi, a great and known writer of all times, has revealed the divine heroic character राम and left the spiritual moral message to human world. The ideals of Sri Rama, if adopted, will definitely raise the man, above the level of animality and enable him to reach divinity. The discipline of personality will help for the spiritual growth.

Bhavabhuti's version is different from that of Valmiki's Ramayana. The vision of Bhavabhuthi in his both महावीरचरितम् and उत्तररामचरितम् has to do with धर्म. Sri Rama's attitude towards धर्म, his particular way of doing his duty and finally the consequences of his having done it, have been effectively picturised by Bhavabhuti, with respect to धर्म in his plays, borders on the heretical, were he not so sublimely subtle and so often ambiguous.

Among the playwrighters, Bhavabhuti occupies a very prominent place. His three works are the masterpieces in Sanskrit Literature. In उत्तररामचरितम् he has revealed the facets of personality, simplicity, gravity, sense of ruling the subjects, possession of self respect, self confidence and duty consciousness of his beloved hero Rāma. In his first play, he has hidden the personality of Rāma and given prominent place according to its title, महान् चासौवीर महावीरः, महावीरस्य चरितं वर्ण्यते यत्र तत् नाटकं - "महावीरचरितम्"। In this play the poet clearly gives hints about the personality of his hero Rāma and his heroic sentiment is very much appreciated.

उत्तररामचरितम् is universally accepted as the best creation. Rightly it is said as उत्तरे रामचरिते भवभूतिर्विशिष्यते। The main scene in Rāmāyaṇa is pathos of क्रौञ्चवध, which melts the heart of sage Vālmiki and influenced his personality and outburst the feelings and emotions, stirs the deepest chords in human mankind. Vālmiki who spells the poem in metrical order with full of emotions and sorrows, शोकःश्लोकत्वमागतः, became the first stanza of the classical period. The story of क्रौञ्चवध may be allegory of pinpointing the fundamental truth. He became the आदिकवि. Then he was compelled to write the story of Sri Rama in the same metrical order which became the आदिकवि।

Bhavabhuti follows the line of Valmiki in his उत्तररामचरितम्. His poetry coming out of his sensitive mind would melt even the stones and break even the diamond which is said to be a king of metals? – "अपि ग्रावा रोदित्यपि दलति वज्रस्य हृदयम्" (उ.रा.च-28)

Here the poet seems to allude to his own power of making even the stones weep by his forcible and touching treatment of the sentiment of pathos. Thus the poet stands with Valmiki in proving the pathos – कारुण्यं भवभूतिरेव तनुते।

Bhavabhuti has thrown the light on the personality of Sri Rama in his dramas and pointed him with brighter colours. He tried to humanise Rāma, the incarnation of lord Vishnu of epic. He brought Rāma, the dramatic hero, as a noble man of human feelings. Rāma's reference and regard for elders is revealed in his willing obedience to their instructions and complete trust.

He sets more prominently Rāma's personality and character as a king, as a husband, as a father, more over as a human being.

As a king he had at tributed the highest place to his duty of propitiating the subjects at every cost and was ready to make the maximum sacrifice even by abandoned his dear wife.

As a husband, though he has abandoned his beloved wife Sita, who understood him for his great virtue of modesty, सुष्टु शोभसे आर्यपुत्र, एतेन विनयमाहात्म्येन revealed while ooserving the paintings of past events, his love for Sita had no comparison. To him she was a symbol of great bliss. He condemned himself for his act of abandoning her. Even after abandoning Sita he remained alone, remembering his past sweet memories, wept and pained for several times. He performed Ashwamedha sacrifice with golden image of Sita during her absence.

As a human being he did not like to punish Shambhooka, a Śūdra ascetic and wished him a place in the highest regions. Rāma though affected by misery as a human Being, he sticked to his duty as a king on seeing Lava and Kuśa, he showed his most paternal affection for them.

With all these aspects the personality of Sri Rama exposed in different colours and reflected vividly.

Madhava the hero of मालतीमाधवम्, acts mostly in accordance with the scheming of Kāmandaki. The selling of flesh to the ghosts however was an action of his own thought.

Similarly Bhavabhuti has thrown light on the personalities of other characters also. The personality of Sita in महावीरचरितम् is a shy maiden. She appears on the stage for a very short period. But the same Sita in उत्तररामचरितम् turned into a matured intellect. As a Hindu woman, she showed atmost respect and happiness to her husband. Though she was abandoned by Sri Rama without any fault of her, she did not utter any harsh word for him.

The personality of Mālatī in मालतीमाधवम् was also matured enough to distinguish between good and bad. To her the prestige of her parents and family were more important than her own life and love.

Thus Bhavabhuti has thrown light on the personality development of his characters and made them ever remembered. He stood unrivalled in his treatment of deep and tender human feelings, a true lover of nature in its beautiful, awe – inspiring and sublime aspects and moods.

16

Bhāravi's Disciplines of Power and Polity based on Personality Development

Shakuntala Hiremath

1. Introduction : Person – Personality

Man is considered to be the crown of creations. '*Person*' means human being who is an unique creation of God. Man's physical body is considered as an extra-ordinary machine, meant for beneficial mission. Man differs from other creatures as he has a capacity to think and decide what is good and what is bad. Man has got the capacity to talk and express his feelings effectively so as to build an impressing public image and place himself particular hierarchy in the society. Man has to get the capacity to smile and also make others smile, be happy by following some respectful decent behaviour in every walk of his life. This itself may be known as personality development.

The word '*personality*' is derived from a Latin word '*persona*' meaning 'mask'. It develops as a decoration and honour along with the age, from childhood every person discovers wisdom practice behaviour learns skill express, love and identifies values respectively and that is his mask, his personality. A person who does not have to wear different mask for others and can confidently show his true self is supposed to develop his good personality. For the welfare of the people, each person is expected to build up his personality by developing good qualities or human values within himself. Not only an ordinary man, but even a king or minister or any higher official should possess such human values for the well-being of their kingdom or nation. In this regard, a great poet Bhāravi, in his *Kirātārjunīya* has unfolded the different disciplines of the personality for the persons possessing political power.

The *Kirātārjunīyam* in the opening canto, expresses that Yudhiṣṭhira during exile along with his brothers and wife Draupadī, appoints a spy to get the news about the reign of Duryodhana. The spy reports the benign rule of Duryodhana who aspires for the stabilizing his governance by winning the hearts of his subjects. On hearing the report, Draupadī and Bhīma got engaged at Yudhiṣṭhira and spoke to him bitterly. But Yudhiṣṭhira consoles them by impressing upon them that pre-mature action in this matter could prove fatal.

The position of the Hindu king in civil list is of a servant who serves the people and gets his salary out of a fraction of the national revenue. With this defined position-shackled with checks and limitations, one can notice the great constitutional power of the *Paura-Jānapada* with a conscience trained to be prone to listen to the public voice. This lofty sense of sacrifice turned the constitutional slave into the moral master. Of all duties of a king, protection of the subjects is of prime importance. Explaining the governance of Duryodhana, Vanecara enumerates the ideals of the king.

2. Governance of Duryodhana

Along with the fact that a king has to come across many difficulties in the execution of political theories successfully. Of course, "uneasy lies the head that wears a crown." Therefore one can come to realize that becoming an ideal king is as tough as the task of rope-dancing. To a rope-dancer, a strict control over his mind and body is absolutely necessary. In the same way, to a successful monarch, proper balance between mind and action, with great control over his sense-organs is basically essential. Manu opines the same regarding this matter that involves himself in the conquest of his sense-organs because that king whose organs are conquered is able to bring the people under his control.[1]

As Vanecara reports, the secret of policies that Duryodhana is undertaking is to become an ideal king. Amongst them, the first and foremost point is developing his personality by having check over his emotions, as well as controlling five sense-organs. The king must be bold enough to have victory over six innate enemies like *Kāma, Krodha, Mada, Matsara, Lobha* and *Moha* which are the main hurdles in the personal achievement of the king. With such an equipment, a king must exercise his duties after dividing the hours of the day and night.[2] So, the idea of successful kingship is basically dependent on the self-control of the king. This idea is supported by the *Manusmṛti* (VII-45-53). The king with strong resolution, must fight against these six internal rivals. The self-possessed king should prefer death to these vices. Because a vicious man when he dies, sinks deeper into hell, while a virtuous man flies to higher heaven. The *Kāmāndikīya Nītisāra* says that a king's rest in his life lies in casting aside the six emotions like *kāma, krodha, lobha, harṣa, mana, mada* and he must cultivate *vinaya* (politeness), which means tolerance.[3] For the success of ideal kingship, top-priority should be given to the nature of tolerance. Regarding this necessity of politeness, Bhāravi states thus :

Vanecara states that Duryodhana's treatment towards his servants as friends, his friends and relatives as his masters, is glaring one. For this, the king has to abandon his egoism. Then only it is possible for him to honour and show affection towards his servants, friends and relatives.[4] Thereby a sense of unity and peace would prevail in his kingdom. The king's position is strengthened only by such unity. Manu illustrates the names of those kings who regained their kingdoms and reached their goal due to their nature of *vinaya*, he sums up his opinion that those kings who are good at conduct who honoured the old, efficient, disciplined men would never perish.

Further, it is elucidated that an ideal king must not fully believe his servants, friends and relatives. The king must always keep an eye on their activities. That eye is, as said by Kauṭilya, the spy (राजानः चारचक्षुषः). As such, Duryodhana has appointed trustworthy guards or confidential agents in order to watch the activities of his spies as well as those of the enemy, and puts on the appearance of being unsuspicious.

The king must pretend as if he has faith in all his servants but in his heart of hearts, he must be very alert and must not suddenly believe and come into the words of his servants or officials. Even in *Nītivākyāmṛta*, it is said that the king must have a clear look at the affairs of both in and out of the state through the special eye called spy. It is actually a sincere spy who becomes the eye-sight of the king.[5] At the same time, he must be grateful to his obedient servants and reward them with riches. Especially the king's spy should always be contented in monetary matters, because it is the fact that no man is the servant of anybody, unless and until his motives get satisfied.

3. King's Personality according to Draupadī

Then, words of Draupadī show another face of the discipline of power and polity based on personality development. Draupadī who is not in a position to tolerate the patience of Yudhiṣṭhira, charges him impatiently with the inefficiency of a king. Because, he is not having any type of feeling after incurring such a deceitful, humiliating and crushing defeat at the hands of his foe. Draupadī also expresses the necessity of self-respect and a sense of anger upto a certain extent.[6]

The saintliness in polity is of no avail because those who are devoid of wrath have no position or value in the society. Neither his friendship nor his enmity is fruitful. Friends never care for his actions, and enemies will never fear his existence. Therefore the king should act according to the circumstances. Then only his personality will create a sense of security and awe among all. Manu has also expressed the need of anger to the king according to the context.[7] Thus, a king should be a blend of both soft as well as hard. Possessing self-respect he must not keep quiet or excuse the humiliations brought by his rivals. Inertia is not suitable for such a king. Draupadī draws Yudhiṣṭhira's attention that he himself is born in Kṣatriya race. He must behave like a *Kṣatriya*, possessing all the qualities like vigorousness, self-respect and a towering personality which can create a sense of safety towards his subjects and of fear towards his enemies.

Yudhiṣṭhira's sense of quietude makes his personality a butt of ridicule. When Yudhiṣṭhira being a king, does not react or safe-gaurd his own kingly authority, state, wealth etc., against his enemy, how then can subjects expect a sense of security from such a king ? That is why Draupadī says –

विहाय शान्तिं नृप धाम तत्पुनः प्रसीद सन्धेहि वधाय विद्विषाम् । (I.42)

4. The Role of prowess according to Bhīma

In the second canto of the *Kirātārjunīya*, Bhīma too speaks about the role of prowess in the attainment of kingdom as well as in the destruction of rivals, Bhīmasena urges Dharmarāja to wreak revenge against Duryodhana. In a hyperbolic expression in praise of Draupadī's speech, he means that her ideas of politics are so vivid that even Bṛhaspati cannot think of them. In the opinion of Bhīma, Yudhiṣṭhira must not pocket an insult at the hands of their enemies but he has to summon his political knowledge to regain their kingdom.[8]

Bhīma wonders as to why Yudhiṣṭhira, though having all lores of knowledge like Polity, Vedas, Economics, is undergoing this deplorable position. The main reason is his quietitude. Though well-versed in carrying four upāyas, why are they not used by Dharmarāja to get rid of the present condition ? Instead of regaining his lost position by making use of the knowledge of four expedients, Dharmarāja's intellect is sinking low like an elephantess getting stuck in the mud.[9]

Bhāravi emphasizes that a king should be well-versed in the four kinds of science. They are (i) *Ānvikṣiki*-Logic and Metaphysics (ii) *Trayī* – the three Vedas (Ṛg., Sāma, Yajur), (iii) *Vārta* – the science of economics and (iv) *Daṇḍanīti* – the science of government or polity. Manu states the necessity of the knowledge of these four upāyas for a king.[10] A King should study the three Vedas. He should be well-versed in the science of polity on his own accord, as it is his custom. He should be well-acquainted with the knowledge of logic and *Ātmavidyā*, teaching as to how to keep up the proper balance of mind. The king should also study Economics which provides him with general knowledge of agriculture, cattle-breeding, trade and commerce and other financial aspects. Kāmāndaka also stresses the importance and the contents of these sciences.[11] Even Kauṭilya and Yājñavalkya have given importance to the necessity of these four lores for the advancement of a king.[12]

Expressing his astonishment at the sober act of Dharmarāja, Bhīma says as to why the great and highly praised prowess of him should deteriorate, when placed under such insults. It is further said that Duryodhana's achievement in kingly affairs is clearly leading to the perfect and eternal prosperity. Under such circumstances it is fair on the part of Dharmarāja to destroy or curb his enemy's prosperity with the exhibition of his valour.[13] And for this, he has to break the terms of gambling. This political strategy is cited in the Manusmṛti. If a king is confident enough of his success in future, then for the time being, he must adopt the policy of conciliation with his enemy.[14] Bhīma says that a king should beat the enemy, to prosper by leaps and bounds lest he should be a victim of public censure for his passiveness. Kāmāndaka too says 'The king who is inactive in the attainment of his position will always be humiliated, and may stand to lose his hard-earned kingdom like *ṣaṇḍa* who is insulted by ladies.'[15]

These fiery words of Bhīma shed light on an important point that the recovery of kingdom from the hands of rivals is secondary but the display of prowess, agility and efforts made by a king to get prosperity is primary. Subjects always love and honour that king who does not sit idle but who carries efforts to regain his lost kingship.

Prowess is highly essential to the king who is ambitious of attaining a cherished lofty position. In Bhima's opinion usually calamities overwhelm that person who is devoid of prowess. Therefore, he urges Yudhiṣṭhira to exhibit his valourous actions to wreak revenge against his foe, as it is the nature of an ideal king to do so. Bhīma also conjectures the objection of Dharmarāja that they have to keep up their words according to the terms and agreements of the dice. So it is better on their part to wait up to the expiry of the period of exile. Thinking thus Bhīma says ṣ

अथ चेदवधिः प्रतीक्ष्यते कथमाविष्कृताजिह्मवृतिना ।
धृतराष्ट्रसुतेन सुत्यजाश्चिरमास्वाद्य नरेन्द्रसंपदः ।। (II.16)

Following the terms and conditions of agreement it is not fair on their part because Duryodhana played them false first in the game of dice. Under such circumstances they might not obey the terms of agreement. Even though the agreement is adhered to by them, the vile-natured Duryodhana will never agree to restore their kingdom. But if unexpectedly he transfers the fortune into their hands, then also it is not praiseworthy on their part. The main reason for this is that many politicians opine that an ideal king should regain or extend the borders of his kingdom, only by the exhibition of his prowess but not having it in the form of donation. Even a lion (II.23) will always accept the meat out of the body of that elephant, which is killed by its own strength. Then Bhīma wonders as to how it should look fair on the part of human king. Like Draupadī, Bhīma also lays more stress on the point of self-respect, sense of anger and vindictive actions.

Further essentially a king, who must have self-respect and expression of reaction in all fury. Because it is for this reason that, the anger of a particular person (king) is just like fire, the man devoid of anger is just like a heap of ashes. People will easily trample on him as nobody fears to walk on the ashes but everyone will get back when anger like fire is there in a person. Therefore a king should always earn his kingdom by his valour and react with revengeful actions towards his fraudulent enemies. Bhāravi sums up that inactivity or idleness and lack of self-respect are the main causes of the downfall of a king. Even in the speech of Bhīma, one finds an echo of Yājñavalkya's words regarding the vital role of human effort in the attainment of their goal. Yājñavalkya says that the attainment of their goal is not wholly dependent on fate (*Daiva*) but the most part of it is dependent on human effort only. So he says that one has to try hard and continuously puts in efforts to reach their goal.[16]

5. Yudhisthira's Personality

On the other hand Yudhisthira's views agree with the other thoughts of Yājñavalkya. The successful undertakings of a king depend not wholly on fate, nor does it depend upon a certain period (*Kāla*), not without reason, but the fulfilment of a king's desire equally depend on the fate (*Daiva*), nature, period (*Kāla*) and valour.[17] Dharmarāja, with his coolness of temper and unshaken mind says that: Bhīma has justified the political ideas. But Yudhiṣṭhira gradually makes his brother Bhīma realize the fact that the enemy's party is too strong to overpower at the current juncture; and any how hasty actions on their part would ruin their cause. So Yudhiṣṭhira shows that the ideas of Draupadī and Bhīmasena expressed on the political affairs of a king, are theorotically correct. But, the display of valour alone will never serve the purpose of the king, but at the same time, the success of a particular political aim equally depends upon the timely display of prowess even though the execution of other state-crafts; like four upāyas as stated by Manu is present. Battle or exhibition of valour towards rivals is not always good. First of all they should also make use of other upāyas like *Sāma* (conciliation), *Dāna* (charity), *Bheda* (dissension or duplicity) and as a last resort *Daṇḍa*' i.e., declaring war against his enemy[18]; Above all, an ideal king has to cultivate '*vinaya*'.

There is a multiplicity of policies to be adopted under different circumstances when his enemy is very strong by attaining the power of saptāṅgas, one must not take hasty steps to exhibit valour in an angry mood in such a situation.[19] Because he feels that 'haste is waste' – सहसा विदधीत न क्रियामविवेकः परमापदां पदम् । (II.30).

These words of Dharmarāja remind of Manu's view that the successful execution of political affairs is very difficult that too by one man, who is devoid of *saptāṅga*[20] Dharmarāja.

'First of all, accurate knowledge of the śāstras adorns the person, self-possession becomes its embellishment, timely display of valour is the ornament, success is brought on by right policy. These lines of Bhāravi remind us of Kauṭilya's idea regarding well-developed personality of a king.[21]

In response to the opinion of Bhīma regarding the idea of breaking the terms of gambling, Yudhiṣṭhira saysṣ

शिवमौपयिकं गरीयसीं फलनिष्पत्तिमदूषितायतीम् ।
विगणय्य नयन्ति पौरुषं विजितक्रोधरया जिगीषवः ।। (II.35)

They must not yield to the impulse of anger but wait for a favourable opportunity. Because, the men who are ambitious of conquest over the force of anger and having well ascertained and must attain their desired aim. Even Kāmāndaka expresses his views on this fact that with regard to political measure, which is very tough to execute under particular circumstances and the result of which is hazy, the intelligent king should not take any hasty political step, tinged with the passion of jealousy. Manu also holds the same, when he says – "Even though the strength of the king is excellent and if it works through passions like jealousy and the valour exhibited by him, it results into the destruction of the three kinds of regal powers i.e., *Prabhuśakti, Utsāhaśakti* and *Mantraśakti*".[22] Bhāravi states thus :

बलवानपि कोपजन्मनस्तमसो नाभिभवं रुणद्धि यः ।
क्षयपक्ष इवैन्दवीः कलाः सकला हन्ति स शक्तिसंपदः ।। (II.37)

Dharmarāja impresses upon Bhīma the fact that a king, who wants to have victory over his enemy, should invariably win his own internal rivals (*Ariṣaḍvarga*) by self possession and *Vinaya* (modesty) as Manu also lays accent on this quality.[23] Yudhiṣṭhira also says that this expression of modesty forever is not good. But the king has to maintain a proper balance between sobriety and severity. He must assume mildness or display severity at the proper time. Then only, it is possible for him to preside over the whole world like the Sun by his luster.[24]

Thus Dharmarāja advising Bhīma says that there is no other way for them to attain success except self-control, as Duryodhana is self sufficient in every sphere of politics to destroy them. So it is not the proper time for them to take revengeful action. Further Dharmarāja also expresses his views on *Kāmaja* and *Krodhaja* lapses (II.33-35). To this idea the opinion of Manu is similar.[25] The king who indulges in *Kāma* (lust) and *Vyasana* (bad habit) or in waywardness will be devoid of wealth and duty. But, that king who is caught up in the hands of fury will fritter away himself. In other words he will be totally destroyed. Therefore Yudhiṣṭhira warns Vāyuputra against restlessness, that may land them in total destruction. He wants Bhīma to understand clearly that if they revolt against Duryodhana by the conceit of arrogance in the force of anger they only meets with loss. More than this if they behave out of the way, they will also lose the company of strong Yādavas who are their real allies. And since, friends are considered as one of saptāṅgas of the state, he does not want to lose them, as they are the real source of victory.

सुहृदः सहजास्तथेतरे मतमेषां न विलंघयन्ति ये ।
विनयादिव यापयन्ति धृतराष्ट्रात्मजमात्मसिद्धये ।। (II.45)

Kāmāndaka states these seven parts of a state in Nītisāra.[26] The author of the Manu code says that the king should not go along a wrong path as far as possible, (M.S.VII.104).24 Otherwise he has to lose saptāṅgas or any one of them. Yudhiṣ ṭhira advises Bhīma as –

अभियोग इमान्महीभुजो भवता तस्य कृतः कृतावधेः ।
प्रविघाटयिता समुत्पतन्हरिदश्वः कमलाकरनिव ।। (II.46)

Besides, Yudhiṣṭhira points out one important loophole i.e., artificial modesty of them. Duryodhana which may come to help them to get their ends fulfilled, by making Duryodhana lose his hold in political field. Such a quality with the help of which he has gained tight hold on his position and attained prosperity will never last long as a result of which his royal power will be curbed. Because many scholars feel that there are two types of modesty (*Vinaya*) (i) which is acquired by one right from nature or by birth, which is known as *prākṛtikavinaya* (original) modesty. (ii) The other one is aquired by practice or by ceaseless efforts, which is called '*kṛtrimavinaya*', (artificial modesty). As the modesty of Duryodhana is an artificial one, one day or the other cat must come out of the bag, because Duryodhana is wicked and haughty by nature. He will definitely lose his balance of mind and will go on the wrong side, and as a result, will lose his control over saptāṅgas. Therefore, they have to wait for such an opportunity and also detect his weak points, by confirming to the terms of compromise.

मतिमान्विनयप्राथिनः समुपेक्षेत समुन्नतिं द्विषः ।
सुजयः खलु तादृगन्तरे विपदन्ता हाविनीतसंपदः ।। (II.52)

Bhāravi concludes that king's real strength and virtue are always tested by the touch-stone of miseries like gold tested in fire. And, it is true that always hardships and disasters add strength to the personality of a king, and make him successful ever.

Reference

1. इन्द्रियाणां जये योगं सातिष्ठेद्दिवानिशम् ।
   जितेन्द्रियो हि शक्नोति वशे स्थापयितुं प्रजाः ॥ Ch.VII, 44, P.33
   J.H.Dave, *Manusmāti*, Vol.IV, Part I, Bharatiya Vidya Bhavan, Bombay, 1985.
2. कृतारिषड्वर्गजयेन मानवीमगम्यरूपां पदवीं प्रपित्सुना ।
   विभज्य नक्तंदिवमस्ततन्द्रिणा वितन्यते तेन नयेन पौरुषम् ॥
   M.R. Kale, *Kirātārjunīya of Bhāravi*, Motilal Banarsidass, Delhi, I.9, p.20
3. आत्मानं राजा विनयेनोपपादयेत् -
   कामः क्रोधस्तथालोभो हर्षः मानो मदस्तथा ।
   षड्वर्गमुत्सृजेदेनमस्मिंस्त्यक्ते सुखी नृपे ॥ (Ch.I. 23. P.9)
   Jwalaprasad Mishra, *Kāmāndikīyanītisāra*, Sri Venkateswara Steam Press, Bombay, 1874.
4. सखीनिव प्रीतियुजोनुजीविनः समानमानान्सुहृदश्च बन्धुभिः ।
   स सन्ततं दर्शयते गतस्मयः कृताधिपत्यामिव साधु बन्धुताम् ॥
   M.R. Kale, *Kirātārjunīya*, I.10, p.23
5. स्वपरण्डले कार्याकार्यविलोकने चारचक्षूंषि क्षितीपतिनाम् ॥
   Nītivākyāmāta Q. M.R. Kale, *Kirātārjunīya*, 1997, p.11

6. अवन्ध्यकोपस्य विहन्तुरापदां भवन्ति वश्याः स्वयमेव देहिनः ।
अमर्षशून्येन जनस्य जन्तुना न जातहार्देन न विद्विषादरः ॥
M.R. Kale, *Kirätärjunïya*, I.33, p.63
7. तीक्ष्णश्चैव मुदुश्च स्यात्कार्य वीक्ष्य महीपतिः ।
तीक्ष्णश्चैव मृदुश्चैव राजा भवति सम्मतः ॥ M.S. VII 140, P.105
8. विषमोऽपि विगाह्यते नयः कृततीर्थः पयसामिवाशयः ।
स तु तत्र विशेषदुर्लभः सदुपन्यस्यति कृत्यवर्त्म यः ॥
M.R. Kale, *Kirätärjunïya*, II.3
9. चतुर्ष्वपि ते विवेकिनी नृप विद्यासु निरूढिमागता ।
कथमेत्य मतिर्विपर्ययकरिणी पङ्कमिवावसीदति ॥
M.R. Kale, *Kirätärjunïya*, II.6
10. त्रैविद्येभ्यस्त्रयीं विद्यां दण्डनीतिं च शाश्वतीम् ।
आन्वीक्षिकीं चात्मविद्यां वार्तारंभांश्च लोकतः ॥
Manusmãti, VII.43, p.31
11. आन्वीक्षिकी त्रयी वार्ता दण्डनीति शाश्वती ।
विद्याश्चतस्र एवैता योगमोक्षाय देहिनाम् ॥
आन्वीक्षक्यात्माविज्ञानं धर्माधर्मो त्रयीस्थितौ ।
आर्थानर्थो तु वार्तायां दण्डनीत्यां नयानयी ॥
Jwalaprasad Mishra, *Kämändikiyanïtisära*, II.2&7, pp.18-19
12. वृत्तोप्नयनस्त्रयीमान्वीक्षिकीं च शिष्टेभ्यः वार्तामध्यक्षोभ्यः दण्डनीतिं वक्तृप्रयोक्तृम्भः ।
R. Shama Sastry, *Arthaáästra* of Kauâilya, Mysore, 1924, Ch.II.2, p.10
आन्वीक्षिकी त्रयी वार्ता दण्डनीति शाश्वती ।
विद्याश्चतस्र एवैता योगमोक्षाय देहिनाम् ॥
Yäjñavalkya-smãti, Prak. 13.311, p.105
13. द्विषतामुदयः सुमेधसा गुरुरस्वन्तरः सुमर्षणः ।
न महानपि भूतिमिच्छता फलसम्पत्प्रवणः परिक्षयः ॥
चिरेण परस्य भूयसीं विपरीतां विगणय्य चात्मनः ।
क्षययुक्तिमुपेक्षते कृती कुरुते तत्प्रतिकारमन्यथा ॥
M.R. Kale, *Kirätärjunïya*, II.8-9
14. यदावगच्छेदायत्यामाधिक्यं ध्रुवमात्मनः ।
तदात्वे चाल्पिकां पीडां तदा सन्धिं समाश्रयेत् ॥
Manusmãti, VII.169, p.132

15. स्त्रीभिः षण्ड इव श्रीभिरलसः परिभूयते ॥

    Kämändikïya Nïtisära, Canto 13.8. p.141

16. दैवे पुरुषाकारे च कर्मसिद्धिर्व्यवस्थिता ।
    तत्र दैवमभियुक्तं पौरुषं पौर्वं दैहिकम् ॥

    Yäjñavalkya-smäti, Prak. 13.349, p.116

17. केचिद्दैवात्स्वभावाद्वा कालात्पुरुषाकारतः ।
    संयोगे केचिदिच्छन्ति फलं कुशलबुद्धयः ॥

    Ibid., Prak. 13.350, p.116

18. साम्ना दानेन भेदेन समस्तैरथवा पृथक् ।
    विजेतुं प्रयतेतारीन्न युद्धेन कदाचन ॥

    Manusmäti, VII.198, p.153

19. अवितृप्ततया तथापि में हृदयं निर्णयमेव धावति ।
    अवसाययितुं क्षमाः सुखं न विधेयेषु विशेषसम्पदः ॥

    M.R. Kale, *Kirätärjunïya*, II.29, p.124

20. अपि यत्सुकरं कर्म तदप्येकेन दुष्करम् ।
    विशेषतोऽसहायेन किं नु राज्यं महोदयम् ॥

    Ibid., VII.55, p.45

21. शुचि भूषयति श्रुतं वपुः प्रशमस्तस्य भवत्यलंक्रिया ।
    प्रशमाभरणं पराक्रमः स नयापादितसिद्धिभूषणः ॥

    M.R. Kale, *Kirätärjunïya*, II.32

22. विद्याविनयहेतुरिन्द्रियजयः कामक्रोधलोभमानमदहर्षत्यागात्कार्यः । कर्णत्वगक्षिजिह्वाघ्राणेन्द्रियाणां शब्दस्पर्शरूपरसगन्धेष्वविप्रतिपत्तिरिन्द्रियजयः शास्त्रार्थानुष्ठानं वा । कृत्स्नं हि शास्त्रमिदमिन्द्रियजयः ॥

    R. Shama Shastry, *Arthaáästra* of Kauâilya, Mysore-1924, VIII, p.11

23. निष्फलं क्लेशबहुलं संदिग्धफलमेव च । न कर्म कुर्यान्मतिमान्महावैरानुबन्धि च ॥

    Kämändikïya Nïtisära, Canto. 11.42, p.124

    अनित्यो विजयो यस्मादृश्यते युध्यमानयोः । पराजयश्च संग्रामे तस्माद्युध्यं विवर्जयेत् ॥

    Manusmäti, VII.199, p.79

24. विनीतात्मा हि नृपतिर्न विनश्यति कर्हिंचित् ।
    वनस्था अपि राज्यानि विनयात् प्रतिपेदिरे ॥

    Ibid., VII.39, p.29

25. समवृत्तिरुपैति मार्दवं समये यश्च तनोति तिग्मताम् ।
आधितिष्ठति लोकमोजसा स विवस्वानिव मेदिनीपतिः ॥
M.R. Kale, *Kirätärjunïya*, II.38, p.136

26. कामजेषु प्रसक्तो हि व्यसनेषु महीपतिः ।
वियुज्यतेऽर्थधर्माभ्यां क्रोधजेष्वात्मनैव तु ॥
Manusmãti, VII.46, p.34

17

Vedānta Deśika's Scheme of Personality Development

R. Laxmi

यद्भक्तिप्रचयात्मके दिनमुखे दृष्टिक्षमः क्षेत्रिणः
क्षिप्रं संसृतिशर्वरी क्षिपति यत्संकल्पसूर्योदयः।
तत्वैरस्रविभूषणैरधिगतः स्वाधीननित्योन्नतिः
श्रीमानस्तु स मे समस्तविपदुत्ताराय नारायणः।।

The scheme of Personality Development is to be found in Deśika's *magnum opus* play Saṅkalpa Sūryodaya. This allegorical drama imbibes more than forty characters, including both male and female. Of these, some twenty characters are grouped under the leadership of king Viveka, the *Nāyaka* of the drama. And, similarly other characters belong to king Mahāmoha, the *Pratināyaka*. Drama is a direct objective and impersonal representation of life on the stage. And the allegorical dramas convey a veiled moral meaning in which various qualities and virtues are personified. In this direction, Vedānta Deśika has portrayed several virtuous characters as against the wicked ones. They are the representations of Personality Development. Among them Viveka is the supreme one because he fights against Mahāmoha the most wicked one. His success in the battle against Mahāmoha is aided by his virtues like right thinking etc.

It is a well known fact from ancient times that attainment of *Mokṣa* is the highest goal of human achievement. It should be the final goal of every man to develop his inner and outer personality. For this purpose, he has to acquire a knowledge of the Absolute or Brahmajñāna. In this paper an effort is made to highlight the significant aspects of Personality Development as depicted by the dramatist through innate virtues possessed by the characters. Because the theme of the play is mainly to show how ethics and Visiṣṭādvaita Philosophy, can help an individual to achieve the highest goal i.e. attainment of *mokṣa*. Among the Caturvidha Puruṣārthas, *mokṣa* is the ultimate one.

In the play, Lord Nārāyaṇa is the Supreme Being. Devotion to Him leads to *mokṣa* and His auspicious boon makes the devotee free from *Samsāra*. Thus he who is imparted within the knowledge of Aṣṭākṣaramantra by a Competent Preceptor, he conquers the demon called *avidyā*.

In the drama, Deśika states that by the study of the scriptures, the pure soul turns away his mind from the pleasures of the world through *niṣkāma karma*, he is eligible to gain the grace of the Lord. He cultivates *bhakti* and steps ahead as *prapanna*. Then the individual soul attains salvation.

When *jīva* adopts the means of realisation, preceptors favour is quite essential to win. Because just as evil spirits bind a *Jīva, Kāma, Krodha, Ahaṅkāra* etc. catch hold of the individual soul, the preceptor protects him and destroys *Kāma, Krodha,* etc. to whom he surrenders with devotion. Through the grace of the preceptor, his path of realisation becomes unobstructed. The seeker should always approach such a preceptor who can remove his ignorance and shower pure knowledge on him. Therefore individual selves seeking knowledge can learn all the truths from such preceptor with care and attention. Thus the role of preceptor in the life of a seeker is very important. Such preceptor instructs to his disciple the essence of Upaniṣadic texts as upheld by Rāmānuja. This shows the importance of the path to Personality Development.

According to the philosophy of Visiṣṭādvaita, *jīvas* are three fold, i.e., *Baddha, Mukta* and *Nitya*. Also there are three kinds of non-sentient things such as *Prakṛti, Kāla* and *Śuddhasattva*. Lord Nārāyaṇa alone can grant all the four objects, i.e., *dharmārthakāmamokṣa*. Just as all rivers meet in the ocean, all beneficient streams of vedic texts have the eternal and natural substratum i.e., the Supreme Being.

In the Visiṣṭādvaita religion, the place of *Garuḍa* is remarkable. It is glorified that *Garuḍa* can make accessible to the seeker the spiritual meditation called *upāsanas* in the *Upaniṣads*. *Garuda*'s *Pañcākṣarimantra* which has *Praṇava* before the Puruṣārthas fruitified. In the Pañcarātra āgamas, it is declared that the Sannaha or equipment and Saṅkalpa or resolve of Lord Hari appear as visible manifestation in the form of *Garuḍa* and Sudarśana *Cakra* respectively.

Goddess *Lakṣmī*, the consort of Lord Nārāyaṇa is given prime importance in the Viśiṣṭādvaita Philosophy. This role of Goddess *Lakṣmī* points to Her nityaniyogittva with the Lord. Her grace is necessary for devotee to realise the knowledge of the Absolute.

So far as the concept of *jīva* is concerned, Vedānta Deśika refers to another type of *jīva* i.e., *Baddha* or bound *jīva*. These *jīvas* are not freed from the empirical existance. The bound *jīvas* are again divided into many groups. The *Puruṣa* or the individual soul who is boosted up by Viveka comes under the group of *dharmapara jīvas* who are devoted to none other than Lord Nārāyaṇa. The *Puruṣa* of this drama may be called *jijñāsu* or the seeker of knowledge. He is a votary of self-realisation and of release from *samsāra*. Self-realisation arises from pure knowledge of Brahman. The votaries of *mokṣa* are the devotees of Lord as well as prapannas i.e., those who have completely surrendered themselves to God and through the means of prapatti attain *mokṣa*. When *jīva* is treading the path of *mokṣa*, he has to offer eight flowers to the Lord, i.e., he has to observe *Ahiṁsā, Indriyajaya, Daya, Kṣamā, Jñāna, Tapas, Dhyāna* and *Satya*. By following all these disciplines strictly, all sins are removed. He should possessed unstinted devotion to Lord Nārāyaṇa alone. Then he should undertake the course of deep meditation of no one but the Lord. Then he becomes eligible to the attainment of eternal bliss in Vaikuṇṭha. At this stage, will of the Lord arises and the *jīva* becomes liberated.

When the *jīva* ascends the steps of meditation, he should win over all the evil effects of the mind, i.e. he should win over *Kāma* by *Virakti, Krodha* by *Kṣṭānti*, *Lobha* by *Tuṣṭi, Moha, Dambha, Darpa, Asūya, Irṣa*, etc. by Viveka. This discipline is highlighted in the whole of the battle scene in the eighth act of the drama. And the seeker can enter into a deep meditation if he has cultivated the qualities like *Śama, Dama, Uparati,* etc. and by the blessings of the preceptor. To a person engrossed in meditation, future sins will not cling and his past sins are destroyed. Finally he attains *mokṣa*.

Vedānta Deśika makes it explicit that all sins of the *jīva* will be destroyed by the will of the Lord. Still *Prārabdha Karma* remains to be experienced. After experiencing all *Prārabdha Karmas*, *Sthūla Śarīra* of *jīva* will be left away after the fall of the body of the *jīva*. The *Sukṣma Śarīra* which he possesses even then, that will be left away after taking bath in the river Virajā. Thus the *jīva* comes out of the prison house of the body constituted of water, blood, flesh, fat, bones, marrow and semen and like a prince emerging from within the hut of the hunter and hastening to climb up the palace of his father, the emperor, the *jīva* ascends to *Paramapada* through the path of *Devayāna* accessible to none else. Then he is escorted to the region beyond *Tamas*. At every step of *jīva*'s path leading to *Paramapada* grace of Lord Nārāyaṇa is essential. This grace is technically called *icchāśakti* of Nārāyaṇa.

King Viveka is portrayed as *Dhirodātta*[1] type of hero in the drama. Dhirodātta or the hero of sublime qualities is one who is *Mahāsattva* or one whose mind does not get disturbed by grief, anger, greed, lust etc. *Atigambhīra* (very sincere boosting), *Kṣamāvān* (patient), *Avikatthana* (not given to boosting), *Sthira* (of firm resolve), *Niguāhāhaṅkāra* (whose self-conceous is concealed due to his modesty), *Dṛāhavrata* (one who accomplishes the work undertaken.

In the present context, the role of the king Viveka is portrayed to have possessed all these qualities of *Dhirodātta* type of hero. Vedānta Deśika gives more prominence to the role of Viveka because all strategies and the actions there of relating to the goal, i.e., the attainment of *mokṣa*. All the scenes in the play centre round king Viveka. There could be some obstacles brought about by the rival hero, Mahāmoha and his supporters, but they see the end in miserable failure due to the irresistible force of Viveka and Saṅkalpa.

So far as Viveka's geneology is concerned, the drama expresses that Buddhi the devoted wife of *Puruṣa* (individual soul) endowed with the three qualities – *sattva, rajas* and *tamas*, gave birth to three families each at a time. When one or the other of *Puruṣa*'s three qualities was predominant in him. The first family consisted of Viveka and others who are averse to his pleasures and pains in life and the other two of Rāga and Mahāmoha who have joined their forces together being associated respectively with rajas and tamas.

Secondly, Viveka is characterised as a man of pure Wisdom. Sumati asks Viveka about the means of liberation. In response to this, Viveka gives a clear picture of the philosophy of Visiṣṭādvaita in essence :

मदनमत्सरमानमयः पुमान् बहुपिशाचगृहीत इवार्भकः।
निगमसिद्धनरेन्द्र निरीक्षणान्निपुणपद्धतिमभ्यवपद्यते।।

S.S. 1-76, p.153.

Because Viveka had cultivated *Sattva guṇas*, he was able to finally overcome the *rajas* and *tamas guṇas* of his rivals.

As Kāma remarks, Viveka is free from all doubts, has studied the Vedānta philosophy thoughtfully and reads about those observances leading to *mokṣa*. He has cultivated the virtues like self-control and practise the repetition of *Aṣṭākṣara* and *Gītā* with unstinted devotion. Viveka cultivating the bright virtue of introspection in the form of Sumati and entertaining the deepest and stanchest love of God though in prosperity, keeps Ahaṅkāra under perfect control and seeks the feet of the Lord. These are essential qualities to achieve the goal. Viveka has all these virtues. This aspect has been portrayed in the following verse :

मुकुलयति विवित्सां मोहविध्वंसमिच्छन् विमृशति निगमान्तान्
वीक्षते मोक्षधर्मान्।
निशमयति च गीतां नित्यमेकान्त्याकत्या गुणपरिषदेवेक्षी
गुप्तमन्त्रो विवेकः।। S.S. I-61, p.123

प्रत्यङ्मुखीं सुमतिदीप्तिमिह प्रचिन्वन् प्राप्तोदयोऽप्या
मितरागबलोपपन्नः
क्षाम्यन्नहंकृतिमयीमवशो हिमानीं भास्वानसौ भजति विष्णुपदं
विवेकः॥ S.S. I-62, p.124-25

In the play, the *Prakṛti* with her power of illusion binds *Puruṣa* or *Jīvātmā* in the chain of births and deaths. This *puruṣa* has given birth to Viveka and Mahāmoha along with their followers. King Viveka aptly pointed out the nature of Mahāmoha as स्वभाव्यमेव शवमुष्टिवद् गृहीतग्रहिता महामोहस्य (S.S.III., p.385). Mahāmoha also makes efforts to win over Viveka. Finally Viveka becomes victorious with the help of his assistants of *Sattva* qualities through the Saṅkalpa or Grace of the Lord.

The character of Viveka and Sumati are portrayed as king and queen in the play. Vyavasāya, the human effort is the commander-in-chief in the battle. Vedānta Deśika has provided a very prominent place to Vyavasāya in the play. For the successful realisation of the purpose of human effort, Divine Grace is very much required. It is true that the final goal can be attained by the Divine Grace only, still the factor of human effort cannot be neglected. On the contrary, Mahāmoha and Durmati work for evil. *Puruṣa* represents the warring element and the final victory of Viveka will bring him good. After the victory of the good over evil, God's grace is bestowed upon the individual soul to save himself from the cycle of births and deaths. This is the final stage of *sādhana* where man attains salvation.

Viveka, the hero of valour possesses exclusive power to destroy *kāma, krodha* etc. while cowerdice fails to achieve the purpose. Viveka takes up a brave fight with the evil forces of Mahāmoha and ultimately they are defeated. Even fighting against Mahāmoha, Viveka did not get hesitated; but with all enthusiasm and courage without loosing self-reliance, he fights with Mahāmoha and becomes victorious. This shows his being *dṛāhvrata* or confident of his work undertaken, which helps development of personality.

Viveka is pictured as *jitakrodha* or as having won anger is another quality needed for Personality Development. Though Viveka is condemned as deceitful, sinner etc. by kāma and vasanta he does not get angry and remained determined with his effort to follow the right path. In another context, an envoy of Mahāmoha approaches Viveka and reads out the message of his Lord :

"If you should disobey the orders, you will be attacked by your wrathful foes, krodha and others, who will rush against you at the dance like knitting of our brow and you will then cease to be." Listening to these words, Viveka quietly says that "this is indeed a blessing to us for having been ever devoted to our drama." Here Viveka's capacity of finding a merit on other's demerit is really remarkable. At the same time he shows another face of composure saying that Righteous indignation is not a sin, for it is praised by those who know the real truth, as being necessary for winning krodha. Deśika has portrayed Viveka as a person of right thinking and far sightedness. At this juncture to achieve his ultimate goal Viveka decides to search for a suitable place for meditation. Ultimately he realises that the most suitable place was not outside but in his own mental furniture or in *daharakaśa*.

When *puruṣa* is attacked by the evil forces, he falls into a pitiable condition. Seeing this, Sumati sometimes expresses her doubt as to whether they could liberate *puruṣa* from the clutches of *Samsāra*. In such context also, Viveka remains patient and asks Sumati the same, filling courage in her heart.

Another quality for Personality Development portrayed by Vedānta Deśika is *sthira* or steadfastness. Viveka had this quality too.

The role of Sumati is an another quality which helps to attain spiritual development. She belongs to *svakīya* type and possesses the qualities like *vinaya*, *ārjava* and *pātivṛtya* etc.

Sumati represents right thinking or understanding. This virtue is essential for acquiring *vairāgya* leading to *Samādhi*. In the play, she is portrayed as ably and timely assisting king Viveka in his attacking king Mahāmoha and his followers and winning a victory over them. The following passage shows her firm conviction :

अस्ति खल्वनभिज्ञकुल सार्वभौम
विवेकहृतकमूलाकर्तृत्वाभिमानादि नानाविधिविषमदृष्टिसहकृत:
कश्चिदस्मत्कुलाभिचारकाङ्क्षिभिरुपनिषदूषरनिष्ठै:
कैश्चिन्निष्टुरैरनुष्ठीयमानो निवृत्तिसंज्ञको धर्म:।
यन्निष्ठस्यपरदोष दर्शनादिष्वन्धबधिरमूकषण्डादिवदत्यन्तम्
वसन्नावस्थानमाकर्ण्यते।। (S.S.I - pp.106-107)

She does not sustain to know the condemnation of Viveka by Vasanta, Kāma and Rati. For instance, kāma condemns Viveka, "that prince of fools, Viveka has suggested a path or dharma called *nivṛtti* which has been followed by some cruel persons who live in the swamps of the *Upaniṣad*s, and who want to practise the wiles of black magic against our race. This path or dharma called renunciation is supported by many perverse thoughts such as saying to oneself, "I am not the author of these actions of mine." We hear that a person who follows the path falls into a painful state in regard to such things as seeking into other's faults, like one who is blind, deaf, impotent, lame and dumb.

For this, Sumati wisely responds that ugly persons attribute the ugliness of their own face to mirrors, clear though they are. The following verse indicates this point :

आर्यपुत्र, विरूपाः खलु जना निजमुखदोषं।
निर्मलेष्वपि दर्पणेषु समर्पयन्ति।। S.S.I. p.129

Here, Sumati points out to Viveka the line of right understanding. Viveka also realised the value of Sumati's words, comes out spontaneously with the priceless attributes of Sumati as *yatārthadarśini, yatārthavādini*. He says "what you say is quite true, my dear, you see the truth always and speak of just what you have seen well." In another context, Sumati expresses pity on *puruṣa* who is likely to fall a prey to king Mahāmoha's forces as broughtout by the following passage.

"आर्यपुत्र कथं स नित्यनिर्मलमहानन्दशान्तस्वयंप्रकाश
सर्वजनदर्शनयोग्य स्वभावः पुरुषो महामोहेन
मानमदमत्सरप्रमुखैरपिदुर्विनीतैर्दुर्वारगर्व संकुलदुरितमोहोर्मि
संघातसंघटनभीषणे दुःखसागरे निक्षिप्तः?" (S.S.I. p.135)

"How was *puruṣa* who in his essential nature is eternal, supremely blissful, spotless and radiant thrown by Mahāmoha, conceit, pride, hatred and others into the ocean of sorrow, dreadful owing to the impact against one another of the great waves of sin mingled with resistless arrogance." He called the virtues of Sumati as *Sukṣmadarśini*. With Viveka, Sumati is equally responsible in achieving the goal. Sumati makes Viveka realises his responsibility of lifting *puruṣa* up from sins and evil forces.

Sumati plays her role till the emergence of Viveka to assist *puruṣa* to obtain Saṅkalpa. She feels supreme delight in the victory gained by her spouse, in the fight with Mahāmoha. Infact, she shares supreme happiness on account of Vivekodaya and rise of Saṅkalpa in *puruṣa*.

Likewise Viveka, the role of *puruṣa* too occupies a prominent place in the drama. Because the entire theme of the drama depends on *puruṣa*'s achievement of the goal. *Puruṣa* is personified as an individual soul. He is the father of both Viveka and Mahāmoha.

Being the son, Viveka always thinks good for his father *puruṣa*. That is why, Viveka makes all efforts to lift him up to salvation.

Puruṣa in his essential nature, is eternal, supremely blissful, spotless and self-effulgent. Yet being thrown by *Mahāmoha, mada* and *matsara* etc. into the ocean of sorrow. This is clear from the following statement of Viveka. We often see the true and essential nature of objects given up by them owing to some circumstances brought about by fate when those circumstances disappear, they resume once again their original and true nature. So this endless cycle of births and deaths called *Samsāra* obscures the true nature of *puruṣa* and it will guide away also.[2]

Puruṣa himself says that he is now without sins and endowed with virtues like Śama and Dama he spends his time in such *Yajñas* as the meditation on the Supreme Being. Thus he is eagerly awaiting the time of fruition. As *puruṣa* is endowed with deep sṛddha or faith he is described as having a dialogue with the role named Sṛddhā. Through their dialogue *puruṣa* comes to know that he should approach Viṣṇubhakti who can lead him to *mokṣa* along with Viveka and Sumati. Viṣṇubhakti informs him, that after passing through *prarabdha karmas* *puruṣa* leaves of his subtle body in the virajā river. Then he will attain the realm of Lord Viṣṇu. *Puruṣa* feels very much blessed by Viṣṇubhakti and others. He then follows his final journey to *vaikuntha*.

Viṣṇubhakti informs the audience as follows : "Now the Lord, who has the whole universe for His body and who is absolutely free from all that is impure, has decided to lead the saintly *puruṣa* along the road to His own city from which there is no return to Samsāra.[3] (In this way, *puruṣa*'s role portrayed as a predominant character in the drama).

Vyavasāya

Another character in the drama is portrayed by Deśika is Vyavasāya or commander-in-chief of king Viveka. His duty is to maintain discipline and to keep up the determination of the mind of *puruṣa* in order to make him reach the goal. He appears in the second, seventh and ninth acts of the drama, the effects of his systematic plans have spread all over the drama.

For the first time he appears on the stage in the second Act. *Puruṣa* is found as being fettered by the noose of karma. As a result all his activities render fruitless. He is wielded by Mahāmoha. Observing this condition of *puruṣa*, Viveka has made an oath to make him free from the bondage of Samsāra. Viveka feels Vyavasāya's help necessary in fulfilling his oath. Therefore, he asks Vyavasāya his help. At this juncture, Vyavasāya makes a remark seeing the condition of *puruṣa*. Viveka has blessed *puruṣa* with the knowledge of Vedānta. Vyavasāya follows Viveka in all his activities just like a shadow.

Vyavasāya, the worthy commander-in-chief of Viveka, stands here with wise and learned men revealing himself to those who are on his side.[4]

Vyavasāya is an adept in vedānta philosophy and always keeps his eye on the philosophical discussions. He ably assist

Viveka in choosing right Guru and Śiṣya for *Samvāda*. He avoids scenes of ego wherever reflected in the drama on the path of *puruṣa*'s realisation of Highest Truth, he stands out as a torch-bearer.

Saṅkalpa

The role of Saṅkalpa is the crest of all characters, because in its absence the drama becomes insignificant. Saṅkalpa means Divine Grace. This is essential to obtain salvation which has been very graphically broughtout in the play. Saṅkalpa is very essential to wipe out the ignorance just as the rise of the Sun dispels the darkness. The nandi verse of this drama brings out this import as follows :

"May Śrīman Nārāyaṇa be pleased to convey me over all the ills of life. Nārāyaṇa whose WILL like Sunrise dispels at once the night of SAṀSĀRA, who is capable of being seen by the *jīva* or embodied soul, when its deep devotion has attained to the state of the dawn of day – Nārāyaṇa, whose Supremacy is self- dependent and eternal, arising as it does from His missiles and ornaments which are symbolic of the various TATTVAS or 'reals' of the universe.

In other words, human effort and Divine Grace are necessary for ultimate success. This grace emerges in the case of a *puruṣa* who is fit to receive it by his meritorious life and sustained effort which qualify him to attain salvation. Saṅkalpa is required at every step to liberation and appears on the stage in the tenth Act.

Saṅkalpa is necessary not only for Salvation but fruitful for everything. The play commences with the keynote character i.e. Saṅkalpa and concludes with the epithet of Nārāyaṇa, Vāsudeva whose Saṅkalpa is absolutely necessary for the attainment of salvation. The beneficial impact of Saṅkalpa is declared by Viṣṇubhakti. To quote:

"How wonderful ! all the quarters of the world and all the intermediate quarters shine with a brilliant light. It looks as if Saṅkalpa of the Lord, who is the lover of companion is approaching."

In fact he stands for the mental activity. In the Pañcarātra Āgamas, it is declared that the equipment (Sannaha) and resolve (Saṅkalpa) of Hari, the saviour of the world, appear as visible manifestations in the form of *Garuāa* and Sudarśana respectively.

Another verse highlights the prowess of Saṅkalpa which is remarkable.

"I will now instantly wake up *puruṣa* from the sleep (ignorance) which had no beginning and create in him a state of awakening (knowledge) which will have no end. He tries to awaken *puruṣa* from Deep Sleep (अध्यास) to self-realisation.

Saṅkalpa is capable of releasing *puruṣa* from the bondage of Samsāra. *Puruṣa* has placed his burden on Him with full faith (*Bharanyāsa*) and dedication and has now steadily fixed his mind on performing *nitya* and *naimittika karmas* without any desire for the fruits thereof. At this juncture, Saṅkalpa respects Viṣṇubhakti when she prostrates. Lord Nārāyaṇa is symbolised in the character of Saṅkalpa. He assures *puruṣa* of salvation. In turn *puruṣa* is grateful to Saṅkalpa.

Another notable character in the play is Viṣṇubhakti. Devotion to Lord Viṣṇu is here personified as Viṣṇubhakti. She enters in the concluding portion of the Ninth Act and introduces herself in the following narration :

"I entertain myself with the graceful dance, service to the Lord and with the proud and exaulted dance of removing all sins."[5] Further she says, "my mother is the spotless understanding of *puruṣa*; my father is *puruṣa* who is ever bent on dharma, contentment is my sister, forbearance is my consort and righteous conduct is my servant, who ever does my bidding. I am myself Vidyā (being *Bhakti* or *Upāsana*) and my sport consists in destroying the sins of the world. I am Viṣṇubhakti and live changeless and I feel sure that Samsāra will come to an end. She also says that she declares a truth that has been stated by great sages who have gained direct vision of the Lord which is most needed for Personality Development.

Puruṣa, who is eagerly thirsty for *mukti* and who is in the grip of such classes of enemies as the senses, the body, sons, wives and the like which are in reality the products of sins, should be released (from these bonds) by me alone, for I am the *līlā* of Lord's grace." She gives her opinion that when, with the help of Divine compassion, she would prompt Saṅkalpa Sūrya to take the necessary action for the salvation of *puruṣa*. It is here clear that without the support of Lord's compassion, Viṣṇubhakti cannot get *puruṣa* anything else.

Viṣṇubhakti has high regard for *Garuḍa*, the charioteer of Lord Nārāyaṇa. She glorifies earnestly *Garuāa* at length. In this regard Saṅkalpa also expresses his joy to see greatness of Viṣṇubhakti. He says that – "she is cherished by those who are endowed with spiritual serenity and the source of the ripe fruit of the creeper of knowledge. She is indeed, the perfect development of the Śrutis and the abiding place of purity. She is the guarantee of heavely bliss and the dawn that dispels the fear of *Samsāra*. She is also the lamps that illumines the truths concerning all things, high and low. Addressing her as revered lady of devotion to Hari he exclaims that she is like a divine ornament to the Ātmā or self.

Viṣṇubhakti knows *puruṣa*'s merits and his efforts to attain liberation. Therefore, whenever Viveka becomes anxious to see *puruṣa*'s condition, Viṣṇubhakti gives him a support and tells something convincingly in favour of *puruṣa*.

The role of Viṣṇubhakti is the ultimate stage of *puruṣa*'s attainment is seen very important. It is she who lifts *puruṣa* up to lead the path to Lord's realm of Vaikuṇāha.

These are some other minor characters who help and support at appropriate time to *puruṣa*, Viveka and to Sumati. They are Śṛddhā and Vicāraṇa, Vedānta Siddhānta and Vāda, Tarka, Samskāra, Sama, Dṛṣṭapratyaya, Nārada and Tumburu.

Sṛddha and Vicāraṇa are the female assistants to Sumati and give courage and support to *puruṣa* in his attainment of Samādhi. In turn, *puruṣa* seeks the help of Sṛddha and asks her to convey to Viṣṇubhakti his eagerness and to attain liberation. Sṛddha may be portrayed as the personification of faith.

Vedānta-Siddhānta and Vāda are personified as Guru and Śiṣya respectively. They appear in the second Act to hold a philosophical discussion. These two characters play their roles effectively in the discourse arranged by Viveka.

Saṁskāra, the son of Anubhava is another interesting and significant character in the play. He is represented as a Divine artist and stands for imagination. He appears on the stage in the Seventh Act.

The painter has not painted the universe here with external materials like the brush and paints, surely under the pretext of painting, he has put forth of his own varied imaginations painted with the brush of joy. He represents the truth of experience.

Tarka's role in the drama is characterised as Viveka's charioteer, Nārada and Tumburu are two divine sages. They are the witnesses of the battle between the forces of Viveka and Mahāmoha. In this battle, kāma is killed by vairāgya, krodha by kāma, lobha by santoṣa and darpa by atidṛṣṭi. In the terrible fight Viveka destroys Mahāmoha and sets *puruṣa* free.

Dṛṣṭapratyaya is Viveka's messenger, Buddhi, the wife of *puruṣa* represents as *puruṣa*'s knowledge of discrimination and intellect.

Besides these minor characters, the play has a few characters who play an assisting role but not seen on the stage. They are Tuṣṭi, Virakti, Titikṣā, Jigupsā, Śama, Dama, Svādhyāya, Anubhava, Toṣa, Maitri, Karuṇa, Mudita, Sahajadṛṣṭi and Sādśadṛṣṭi.

So far it is dealt with virtuous characters who help development of personality. On the contrary, these are counter parts of virtuous characters, lead by Mahāmoha and assisted by kāma, krodha and others. But they are defeated at the final analysis on account of the determination or Saṅkalpa of Lord Nārāyaṇa.

Conclusion

According to the scheme of Vedānta Deśika in *Saṅkalpa Sūryodaya* the following conclusion may be made.

The path of *Bhakti* and *Prapatti* is essential to give the grace of the Lord. It is called *Mahāviśvāsa*. This idea of *Mahāviśvāsa* is so sweet that the imagination of Vedānta Deśika is realised in practice.

मिथः कलहकल्पनाविषमवृत्तिलीलादया-
परिग्रहणकौतुकप्रथितपारवश्यः प्रभुः।
स्वलक्षितसमुद्गमे सुकृतलक्षणे कुत्रचित्
धुणक्षतलिपिक्रमादुपनिपातिनः पाति नः ॥ S.S. I-67, p.138

As explained in the Pañcarātra Āgama, Saṅkalpa or Divine will is *Kriyāśakti* or power of action of the lord. To quote the relevant verse which substantiates the truth i.e. the great destroyer of the ocean of *Samsāra*.

क्रियाशक्तिं केचिद्दनुजमथनीं हेतिमपरे
मनस्तत्वं चान्ये मधुविजयिनस्तामभिदधुः।
तमेवैके तत्तत्पदपिषयजुष्टं तदिह नः
सदोत्तुङ्गः प्रादुर्भवसि भवसिन्धुप्रमथनः।। S.S. X-57, p.846

Devotion to God is ordained as the Preparation for the rise of Saṅkalpa Sūrya. To cite the relevant verse which leads as follows :

प्रकृतः क्रियया धिया च योगः परमैकान्त्यपरिष्कृतस्य पुंसः।
निधिदर्शनवन्निरूढहर्षं प्रणिधत्ते विद्वादं परप्रकाशम् ।।
S.S. X-28, p.819

Mokṣa is the ultimate goal of life. The person who practices Bhakti and Prapatti does attain *Mokṣa* at the dawn of the Divine Will regarding the nature of *Mokṣa*. A liberated soul is always engaged in *Bhagavat-kainkarya*.

The characters entertained in the allegorical drama speak of two faces of life one being the positive the other negative The characters like Viveka etc. play a very important role in the act of Personality Development. Though the vile characters like Mahāmoha and so on bring about many obstacles on the path of successful life of any person, yet firm conviction and a sense of righteousness make the person go ahead of acquiring cherished goal.

References

1. महासत्तवोऽतिगम्भीरः क्षमावानविकन्थनः
स्थिरोनिगूढाहङ्कारो धीरोदात्तो दृढव्रतः।।

Dhanañjaya, Daśarūpakam, Motilal Banarasidas, Delhi, 1979, II-4, p.137.

2. स्वतः प्राप्तं रूपं यदिह किल भावेषु तदपि त्यजन्तस्ते दृष्ट्वा नियतिधटितोपाधिवद्यातः प्रकृत्या तिष्ठन्ति ह्युपधिविगमे ते च तदसावनादिः संसारः पुरुष रुपन्द्धे गलति च।।
S.S. I-66, p.136

3. स्वयं व्यक्तक्षेत्रे विपिनविषये वा विधिवशात् प्रशस्ते दृष्टे वा क्वचन समये त्यक्तवपुषः।
मुकुन्दस्त्रय्यन्तप्रथितमहिमा सोऽयमनघान् प्रपन्नानुद्धृत्य स्वपदमनपायं शमयति।।
S.S. X-90, p.880

4. विवेकस्य गुणमेयान् व्यवसायश्चमूपतिः।
स्वपक्षे तिष्ठमानेभ्यः स्वयमागत्य तिष्ठते।। S.S. II-35, p.247

5. अहं वैकुण्ठदास्यैकलास्थलीलाविनोदिनी।
विश्वकिल्बिषसंहार विभ्रमारभटीनटी।। S.S. X-1, p.795
अम्बा मे पुरुषस्य बुद्धिरनघा तातः स धर्मोत्तरः
संतुष्टिः सहजा क्षमा प्रियसखी सद्वृत्तिराज्ञाकरी।
विद्यैव स्वयमस्मि विश्ववृजिन प्रध्वंसनं क्रीडितं साहं
प्राणिमि विष्णुभक्तिरचला संतिष्ठते संसृतिः।। S.S. X-2, p.796
महाभाग, अहं किल परमपुरुषसंकल्पः परमैकान्ति परिषदग्रगण्य-मनन्त सुकृतदुष्कृतनिगलयुगल विगलनपूर्विकया परमपदपर्यङ्क-परिष्कारपरब्रह्मसेवापर्यन्तया भक्तिपरिपाकसंपदा संघटायितुं तदेकवल्लभया कृपणजनविषयकृतपक्षपातया कृपया नियुक्तश्चिर प्रार्थितदर्शनं भवन्तमुपगच्छामि। तदिह निकटवर्तिन्यां निःश्रेयस संपदि निर्विशङ्केन भवता। भवितष्यम् S.S.-X, p.841-42

18

श्रीमध्वाचार्याणां ग्रन्थेषु व्यक्तित्वविकसनम्।

V.B. Tadakod

व्यक्तित्वं नाम व्यक्तिनिष्ठबाह्याभ्यान्तरात्मकं चलनशीलसंघटनाजालम्। व्यक्तित्वं च सङ्कीर्णं सत् मानसिकत्वभौतिकत्वाभ्यां भिन्नम् व्यासज्जवृत्ति। व्यक्तिगतानां नानाविधानां गुणलक्षणानां संग्रहः व्यक्तित्वं न भवति किं तु तेषा समेषां गुणानां सम्मेलने विशिष्टा रचना। मृत्शिलाइष्टिकादीनों यथा कथंचित् मेलनं भित्तिर्न भवति। एवं गुणलक्षणानां वाह्याभ्यन्तराणां विशिष्ट संयोजनात्मकस्य व्यक्तित्वस्वरूपस्य विकासः कथं संजायते इत्यापि विप्रतिपत्यप्रतिपतिप्रतिबद्धः प्रतिभाति।

भारतीयानां आस्तिकदार्शनिकानां मते अत्मा देहातिरिक्तः। देहातिरिक्तस्यापि आत्मनः विकासः देहं विना न घटनाकोटिमाटीकते। ''शरीरमाद्यं खलु धर्मसाधनम्''। शरीरस्य शारीरिकस्य च अभिवृद्धिः आत्मविकासः। आस्तिकदार्शनिकानां मते व्यक्तित्वविकसनं द्विधा भवति। लौकिकं पारलौकिक च। पारलौकिक विकासोऽपि ऐहिकाविकास अविनाभूतः। यद्यपि एते दार्शनिकाः पारलौकिक विकास एवं बद्धदीक्षाः। लौकिकविकासः आनुषंगिकः। ''कथितं कृषेरिव पलालकुलम्''। आध्यात्मिकविकासः परमात्मकेंद्रीकृतः। आधिभौतिकविकासः जीवात्मकेंद्रीकृतः।

द्वैतमताचार्याणां श्रीमध्वाचार्याणां भक्तिप्रधानं दर्शन परमात्मैकनिष्ठम्। अनादिनित्योपि जीवः परमात्माधीनः नित्यं अनादितः। सदा परमात्माधीनस्य जीवस्य कर्तृत्वं अस्ति वा न वा इति प्रथमतः संशीतिः संजायते। मध्वाचार्याणां अभिप्राये जीवस्य कर्तृत्वं अस्ति एव। "जीवस्य कर्तृत्वाभावे शास्त्रस्य अप्रयोजकत्वापत्तेः" (ब्र. सू. भा. 2.3.33) कर्त्ता शास्त्रार्थत्वात् इति सूत्रानुसारं जीवस्य कर्तृत्वं अंगीकार्यमेव। अन्यथा अहरहः प्रत्यक्षेणैव कर्तृत्वं सिध्दम्। प्रत्यक्षैकगम्यानां विषये प्रत्यक्षं प्रामाणमूर्धन्यम्। एताहशं च कर्तृत्वं पराधीनं भवेदेव। पराधीनमपि कर्तृत्वं कर्तृत्वं न जहाति। एवं आत्मनः विकासार्थं अवश्यं आत्मास्तित्वं द्वैतमते स्पष्टम् अंगीकृतं। अंगीकर्तव्यं च। स्वव्यक्तित्वं जीवः न कदापि जहातीति आत्मविकासस्य परमोत्कर्षः। "आत्माभावे पुमर्थः कः इष्टस्यात्मावधिर्यतः (अनुव्याख्यानं 4.2.1)। आत्मनस्तु कामाय सर्वं प्रियं भवति खलु। सर्वेषामपि लौकिकानां अयमेव अनुभवः। ये तु अलौकिकाः भगवन्निष्ठमोक्षाख्यपरमपुरुषार्थाकांक्षिणः तेषामपि ईदृशी काचित् व्यवस्था–

"मुक्तिर्हित्वान्यथारूपं स्वरूपेण व्यवस्थितिः" (ब्र.सू.भा. 1.1.17)।

स्वस्वरूपानंदाविर्भावेण स्थितिः मुक्तिः। लौकिकं विकासं हित्वा त्यक्त्वा पारलौकिकोन्नत्यारुरुक्षा नैव युज्यते। अतः आस्तिकदार्शनिकैः अपि लौकिक व्यक्तित्वाभिवृध्यर्थं दत्तैव दृष्टिः। इयमेव साधनं, उपासना, योगः, इत्यादि शब्दान्तरजालैः अभिधीयते। श्रीमध्वाचार्यैः विरचिताः सप्तत्रिंशत् ग्रंथाः प्रसिद्धाः। प्रस्थानत्रयभाष्याणि, भागवततात्पर्यनिर्णयः, महाभारततात्पर्यनिर्णयः सदाचारग्रंथाः, स्तोत्राणि, प्रकरणानि इत्यादिप्रकारतया विभक्ताश्च ते ग्रंथाः। एष हि तेषां आघोषः–.

"कुरु भुंक्ष्व च कर्म निजं नियतं हरिपादविनम्रधिया सततं"।
(द्वादशस्तोत्रं 3.1)

ब्रह्मापरोक्षज्ञानानन्तर क्रियमाणानां कर्मणा मोक्षे आनंदाविर्भावोत्कर्षप्रापकत्वं अंगीकुर्वाणानां एतेषां मते अधिकारिणां जीवाना तत्पूर्वमपि कर्म अवश्यक

इति किमु वक्तव्यमस्ति। आविकासार्थ अंतःकरणशुद्ध्यर्थ स्वोचितं कर्म कर्तव्यमेव। व्यक्तित्वविकासः कर्म विना कथं उपपद्यते। तत्रैव द्वादशस्तोत्रे निरूपितं यत्-

"तदलं बहुलोकविचिंतनया प्रवणं कुरु मानसमीशपदे"।

ईशपदे मनसः प्रावण्यं प्राप्यमेव। लोकविचिंतनं बाहुल्येन न करणीयं लौकिकचिंतनं नैव करणीयमेवेति नास्ति। तत्वविवेकाख्य प्रकरणग्रंथांते श्री मध्वाचार्याणां अयमादेशः।

"य एतत्परतंत्रं तु सर्वमेव हरेः सदा।
वशमित्येव जानाति ससारान्मुच्यते हि सः"। इति।

अत्र परमात्मपरतंत्रतया सकलमपि जगत् यथाशक्ति ज्ञातव्यमेव भगवन्माहात्म्यस्य द्वादशस्तोत्रे इदमपि अभिहितम्--

"यदि नामपरो न भवेत्स हरिः कथमस्य वशे जगदेतदभूत्।
यदि नाम न तस्य वशे सकलं कथमेव तु नित्यसुखं न भवेत्"।

भगवदधीनतया जगदवगंतव्यं तथा पराधीनं कर्तृत्वं स्वनिष्ठं अवगंतव्यम्। जीवस्य लोके एकान्तसुखाभावान्यथानुपपत्या पराधीनकर्तृत्वं सेत्स्यति। एतादृश कर्तृत्वोपेतः जीवः प्रयत्नं विना नैव उन्नतिं प्राप्नोति।

"महाप्रयत्नवर्जिताः हरेरनुग्रहोज्झिताः।
निजानुभाववर्जिताः जना न जग्मुरुन्नतिम्।
प्रयत्नमेकमग्रतो विधाय भूतिमाप्नुमः" (म भा तानि 21.17.18)

महाभारततात्पर्यनिर्णये भीमसेनवाक्यमिदम्। स्वप्रयत्नाधाने नैर्भर्यमत्र प्रकटितम्। सर्वमपि दैवाधीनमिति मत्वा प्रयत्नवर्जितैः न अस्माभिः भवितव्यमिति अयं संदेशः प्रयत्नात् पलायनवादं नितरां निराकरोति।

कार्यसिद्ध्यर्थ अवश्यं प्रयत्नः करणीयः। सामग्रीसंपादनाय यत्नं विना नान्योऽस्ति उपायः। सर्वासां सामग्रीणां सत्वे कार्यं भवत्येव। सामग्रीणां सत्वे

उदृष्टाभावेन कार्य विघटितं न कुत्रापि दृष्टम्।[1] एवं प्रयत्नैकासादनीयश्चायं आत्मविकासः नैकविधः। व्यक्तिगततया, मानसिकतया, सामाजिकतया, धार्मिकतया, आध्यात्मिकतया बहुधा भवेत्। आध्यात्मिकविकासः परलोकसंबंधीति नात्र तद्विचारस्तन्यते। लौकिकविचाराश्च पारलौकिकानुषांगिकतया विहिता अपि लौकिकत्वं न परित्यजन्ति। स्वनिष्ठतया व्यक्तिविकासः भौतिकः मानसिक इति द्विधा भवति। सदाचारस्मृतिग्रंथे श्रीमध्वाचार्यैः बाह्याभ्यान्तरशुद्धिविचारः आरोग्यादिप्रदः स्मृत्यनुसारेण विहितः। प्रातरारभ्य रात्रिपर्यन्तं हरिस्मरणपूर्वकं यथा वर्तितव्यमिति उपदिष्टम्। व्यक्तित्वविकासाय ज्ञानसम्पादनस्य महत्वं च उक्तं श्रीमध्वाचार्यैः अनुव्याख्यानाख्ये ग्रन्थे ब्रह्मसूत्रव्याख्यनात्मके।

"श्रवणादिविना नैव क्षणं तिष्ठेदपि क्वचित्।
अत्यशक्ये तु निद्रादौ पुनरेव समाचरेत्।।

अभावे निर्णयज्ञस्य सत्शास्त्राण्येव सर्वदा।
श्रुणुयात् यदि सज्ञानप्राचुर्यमुपलभ्यते।।

महद्भ्यो विष्णुभक्तेभ्यो यथाशक्ति च संशयान्।
छिन्द्यात् स्वतोधिकाभावे स्वयमेव समभ्यसेत्।।

ब्रूयादपि च शिष्येभ्यः सत्सिद्धान्तं अहापयन्।
(अनुव्याख्यान 3.3.9)

शास्त्रज्ञानसम्पादनार्थ श्रवणादिकं निरन्तरतया कर्तव्यम्। यः कोऽपि ज्ञाने स्वाधिकः तस्मात् संपादनीयमेव ज्ञानम्। तदभावेऽपि यथाज्ञप्ति शास्त्राध्ययनं कर्तव्यं स्वेनैव। न केवलं एतत् शिष्यां तर्थव बोधनीयाः मनोनिग्रहः व्यक्तित्वविकसने अत्यावश्यकः।

"किं तेन मनसा कार्यं यन्न तिष्ठति केशवे।
मनो मुक्तिफलावाप्तौ कारणं सुप्रयोजितम्" (कृ म)।

शमो मन्निष्ठिताबुद्धिः दम इन्द्रियनिग्रहः इत्युक्त्यनुसारेण मनसः इन्द्रियाणां च निग्रहः व्यक्तित्वविकसने महत् स्थानं लभते।

सामाजिकतया व्यक्तित्वविकसनोपाया: तत्र तत्र निरूपिता:।

"सद्भिर्हि संगतिरिहैव सुखस्य हेतु: मोक्षैकहेतुरथ तद्विपरीतमन्यत्।

तस्मात् व्रजेम सह पांडुसुतैर्हि शक्र प्रस्थंत्वितिस्म धृतचेतस आह धर्म:"। (म.भा.ता.नि 19.217)

अत्र च सत्संगति: इहामुत्र सुखहेतुतया वर्णित:। कृष्णामृतमहार्णवे-

"समानां विषमा पूजा विषमाणां समा तथा।
क्रियते येन देवोऽपि स्वपदात् भ्रश्यते हि स:"।

कृष्णामृतयहार्यव 209

समाजे समानां विषमं गौरवं नैव करणीयं विषमाणां च समानतया नैव करणीयम्। एवं चेत् स्वपदभ्रंश एव फलं भवेत्। लोके च तत्तत् योग्यानुसारं सर्वेऽपि सम्मानार्हा:। तत्रापि तरतमभावं: स्वीकार्य:।

"वित्तं बंधु: वय: कर्म विद्या चैव तु पंचमी।
एतानि मान्यस्थानानि गरीयोह्युत्तरोत्तरम्"। (कृ म 210)।

उत्तरोत्तरं गरीयस्तं एतेषां प्रतिपादितमिति विद्या या: परमगौरवात् सम्पादितम। एवं यद्यदस्माभि: साधनीयं तदखिलं सकालिकमेव कर्तव्यम्।

"यावत्स्वस्थमिदं पिंडम् निरुजकरणान्वितं।
तावत्कुरुष्वात्महितं पाश्चात्तापेन तप्यसे"। (कृ म 116)।
पश्चात्तापात् वरं पूर्वताप:।

एवं श्री मध्वाचार्याणां ग्रंथेषु आधुनिकसमाजविज्ञानिनां मानदंडेनापि व्यक्तित्वविकासनोपयोगि उपायजातं समुपलभ्यते। समस्तं जगदेव भगवत्सृष्टम् अस्य पुरुषस्य व्यक्तित्वविकसनाय अलम्।

सन्दर्भ ग्रन्थ सूची

1. अहष्टस्य च ब्राह्मसामग्रीसत्त्वे स्वाभावापराधेन कार्यनिरोधकत्वादर्शनात्। ब्रह्मसुत्रभाष्यटीकातत्त्वप्रकाशिका 2.9.6.18

19

Personality Development in Sculpture

Madhumati S. Shivapuji

The concept of Personality Development is multi-dimensional one. There are many direct and indirect representative elements of Indian culture, influencing the growth of human beings and the society around them. Penance, Meditation, Truthfulness, Non-violence, knowledge and the like, being the indirect elements help in great deal, influencing progressive life-style of the human beings. On the other hand, some other elements like doctor's treatment to a patient, of helping a diseased one, etc., are the direct repersentations to influence one's psychosis and lead to the better position in society. However, indirect means take more time to awaken human psychosis, where as direct representations touch the root of human intellect and penetrate human behaviour to bring the person to the path of righteousness securing exalted position in the family and society. Of such direct representatives, sculpture plays an important role in personality development.

Sculpture of any background, indeed throw much light on rich heritage of Indian culture. The sculptures of olden days were not only artistic but also exhibit their deep scientific knowledge of sculpture in the background of Indian ethics, formulated on the basis of four Puruṣārthas such as, *Dharma, Artha, Kāma* and *Mokṣa*. Verily personality development is based on these puruṣārthas. The *Artha* and *Kāma* based on *Dharma*, certainly lead one to the attainment of *Mokṣa* which itself is eternal goal of all individuals. Sufficiently enough, the sculpture exhibited inside and outside the temple, fort, place during the ancient period, are the causal factors of personality development, through the media of puruṣārthas. At this juncture a question may arise here, what are the characteristic features of the puruṣ ārthas ? Hence, here follows an explanation of puruṣārthas in brief.

Dharma Puruṣārtha

The word '*Dharma*' is used to mean Justice (*Nyāya*), what is right in a given circumstance, moral values of life, pious obligations of individuals, righteous conduct in every sphere of activity, being helpful to other living beings, giving charity to individuals in need of it or to a public cause or alms to the needy, natural qualities or characteristics or properties of living beings and things, duty and law as also constitutional law.

Mahābhārata the great epic which is acclaimed as the *Mānava Kartavya Śāstra* (code of duties of human beings) contains a discussion of this topic. On being asked by Yudhiṣṭ hira to explain the meaning and scope of *Dharma*, Bhīṣma who had mastered the knowledge of *Dharma* replied thus :

ताद‍ृशोऽयमनुप्रश्नो यत्र धर्मः सुदुर्लभः ।
दुष्करः प्रतिसंख्यातुं तत्केनात्र व्यवस्यति ।।
प्रभवार्थाय भूतानां धर्मप्रवचनं कृतम् ।

यः स्यात्प्रभवसंयुक्तः स धर्म इति निश्चयः ।।

[*Shāntiparva* – 109.9.11]

It is most difficult to define *Dharma*. *Dharma* has been explained to be that which helps the upliftment of living beings. Therefore, that which ensures the welfare of living beings is surely *Dharma*. The learned sages have declared that which sustains is *Dharma*. *Karṇa Parva* (Ch.69 verse 58) enlogises *Dharma* in the following words :

धारणाद् धर्म इत्याहुर्धर्मो धारयते प्रजाः ।
यत् स्याद् धारणसंयुक्तं स धर्म इति निश्चयः ।।

Dharma sustains the society, *Dharma* maintains the social order *Dharma* ensures well being and progress of Humanity, *Dharma* is surely that which fulfils these objectives.[1]

Origin of Dharma

Dharma was formulated as the solution to the eternal problems confronting the human race, originating from natural human instincts.

अकामस्य क्रिया काचिद्दृश्यते नेह कर्हिचित् ।
यद्यद्धि कुरुते किञ्चित् तत्तत्कामस्य चेष्टितम् ।। [Manu: II:4]

There is no act of man which is free from desire; whatever a man does is the result of the impulse of desire.

In verse above, analysing the human instinct, Manu states that the force behind every action of human being is his desire (*kāma*). Then the next question was what were the natural desires of man ? The natural desire of man was found to be the desire to have enjoyment of wealth i.e., material pleasure (*artha*) as also emotional and sexual enjoyment. *Artha* is explained by *Vātsyāyana*[2] as connoting material wealth such as gold, cattle, corn, including education or knowledge (intellectual property) necessary to earn wealth. The source of all evil actions of human beings was traced to desire for material pleasure which in turn gave rise to conflict of interests among individuals.

Dharma or rules of righteous conduct was evolved as a solution to this eternal problem arising out of the natural instinct of man. In *Shāntiparva* of the *Mahābhārata* (Ch.59-14) after explaining that an ideal state of affairs did exist when people protected each other acting according to *Dharma*, Bhīṣma proceeded to state that when a few persons began to deflect from the path of *Dharma* being over powered by sensual desires, passion and greed for wealth and material pleasure and, being physically stronger, began to harass the weaker ones, a remedy to this situation, the three-fold ideals called *Dharma*, *Artha* and *Kāma* (*Trivarga*) were laid down for the welfare and happiness of the people and the state was established with a king as its head. He was empowered to ensure the implementation of the *Trivarga* Doctrine.

The object of laying down the three-fold ideals was that *kāma* (desire) for material pleasure (*Artha*) must be entertained and enjoyed only in conformity with *Dharma* and not otherwise.

'*Dharma*' is thus a collective term for the entire code of righteous conduct, covering every sphere of human activity, and in every capacity or role of an individual, in relation to other individuals.

Artha Puruṣārtha

Artha occupies the second place in the *trivarga*. It is necessary for a man to lead a happy life. Here, the term *artha* denotes the whole range of tangible objects that can be possessed and enjoyed. Further, it refers to all the means necessary for acquiring mundane prosperity. *Artha* is essential not only to lead the life comfortably, but also to perform religious deeds. One should not steal other's property. One should not enjoy other's wealth. Thus the acquisition of *artha* is controlled by *dharma*. Manu declares that among all the modes of purification, purity in (the matters related to) wealth to be the best; for, he is pure who gains wealth with clean hands.[3] Man's existence becomes meaningful only when he acquires wealth. Without wealth, all the virtues of man vanish into nothingness and even a good lineage does not bring status. Without wealth one cannot practise *dharma* and *kāma*. Hence, *artha* is considered as one of the human goals by ancient Indian thinkers. The texts on the *arthaśāstra* describe the correct and the moral ways of earning and expanding the wealth which will help to maintain the stability of entire society.

Kāma Puruṣārtha

Kāma is the third *puruṣārtha*. The Sanskrit term *kāma* has a wide connotation. It refers to all the desires of a human being. It denotes love as well as lust. This word however directly refers to sex. *Kāma* is essential for the all-round development of a man or woman. *Kāma* relates to both individual and social elements. It is the basis of mating, marriage and progeny. *Kāma* should be practised as per the dictums of *dharma*. Then and then alone, it will help both the individual and the society. The scope of *kāma* is wide. It includes good food, good drink, pleasant and charming company, fine clothes, perfumes, ornaments, garlands, decorated room or bed and the like. A man is the source of *kāma* for a woman, and a woman is the source of *kāma* for a man. Hence both man and woman should understand the merits and demerits respectively. In this connection, the texts on *kāma* help understand each other. The correct practice of *kāma* will make both man and woman happy. This happiness helps them in their individual development as well. To attain complete happiness, one has to study the *kāmaśāstra*. Indians knew that *kāma* is an instinct and it is not possible to suppress it. Hence, they considered it as one of the *Puruṣārthas*. Here follows an illustration of salient features of these *Puruṣārthas* by means of sculptures.

1. The Sculpture of Gajendramokṣa

This appears on the northern wall of Daśāvatāra temple at Deogarh in Uttarapradesh. This scene tells the legend of Gajendra's liberation in which Viṣṇu liberates the king of elephant from the fatal control of Nāga-serpent. Viṣṇu is rushing to the place, riding His mount Garuḍa then, the human-faced Nāga relaxes his grip and worships God Viṣṇu.

This episode of Gajendramokṣa occurs in the eighth skanda of *Bhāgavata Purāṇa* (8.2 to 4 adh.). As explained therein, the elephant-king is attacked by a crocodile, but not the serpent, as shown in the sculpture above.

This sculpture of Gajendra's releasing by Lord Viṣṇu speaks of two puruṣārthas, one is *Dharma* and other is *Mokṣa*. The reflective ideas under the *dharma* aspect include, 1) protecting individual from the danger, 2) self-conceit of one's own power invites his own downfall. 3) Total surrender is one of the means of liberation. To be precise, as laid down in the sastric texts, *dharma* or righteousness conveys that a person whosoever is, when is encircled by many dangers resulting into the death, should be protected with all efforts. However, the Lord of elephants when came under the clutches of serpent/crocodile fell into such a weak position, that his survival itself has become a question. At the ardent request of Gajendra, Lord

Plate-1: Sculpture of Gajendra Mokṣa

Nārāyaṇa rushed to the place to protect his devotee and did so. No doubt, the elephant and Lord Nārāyaṇa are the entities not of phenomenal level; former one is a devotee and latter is devoted. Lord Nārāyaṇa Himself gives here lesson to the Universe.

Another aspect of *dharma* with regard to self-conceited person is suggested here. The Lord of elephants referred to here, is a cursed Gandharva. As such, he should have been very modest throughout his life. On the contrary, the elephant grew haughty and self-conceit. However, such qualities define one's character and makes the person fall into the pit of difficulties. A man of discriminative wisdom keeps himself away from such defective influence. But, the elephant becoming a victim of his own blemishes, caught by a clutch of death. This incident thus gives a lesson on dreadful effects of self-conceites.

This episode remarks the path of salvation as the lord of elephants totally surrenders with firm devotion to Lord Nārāyaṇa. Every individual has to bring into action that whatever the deeds accomplished by the individual should be surrendered to the Supreme Reality. This is well supported by the *Upaniṣads* and the *Bhagavadgītā*. Such practice of total surrender makes a person attain liberation as in the case of Gajendra. In this manner, the sculpture of *Gajendra-mokṣa* presents an admixture of *dharma* and *mokṣa* puruṣārthas.

2. Sculpture of Bhagīratha above the Arjuna-ratha

This sculpture related to one of the five rathas found in the *Mahābalipuram* represents *Arjuna's penance*. On the top of this sculpture, there finds a figure of man standing with his arms held high over his head, balanced one foot, every bone of his ribeage visibly jutting out. Undoubtedly, this man is none else than Bhagīratha. King Bharata descended from Lord Viṣṇu Himself, belonged to the race of Hariścandra, had made heavenly Ganges flow on the earth, for purifying his ancesters[4], burnt to ashes by the fire of anger of sage Kapila.

Plate-2: Sculpture of Bhagiratha above Arjuna Rath

This sculpture may be considered to convey *dharma* puruṣ ārtha. Being the great grandson of the king Sāgara, Bhagīratha should have to execute his duty of serving his ancesters by means of protecting them from entering the hell due to Kapila's curse. In addition, it was righteous duty of Bhagīratha to see them attain heavenly regions by the holy touch of divine Ganges. For which, he performed severe penance to please God Brahmā and Śiva. Not only his ancesters, the whole of the mankind in future should take the benefit of taking bath in the Ganges. These two motives fulfiled by Bhagīratha, signify the codes of *Dharma* Puruṣārtha. This is the purpose behind the sculpture seen above.

3. Sculpture of Trivikrama

This sculpture of *Trivikrama* is found in the premises of second cave at Badami. Lord Viṣṇu in the form of Trivikrama has held His left leg up, with a view to measuring Antarikṣa. When the supreme demon-king Bali honoured Lord Viṣṇu in the form of celibate Vāmana, he gave a word of offering the space equal to the measurement of three steps of Divine Vāmana. Here, the act of *dāna* performed by king Bali with firm devotion, is a hall-mark of his purity of mind. Despite, the demon-preceptor Śukrācārya dissuaded Bali from his act, the latter did not listen to the former and fulfiled the proposal of the celibate.

This sculpture marks the following points:

1) Bali's unstinted devotion;
2) Bali's purity of mind;
3) Bali's longing (*kāma*) for executing righteous deeds;
4) Bali's deep sense of welcoming the guest whosoever;
5) Bali's sacrifice of entire Universe at the cost of his own life;
6) Lord Viṣṇu's incarnation as Vāmana to remove the ego of Bali.

These qualities invariably come under *Dharma* and *Kāmapuruṣārthas*. Bali's longing for meritorious deeds is not

Plate-3: Sculpture of Trivikrama

an obstruction to *Dharma*. (धर्माविरुद्धो कामः). And *Kāma* goes along with *Dharma*; such efficacious *kāma* does lead to one's personality development.

In this manner, though the Supreme king Bali, born in the race of demons, was aware of his own personality; as such, he strived hard to uplift himself by sacrificing his own life. A visitor when looks at such sculpture, would entertain these feelings mentioned above.

4. Sculpture of Varāharùpi Viṣṇu

Plate-4: Sculpture of Varaharupi

Similarly the sculpture of Varāharùpi Viṣṇu found in Halebidu, is the suggestive of *Dharma* puruṣārtha. In precise, when the whole of the earth was made drowned in the bottom of the ocean, Lord Viṣṇu came forth to protect Godess of Earth in the form of Varāha. Placing the entire earth on his strong teeth, Varāharùpi Viṣṇu killed the demon king Hiraṇyākṣa. Then he lifted the earth and placed it in its former place.

In this manner, this sculpture gives a lesson on protecting the person from difficulties. However, the protection to weaker ones is one of the righteous deeds coming under *Dharma Puruṣ ārtha*. Thus, he who observes the sculpture, would be influenced by this message.

5. Sculpture of Rāma Setu

A stone relief work shown in the picture, is found at Prambanan temple in Java, Indonesia which was built during 10th century A.D. This sculpture narrates an incident of monkeys' building a bridge across the ocean to Lanka.

Plate-5: Sculpture of Rama Setu

As explained in the *Rāmāyaṇa*, Rāma was to fight against Rāvaṇa. He along with his army had to cross the ocean of the length of hundred yojanas, to reach Laṅkā. For this purpose, Sugreeva the chief of army and his mighty monkeys, in consultation with Rāma, took a dicision to construct the bridge. Accordingly under the leadership of Sugreeva, the mighty monkeys constructed the bridge using big boulders and mountains. Afterwards Rāma accompanied by his army went to Laṅkā, fought with Rāvaṇa and killed him. Thus the present sculpture reminds of *Setu bandha* incident.

This sculpture speaks of righteousness of Rāma. As a king it was duty of Rāma to protect his kingdom and his subjects, also it was his duty to establish *dharma* on the earth. But Rāvaṇa was great obstruction, therefore killing Rāvaṇa was one of the duties of Rāma. Thus, one can say that the incident shown in the sculpture may be treated as suggestive of *dharma* concept, which is one of the ingredients of personality development.

6. Sculpture of Vāli-Sugrīva Combat

This stone base relief is situated at Banteay Srei in Cambodia. It depicts the combat between Vāli and Sugrīva (middle), to the right, Rāma fires his bow, and to the left Vāli lies dying, hit by Rāma's arrow.

A close observation of this sculpture makes it evident that the disciplines of *Dharma, Artha* and *Kāma* are reflected in it. In precise, Rāma's killing Vāli is to protect Sugrīva who was banished by his brother. However Sugrīva had surrendered to Rāma and asked for his protection. Undoubtedly it was a prime duty or *Dharma* of Rāma the sovereign king to protect the surrendered one. Secondly, Sugrīva's fulfilment of desire of acquiring kingdom points to both *Artha* and *Kāma*.

Plate-6: Sculpture of Vali-Sugriva Combat

In this way, the *devatā-śilpa* or *mānuṣa-śilpa* seen on the walls of the temples are the suggestive of ethical codes of conduct hidden in the womb of puruṣārthas. Any person whosoever visits the temple and observes the silpas, surely is influenced by not only their beauty, but also reads their perspectives of ethics in furtherance of personality development. On the basis of such illustrative examples of sculpture, it may be viewed in a nutshell that ancient sculptures through the episodes in the *Rāmāyaṇa, Mahābhārata, Purāṇas, Jātakas,* etc. stand themselves as rich treasures of Indian culture weaving into which a finer and synthetic threads of personality development.

Reference

1. A.S. Nèrèyaça Dixitalu V state of A.P. 1996 S.C.C548 Paragraphs 59 to 79.
2. Kèmasvatra, 1.20

3. सर्वेषामेव शौचानामर्थशौंच परस्मृतम् ।
   योऽर्थे शुचिहि स शुचिर्न मृद्वारि शुचिः ॥ [मनु – V-106]
4. This story occurs in the Rämäyaça, (Bälakäçàa), *Mahäbhärata* (Vanaparva ch.108), *Brahmäçàa Puräça* (Ch.97), *Bhägavata Puräça* (9th Skanda), *Padma Puräça* (part 4. chap. 21).

20

Paragonic Efficiency of a King in Sanskrit Inscriptions

Keyur R. Karagudari

Our nation enjoys an ample of epigraphical wealth strewn over the whole of its territory. Inscriptions may be generally defined as the documents, incised on some hard permanent material like stones or copper plates etc, in the form of letters or other conventional signs for the purpose of conveying some information or preserving a record. These inscriptions are not only the most important one amongst all the sources for writing about the history of ancient India but also provide a copious and authentic data about various aspects of life in early times.

There are a large number of inscriptions written in Sanskrit language. These Sanskrit inscriptions form a considerable part of the Sanskrit literature. Amongst all inscriptions found in India Sanskrit inscriptions stand in the first place in respect of both quantity and quality. A meticulous analysis of these Sanskrit epigraphs can reveal a lot of information regarding the social, economic, political and cultural conditions of their respective times. The present paper is a small endeavour to reveal certain exemplary traits of the efficient kings of India as reflected in Sanskrit inscriptions.

The king, in all times, has been expected to be a paragon of virtues, a paragon of efficiency and role model to his subjects as it is very well known that 'यथा राजा तथा प्रजा:'. The Bhagavadgītā also says,

यद्यदाचरति श्रेष्ठ: तत्तदेवेतरो जन:।
स यत्प्रमाणं कुरुते लोकस्तदनुवर्तते।। -Bhagavadgītā III, 21

So the ethical status and the total welfare of the entire society depend upon the personality of the ruling king. That's why the Mahābhārata also says, 'राजा कालस्य कारणम्'. The Nītiśastra also says that one should seek a good king before achieving the wordly objects-

'राजानं प्रथमं विंदेत् ततो भार्यां ततो धनम्'.

As per the personality development is concerned, a very noticeable example in this regard is the great Mouryan emperor Aśoka, who is credited with the forerunnership of the novel tradition of writing inscriptions. Unlike the later generations of kings, Ashoka had a different objective for engraving the inscriptions whereby he wanted to propagate the precious doctrines of Dharma and Samavaya among his citizens. Through the inscriptions sponsored by him all over the country he ruled, he extended many classic tips of personality development to his subjects and himself practiced them too. But, as his inscriptions are in Prakrit language, they have not been discussed here in this paper.

If the king is efficient and a staunch adherent of righteousness then his subjects will feel secured and carry out their duties honestly and practice the virtuous deeds. Endorsing this, the Guḍnāpur inscription of Ravivarma[1] of the Kadamba dynasty says that in the kingship of Ravivarma the people were totally free from fright and felt as if they were on the lap of their father.

तयोस्त्वभीतिरसा यस्मिन्स्वधर्मे व्यवस्थिता: सुखमवापुर्दानभोगरता: पित्रोरिवांकस्थिता: प्रजा:।

The most anticipated quality in the king is his abounding and incessant love and care towards his subjects. Subjects are the true relatives of the king not his cousins or etc, say the inscriptions-

'प्रजाभिस्तु बन्धुमन्त: राजान: न ज्ञातिभि:'.

The king should crave after to win the faith of his subjects. The Kaśākuḍi copper plates of Nandivarman of Pallava dynasty say that the kings experienced an increase in the affection of their subjects and possessed faultless riches and virtues and therefore resembled the science of grammar in which the crude form, affixes and augments are treated but in which the rules on guna and vriddhi are not without exceptions.

'शब्दागम इव प्रकृतिप्रत्ययागमोपेता निरपवादवृद्धिगुणाश्च'

One of a king's major concerns was to have a good reputation among his citizens. Many inscriptions show how some kings were dedicated to serve the humanity and how did they strive to uplift the people in distress. The Allahabad inscription of Samudragupta[2] describes that the king had taken a consecration to helping the poor, orphan and disabled people-

'कृपणदीनानाथातुरजनोद्धरणमन्त्रदीक्षाभ्युपगतमनस: समिद्धस्य विग्रहवतो लोकानुग्रहस्य'...

Skandagupta's relationship with the general people is explained thus "... he made his subjects happy first by conversation accompanied by a smile and presents of honours by unrestricted mutual visits to each others' houses among his people by holding domestic functions calculated to promote cordiality. Many other kings are said to have cherished such an amiable relationship with their citizens. They would look after the needs of the people. They built wells, ponds and canals etc to accomplish the need of water. The king Rudradaman repaired the historical lake '*Sudarśana*' to meet the agricultural requirements. The Talagunda inscription of Kakusthavarma[3] attests that the king's aspirations were-

अर्थिषु दया सम्यक्प्रजापालनं दीनाभ्युद्धरणं द्विजाभ्यर्हणम्... etc.

On the other hand king should not torment his subjects for collecting taxes as the Viduranīti says-

यथा मधु समादत्ते रक्षन् पुष्णाणि षट्पदः।
तद्वदर्थान्मनुष्येभ्यः आदद्यादविहिंसया।।

The Junagadh inscription of Rudradāman[4] states that the king accomplished a highly expensive project of repairing the gigantic Sudarshana lake within a short period without levying any tax like *kara*, viṣṭi etc on his subjects.

महाक्षत्रपेण रुद्रदाम्ना..... अपीडयित्वा करविष्टिप्रणयक्रियाभिः पौरजानपदं जनं स्वस्मात्कोशान्महता धनौघेन अनतिमहता च कालेन त्रिगुणदृढतरविस्तारायामं सेतुं विधाय सर्वतटे सुदर्शनतरं कारितम्।

Another one of a king's most ideal qualities was donation. A majority of inscriptions are to record the donations made by the respective kings. Kings made lavish donations of cows and land as they were believed to be most meritorious among all kinds of donation. Many inscriptions, quoting Manu, say-

त्रीण्याहुरतिदानानि गावः पृथ्वी सरस्वती।
आशतं तारयंत्येते ज्ञानवाहनदोहनैः।।

Kings were very magnanimous in making donations. Many inscriptions extol the kings as they even humiliated the heavenly trees of Kalpadruma or kalpalata in conferring the solicited things. The common expressions cited in inscriptions are-

हस्तापजितद्युशाखी, वितरणे संचारिकल्पद्रुमः, भूलोकचिन्तामणिः etc.

One should make donations without any expectations. There should be a real sense of 'इदं न मम'. A verse from Pāṇḍarangapalli copper plate inscription[5] of king Avidheya of Rashtrakuta dynasty draws our attention towards the king's disposition regarding donations.

अर्थितमात्रदानस्य तस्य दातुर्गुणोचितम्।
कृतं प्रणयिलोकस्य स्वस्त्याद्यपि दुनोति यम्।।

i.e. even the benedictions like *'svasti'* and other approbations, befitting his merits, offered by suppliants to that donor, who makes gifts as soon as they are asked for, afflict him.

And another noble and unique characteristic of Indian kings is to protect and upgrade the righteous exploits made by others, even by one's own enemies. Inscriptions asseverate that-

शत्रुणापि कृतो धर्मः पालनीयः प्रयत्नतः।
शत्रुरेव हि शत्रुः स्यात् धर्मः शत्रुर्न कस्यचित्।।

Keeping aside a very few exceptions, no Indian king annihilated the monuments or public welfare projects constructed by their ancestors or rival kings. The imprecatory verses in the inscriptions affirm that protecting the grants is much more meritorious than making grants and one can achieve *achyutapada* from this-

दानपालनयोर्मध्ये दानाच्छ्रेयोनुपालनम्।
दानात्स्वर्गमवाप्नोति पालनादच्युतं पदम्।।

The Jambgaon plates[6] of Indra III of Rashtrakuta dynasty attest that one should not venture upon undermining the pure fame of others-

अतिविमलमनोभिरात्मनीनैर्न हि पुरुषैः परकीर्तयो विलोप्याः।

The king should not even disturb the donations made by himself. He should not acquire the land donated to brahmanas and should not even levy taxes upon that land. Kings must treat that land as their own sister, say the inscriptions-

एकैव भगिनी लोके सर्वेषामेव भूभुजाम्।
न भोज्या न करग्राह्या विप्रदत्ता वसुन्धरा।।

And the donee was allowed to enjoy all the wealth and natural resources like निधि, निक्षेप, पाषाण, जल etc possessed by that land. This shows that the kings really followed the upanishadic injunctions like श्रद्धया देयम्, श्रिया देयम्, ह्रिया देयम्, भिया देयम्, संविदा देयम् etc.

An ideal king should be endowed with many more virtues like humbleness, generosity, truthfulness, sacrifice etc. The Musunika copper plates[7] of Devendravarman III of Eastern Ganga dynasty list the pleasing qualities of the king thus-

'नयविनयदयादानदाक्षिण्यशौर्योदार्यसत्यत्यागादिगुणसम्पदाधारभूतः...'

The Prakasha inscription[8] of Simhana's time says that the kings of the family of Prabhuvara and Abhrashyama possessed many virtuous qualities as their *kulavrata* and did not left them even in disasters-

दानं दया तपः सत्यमेतद्येषां कुलव्रतम्।
आपद्यपि च कष्टायां न त्यजन्ति कदाचन।।

The inscription also explains how righteous the kings were, in the following verse-

अधीतं कर्मणे येषां तथा कर्म विमुक्तये।
यशसे जीवितं येषां प्रजायै दारसंग्रहः।।

This verse resembles a famous verse from the *Raghuvaṁśa Mahākāvya* of *Kālidāsa* describing the greatness of the kings of Raghu lineage-

त्यागाय सम्भृतार्थानां सत्याय मितभाषिणां।
यशसे विजिगीषूणां प्रजायै गृहमेधिनाम्।।

The king should amass pelf only in a scrupulous way. The Junagadh inscription of Rudradaman[4] states that the king always earned wealth in genuine manner-

'यथावत्प्राप्तैर्बलिशुल्कभागैः
कनकरजतवज्रवैडूर्यरत्नोपचयनिष्यन्दमानकोशेन....'

The kings should never entertain their minds in nefarious deeds, says an inscription from Sirpur[9]

'पश्यन्तस्तदिमं मनः कुरुत भो पापेषु मा भूमिपाः।'

Many kings showed their immense gratitude and respect to their parents. Following are the common expressions often found in inscriptions that manifest this fact-

मातापितृपादानुध्यातः, मातापित्रोरात्मनश्च पुण्ययशोवृद्धये... etc.

The rulers who maintained peace during their reigns are generally found to be virtuous. They did not encourage social inequality. The Junagadh inscription of Rudradaman[4] states that any one irrespective of caste was allowed to approach the king for protection and help-

सर्ववर्ण्यैरभिगम्यः रक्षणार्थम्...

Education plays an important role in personality development of an individual and thereby that of the entire community. The kings were highly literate and also promoted education during their rule. They encouraged scholarship, built and developed several educational institutions like *Agrahara, Brahmapuri* and *Ghaṭikāsthāna* in order to spread literacy and to enhance the intellectual, cultural and moral level of the citizens. According to *Arthashastra* of Koutalya, an ideal king should be well educated, eloquent and endowed with a sharp intellect, a strong memory and a keen mind. He should be well trained in all arts. Exemplifying this, many kings in history were well versed in several branches of learning. For example, the Choudala inscription of Harihara of Vijayanagara dynasty describes a chief named Madhava, who ruled over Goa, that he was well versed in all the Upaniṣads, he published the Shaivagamas, authored many elegant works, preached the Neetishastra and so on.

'स च निर्जिताखिलभूपालः सर्वोपनिषदां व्याकर्ता, शैवागमानां प्रकाशयिता, काव्यानां कर्ता, महादानानां विधाता, नीतिशास्त्रस्योपदेष्टा, सकलगुणालंकरो माधवराजो गोवापुरवरसिंहासनमधितिष्ठति।'

Thus many kings even after their death remained immortal due to their such noble qualities and deeds, says an inscription from Prakasha[8] -

प्रजासु शान्त्या विनयेन साधुषु द्विषत्सु शौर्येण नयेन राजसु।
त्यागेन सर्वत्र च यः प्रकाशते लोकान्तरस्थोऽपि गुणैरिह स्थितैः।।

The kings aspired after the *Trivarga* i.e. *Dharma, Artha* and *Kāma* but the ultimate goal of life was *Moksha*, the liberation. Talagunda inscription[3] of Kakusthavama states-

भ्रातास्य चारुवपुरब्धिगभीरनादो मोक्षत्रिवर्गपटुरन्वयवत्सलश्च।

Though the kings lead luxurious life they should always be aware of the mortality of life, say the inscriptions-

'विद्युल्लोलान्यैश्वर्याणि परिकलय्य तृणाग्रलग्नजलबिन्दुचंचलं च जीवितं समालोच्य...'

I would like to conclude with a verse from a Chola inscription that describes what best can be caused to the society if the king is efficient.

शौर्यं सावधि रूपिणी चतुरता सालम्बना धीरता
सौजन्यं च सनाथतामुपगतं राजन्वती मेदिनी।
सस्थाना कविता कलाकुशलता जाता समेताश्रया
यस्मिन्विस्मयनीयतामुपगता कीर्तिर्दिगन्तेष्वभूत्।।

In him valour achieved its goal, skill was incarnate, courage gained a steady hold, goodness found a protector, the earth had a good king, poetic art attained a proper seat, skill in the fine arts found a common shelter and his fame caused astonishment in all quarters.

Thus king has to develop his personality that heartens his subjects for their personality development indeed. King should carve his character in order to set himself as a paragon to his citizens. He should be an ardent supporter of righteousness and justice. The king who develops his personality by developing all such above discussed qualities is treated by his subjects as God on the earth. The Allahabad inscription[2] of Samudragupta describes the king as-

सुचिरस्तोतव्यानेकाभ्दुतोदारचरितस्य लोकसमयक्रियानुविधानमात्रमनुष्यस्य, लोकधाम्नो देवस्य'

Thus the personality development of king is very much obligatory for the overall development of all the people.

References

1. B.R.Gopal, *Corpus of Kadamba Inscriptions* (1985)

2. C.I.I (Revised) Vol III, pp 203 ff
3. *Epigraphica Carnatica* Vol. VII, Sk 176
4. *Epigraphica indica* Vol. VIII, p. 42
5. *Epigraphica indica* Vol. XXXVII, Part I, pp.20
6. *Epigraphica indica* Vol. XXXVI, pp. 223
7. *Epigraphica indica* Vol. XXX, pp. 23
8. *Epigraphica indica* Vol. XXXVI, pp. 19
9. Balachandra Jain, उत्कीर्ण लेख, pp.36

21

Personality Development in Bhasma Dhāraṇa-mantra

R.R. Shastri

व्यक्तित्वविकसनम् मातुः गर्भप्रवेशादारभ्य भवति। प्राचीनग्रन्थाः एतत् पितुः शरीरे मासत्रयात्पूर्वमेव प्रारभ्यते इति कथयन्ति।। परन्तु अनन्तजीवाणूनां मध्ये एको वा द्वौ वा मातुः गर्भे जन्मावकाशं अकस्मात् लभते। प्रतिक्षणमपि हृदयस्पन्देनेन साकमेतत्! भवदपि अस्मत्सनातनधर्मः पञ्चस्तरेषु विभजते। मनोविज्ञानी Sporlt महाशयः कुटुम्बं, शाला, कलाशाला ततश्च विवाहः, उद्योगः, समाजः इत्येवं बहवः व्यक्तित्वविकसने प्रभावकरा अंशाः इति कथयति।। Havigurston महाशयस्य प्रकारेण चतस्रः अवस्थाः ।। अस्मत्प्राचीनास्तु प्रतिदिनं उपनीतवटोः भस्मधारणसमये प्रोच्यमाने मन्त्रे पञ्चावस्थाः उक्तवन्तः । सः भगवान् परमेश्वरः पञ्चलक्षणामूर्तिः इति वर्ण्यते। अत्र पञ्चमूर्तिः नाम पञ्चमूर्तयः पञ्चशरीराणि, यस्य भगवतः इत्यर्थः। स च जीवोऽहं, सोऽहम् इति, शिवोऽहम् इति चानुसन्धाने सति जीवस्यैव पञ्चावस्थाः इति ज्ञायते।। ताश्च पञ्चावस्थाः जीवस्य सद्योजातावस्था, कौमारावस्था, गार्हस्थ्यावस्था, वानप्रस्थावस्था ततश्च सन्न्यासाश्रमे सर्वत्यागावस्थेति।

1. सद्योजातावस्था अथवा शैशवावस्था -

सद्योजातं प्रपद्यामि सद्योजाताय वै नमो नमः।

भवे भवे नातिभवे भवस्व मां, भवोभ्दवाय नमः।। इति।

वर्धमानस्य वैभवं बाल्ये एवेतिरीत्या बहवः शैशवे एव स्वभावीजीवनवैभवं प्रदर्शयन्ति। स्वामीविवेकानन्दस्य वा महात्मागान्धीमहाशयस्य वा जीवनं पश्यन्तु। बाल्ये शिशवः चलनं अभ्यस्यन्तः भाषणप्रयत्नवन्तः, आहारं स्वीकुर्वन्तः, मुग्धावस्स्थां यापयन्ति। आरम्भे अंहकारः, सुप्तः सन् क्रमेण वर्धते। Sigmond Freud Id, Ego, अवस्थात्रयं कथयति। तन्मतानुस्सारेण - Id इति संवृद्ध्य Ego भविष्यतीति। नाम-अस्मि, अस्मि इति बहुषु कार्येषु वर्धमानः भावः क्रमेण 'अहंकारः' भवति। Id एव Is अथवा Ist (German) नाम संस्कृते अस् धातुः। सः इदमेव अग्रे Super-Ego भविष्यतीति कथयति।

सः तु Id अवस्थायां कृतानां किञ्चिदपि स्मृतौ संस्कारः नावतिष्ठतीति कथयति।। वर्षत्रयपर्यन्तं प्रायः न कस्यचित् मानवस्य कृतं यत्किमपि स्मृतिपथे न तिष्ठति। अहङ्कारः (अस्मिताभावः), यदा भवति तदैव स्मृतिपथे धारणाय संस्काराः समर्थाः भवन्ति। शैशवावस्थां तदा च शिशुः परित्यजति।। बुद्धिमान् शिशुः कुमारावस्थामतिशीघ्रं प्राप्नोति। Super Ego अथवा अत्यहं सर्वत्र त्याज्यमेव वस्तुतः। परन्तु Freud तदेव कार्यकारीति कथयति।।

2. वामदेवावस्था अथवा कुमारावस्था

वामदेवाय नमो ज्येष्ठाय नमः श्रेष्ठाय नमो रुद्राय नमः कालाय नमः कलविकरणाय नमो

बलविकरणाय नमो बलाय नमो बलप्रमथनाय नमः सर्वभूतदमनाय नमो मनोन्मनाय नमः।।

वामदेवः नाम देव इव सुन्दरः इत्यर्थः। वामः (सुन्दरः) देव इव इति व्युत्पत्तिः। कुमारभावस्यापि अयमेवार्थः कुः भूमिः। कौ मारः इव कुमारः।

साक्षान्मन्मथभावः। एकस्य जीवने सौन्दर्यपराकाष्ठा कुमारभावे एव भवतीति सैव वामदेवावस्था। प्रायः अहंकारः वर्धमानः यौवने उष्णरक्तीतिपदवाच्यः भवति। अस्यामवस्थायां शरीरमनसोः समप्रमाणेन वृद्धिः आवश्यकी। अस्यामवस्थायां केचन शरीरदौर्बल्यं, अन्ये च मानस-दौर्बल्यमनुभवन्ति। मनश्चास्यामवस्थायां अतिसूक्ष्मं भवति। अहङ्कारः दृढ़ः इति कृत्वा अधिकाः विषयाः स्मृतिपथे तिष्ठन्ति। नाम धारणशक्तिः अत्यधिका भवति। स्वयं सर्वेषामप्युत्तरदायीति अस्यामवरस्थायां बालकाः चिन्तयन्ति। स्वस्वशक्तिसामर्थ्यज्ञानहीनाः कुमाराः भवन्ति। अग्रिमाध्ययनं परित्यज्य परिसरपरिस्थितिवशादार्थिकसमस्यावशादुद्योगमल्पभरण्यकमपि कुर्वाणाः पश्चात्तपन्ति। अत एवास्यामवस्थायां विशेषावधानं आवश्यकम्।

3. **अघोरावस्था अथवा प्रबुद्धावस्था**

एतदवस्था परिसरसमस्यानां उत्तरदायित्वावस्था। यदि भवति विवेकी विवाहार्हः भविष्यति। अतः मन्त्रःअघोरेभ्योऽथघोरेभ्यो घोरघोरतरेभ्यः। सर्वेभ्यः सर्वशर्वेभ्यो नमस्तेऽस्तु रुद्ररूपेभ्यः।। न घोराः (भयानकाः) अघोराः। न घोरं (भयं) अस्मै कस्यचिदित्यपि साधु। अस्यामवस्थायां मानवः कस्यापि न बिभेति। स्वयं भयानकोऽपि न भवेत्। घोरतरेभ्योऽपि प्रसंगेभ्यः एते एव घोराः सन्तः समस्याः परिहरेयुः। समस्या-परिहारकाः सन्तः रुद्ररूपा एते। तथापि शिवकारकाः कल्याणगुणपूर्णकर्मकरणशीलाः। मानवजीवने पुरुषो वा स्त्री वा अर्थेन, शरीरेण, मनसा च प्रबलः सन् (अथवा प्रबला सती) विवाहेच्छां प्रकटयति। उत्तरदायिता अस्यामवस्थायां अत्यन्तं आवश्यिका।

यस्मान्नोज़िते लोकः लोकान्नोद्विजते चयः।
हर्षाभयोद्वेगेः मुक्रो यः सच मेप्रियः।। (भगो-12-15)
जनकः ब्रह्मज्ञानीत्यस्य अयमेवार्थः।

4. तत्पुरुषावस्था अथवा वार्धक्यम्

वस्तुतः मानवः यदा वृद्धो भवति तदा तस्य (भगवतः) पुरुषः भवति। इतः परं मम लयो भवतीति प्रज्ञा यदायाति तदा समाजसेवायां निरता भवन्ति। इतः पूर्वं योऽहङ्कारः आसीत्, सः विनश्यति। मानवः नानासमस्यासु संलग्नः स्वस्य परिमितत्वं परशक्तेः अपरिमितत्वञ्च अनुभवत् प्रायः सर्वः तत्पुरुषः भवति। अतः भक्तिप्राधान्येन जीवनं कुर्वन् सर्वोऽपि तत्पुरुष एवं भवति। गार्हस्थ्यजीवनं अघोरावस्थाया श्चेत्, वानप्रस्थानाम् जीवनं तत्पुरुषावस्थाया भवति। वस्तुतः एतदेव सुन्दरजीवनं भवति, यतः एतस्यामवस्थायां गीतोक्तः कर्मण्येवाधिकारस्ते मा फलेषु कदाचनेति भावः समुल्लसति। अपवादाः भवेयुः। सामान्यतः एवं भवेदिति शास्त्रं कथयति, अतः मन्त्रः "तत्पुरुषाय विद्महे महादेवाय धीमहि। तन्नो रुद्रः प्रचोदयात्

5. ईशानावस्था-

ईशानः सर्वविद्यानां ईश्वरः सर्वभूतानां ब्रह्माधिपतिर्ब्रह्मणोऽधिपतिर्ब्रह्मा, शिवो मेऽस्तु सदाशिवोम् इति पञ्चमो मन्त्रः। पञ्चमावस्थां जातस्य जीवस्य कथयति। भगवति लयभावः। साक्षाभ्दगवत्स्वरूपाः सम्पूर्णतया स्वार्थं परित्यज्य प्रकृतिभावमनुतिष्ठन्तः मुक्ताः मोक्षसुखमनुभवन्तः भवन्ति।

जीवस्य जननसमये विकृतिभावमापन्नाः पृथिवी-अप्-तेजो-वायु-आकाशरूपेण देवता-भावमापन्नाः सृष्टिस्थितिलयकारणीभूताः पञ्चप्रकृतितत्त्वविशेषाः मानवस्यापि देवपदवीं दातुं समर्थाः विशिष्टाः भवन्ति ईशानावस्थायाम्। जीवन्मुक्ताश्च केचन प्राकृतशरीरे विद्यमाना अपि विक्षेपशक्तेः वेगेन केवलं जीवन्ति।। अतः व्यक्तित्वविकसनस्य अन्तिमं स्तरमेतत् यत् जातस्य लयीभवनम्।

22

Personality Development in Nutshell

A.H. Chachadi

Sanskrit literature is a treasure house of knowledge unparalleled in any other language of the world. The vastness depth and versatility of the language surpass any other literature. Let us divide the Sanskrit literature in to two parts.

I. Veda, Upanishads, Brahmanas, Puranas including Ramayana and Mahabharata.

II. Kavyas dramas and other prosaic literature also include recent thinkers like Kuntilya and others.

Personality development is a broad term which encompasses a vast arena of human endeavour. For the purpose of our discussion, I define Personality development as a continuous effort of human beings to evolve themselves as complete men or women as a response to the changing demand of the world. Personality development needs to be defined in this backdrop.

Personality development is a term drawn from Greek and Latin where 'Persona' means a mask. In essence, Personality development is a choice of which mask to wear. The route used in ancient Sanskrit literature is what is called as modelling in present day research. In Mahabharata as well as Ramayana known as illustrative philosophies which are in essence extension of vedic tenets, you have a vast number of role models available around which one can cast oneself. The stories are so complete that one can cast himself or herself in any mould and can know the effort involved and the likely end result.

As you all very well know the main characters in Mahābhārata, which is a more recent happening and as a result more appealing, are Pāṇḍavas and Kauravas of which Pāṇḍavas represent various kinds of virtues. Kauravas represent vices. To illustrate; Dharmarāja represents Dharma, Bhimasena represents virtues such knowledge, sacrifice, devotion, courage, steadfastness, strength, intelligence and sound reasoning. Arjuna symbolizes Śravaṇa Manana Nidhidhyāsana i.e., listening discipleship and studiousness and an ability to incorporate the knowledge; similarly Nakula and Sahadeva represent character and humbleness. Similarly Duryodhana is a symbol of ignorance. Duśyasana is a symbol of wrong knowledge or misplaced knowledge lastly Śakuni is a symbol of suspicion, all the other 97 brothers represent the other vices that follow.

Through this, a message is given as to which are the virtues to be emulated and which are vices to be avoided. In both the camps, there are several other characters which need to be taken note of. If there is Kunti, Lord Kṛṣṇa, Balarāma, Subhadrā, Draupadi, Drupada and various others in the virtuous camp there are characters like Dhritarashtra, Gandhari, Bhishma, Droṇacārya, Kṛpācārya, Ashwatthāmacārya, Vidura. Each one of them symbolize certain virtues as well as vices except Vidura who is virtuousness personified. If we were to eternalize these characters by model building, it would have been very easy for preceptors to choose any one of them or a combination of them. If we look across to any section of society, we can identify people belonging to both the camps. In this context, it can be said that men and women and their personalities are an outcome of deliberate choices these characters have made either out of their basic nature or circumstances surrounding them.

List of Contributors

Dr. S.Ranganath, Prof. & Head, Dept. of Sanskrit, NMKRV College, Bangalore

Dr. Shankar Bhat, Dr. A.V.Baliga College of Arts & Science, Kumta

Dr. B.L.Nadoni, Professor of Sanskrit, Karnatak University, Dharwad.

Dr. R. Laxmi, Associate Professor, Dept. of Sanskrit, Smt. K.S.J. Arts & Dr. S.M.S., Commerce College for Women, Dharwad - 580 008

Archana G. Murgod, Research Scholar, Department of Sanskrit, Karnatak University, Dharwad - 580 003

Dr. C. Shivaraju, Reader & Chairman, Dept. of Sanskrit, Jnanabharathi, Bangalore University, Bangalore-560056

Dr. Shripad Bhat, H.O.D. 'Shree Balmukund', Lohia Centre of Sanskrit and Indological Studies', Tilak Maharashtra Vidyapeetha, Pune - 411030.

Dr. Umesh. G. Shastri, Associate Professor of Sanskrit, Dr. A.V. Baliga College, Kumta - 581343, Uttara Kannada District, Karnataka.

Dr. K. Narayan Bhat, Reader, Dept. of Sanskrit, University of Mysore, Mysore.

Keyur R. Karagudari, Research Scholar, Department of Sanskrit, Karnatak University, Dharwad

Dr. M.N. Joshi, Professor of Sanskrit, P.G. Dept. of Sanskrit, Karnatak University, Dharwad

Dr. V.K. Hampiholi, Principal Grade I, Dr. A.V.Baliga College of Arts and Science, Kumta: 581343

Dr. V.B. Tadakod, Associate Professor, Dept. of Samskrit, J.S.S. College, Dharwad.

Dr.V. Girishchandra, Asst. Professor, Dept. of Sanskrit, Karnatak University, Dharwad – 580003

R.R. Shastri, College of Arts and Science, Hannavar (N.K.)

Shri Bhimsenacharya Pandurangi, Asst. Professor, Basaveshwar College, Bagalkot.

Mrs. Ashwini S. Patil, Dept. of Sanskrit, Karnatak University, Dharwad

Dr. A.H. Chachadi, Professor & Director, Kausali Institute of Management, Karnatak University, Dharwad - 580003

K. B. Archak

Sujata M.N.

Shakuntala Hiremath

Madhumati S. Shivapuji